The Power of Lies

ALSO BY JOHN KUCICH

Excess and Restraint in the Novels of Charles Dickens

Repression in Victorian Fiction:
Charlotte Brontë, George Eliot, and Charles Dickens

The
Power
of Lies

Transgression in Victorian Fiction

John Kucich

CORNELL
UNIVERSITY
PRESS

Ithaca and London

First published 1994 by Cornell University Press.

Library of Congress Cataloging-in-Publication Data

Kucich, John.
The power of lies : transgression in Victorian fiction / John Kucich.
        p.   cm.
Includes bibliographical references (p.   ) and index.
ISBN 0-8014-2842-4 (cloth: alk. paper)
ISBN 0-8014-8089-2 (pbk.: alk. paper)
1. English fiction—19th century—History and criticism.
2. Truthfulness and falsehood in literature.   I. Title.
PR878.T78K83   1994
823'.809353—dc20   94-11987

Printed in the United States of America

Contents

Acknowledgments

My education in lying has been advanced by a great many people, in both private and professional life—people whose exemplary mendacity has been far more enlightening for me than academic study. At the risk of appearing overearnest, I will respect taboos and leave all these most important of mentors nameless.

In purely scholarly terms, I am indebted to John McGowan, more than to anyone else, for his advice at crucial stages of this project. His comments on both the first chapter I wrote and on the Introduction—as well as his friendship and intellectual support over the past twenty years—have been invaluable. It has been my great good fortune to be on the same wavelength with someone so generous with his time and ideas.

Many others have given me detailed commentary on sections of the manuscript. Individual chapters have been carefully read and improved by Margaret Higonnet, J. Hillis Miller, Dianne Sadoff, Paul Sawyer, Bob Super, and Martha Vicinus. Comprehensive readings have come from Ina Ferris, David Riede, and Harry Shaw. I am grateful as well to those who read various parts of the book and lent me their encouragement, especially James Eli Adams, Austin Booth, Jerome Bump, Bob Caserio, Sheila Emerson, Jonathan Freedman,

Wendy Jones, Kerry Larson, Joseph Litvak, Erin O'Connor, Adela Pinch, Hilary Schor, and Athena Vrettos. I also received special help and advice at the outset from Nancy Armstrong, Patrick Brantlinger, and George Levine. Both Charles Baxter (who alerted me to, among other things, Napoleon's famous "perfidious Albion!"—a phrase I could never figure out how to use until now) and Anne Herrmann helped me considerably without even knowing it, by being stimulating and supportive in many different ways. My debt to a number of anonymous readers at various journals, whose insightful reports guided me in the revision of early drafts, is also very deep.

On the technical side, Austin Booth made my work much easier with her expert research assistance and a steady flow of reliable advice. The librarians at the Bath Reference Library made a short stay immensely useful, and I had a great deal of help from the staffs of the British Library and the Harlan Hatcher Graduate Library in Ann Arbor. I also thank the University of Michigan, in general, and Bob Weisbuch, in particular, for research funding and precious leave time. The John Simon Guggenheim Memorial Foundation has my eternal gratitude for the yearlong Fellowship that enabled me to get the project started.

No one, however, has given me more unwavering support (both intellectual and emotional) during the writing of this book than Katie Marien, and I hope she thinks—at least occasionally—that it was all worth it. Some day I'll have the courage to ask her, since, over the years, I've found that I could always count on her for the truth.

Finally, I thank Melody Pentz—the physical therapist with an answer for everything—whose boundless creativity and responsiveness kept me sane enough, during a very difficult time in my life, to keep working.

Permission has been granted by the Johns Hopkins University Press to reprint revised portions of an earlier version of Chapter 1, which appeared as "Transgression in Trollope: Dishonesty and the Antibourgeois Elite," *ELH* 56 (1989), 593–618. The University of Texas Press has granted permission to reprint revised portions of an earlier version of Chapter 3, which appeared as "Transgression and Sexual Difference in Elizabeth Gaskell's Novels," *Texas Studies in Literature and Language* 32 (1990), 187–213. The University of Illinois Press has granted permission to reprint revised portions of Chapter 5, which appeared as "Moral Authority in the Late Novels: The Gendering of Art," in *The Sense of Sex: Feminist Perspectives on Hardy*, edited by Margaret R. Higonnet (1993). I am grateful to all involved.

JOHN KUCICH

Ann Arbor, Michigan

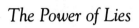

The Power of Lies

Introduction

T his book is about Victorian England's fascination with lying—or, more properly, with slippery distinctions between
lying and truth-telling. It is also about the way this fascination with ethical boundaries shaped Victorian attitudes toward social
distinctions, particularly—but not exclusively—those of class and
gender. Victorian literary criticism of recent years has been steadily
drawn to the play of boundary phenomena—public and private,
performative and secretive, criminal and legal, healthy and ill,
masculine and feminine. Although I share the inclination of many
critics to find the breakdown of these boundaries more interesting
than the boundaries themselves, I have resisted the common tendency to interpret such breakdowns as symptoms of conceptual
crisis. I am more interested in how the transgression of conceptual
boundaries is socially and symbolically productive. In this sense, I
find Victorian blurrings of the honesty/dishonesty distinction to be
a crucial instrument of symbolic transformation, which could be
used to rearticulate lines of class and gender conventionally mapped
through ethical oppositions. This symbolic productivity was enormously important in all phases of Victorian culture, but it was
particularly useful to the social strategies of certain middle-class
elites: professionals, cultural intellectuals, writers.

I have not approached Victorian ethics simply as a philosophical system, but, rather, as a reservoir of ideological content. My concern with ethics is rooted in the conviction that, as Alasdair MacIntyre puts it, every ethical system "presupposes a sociology."[1] There would be little point in demonstrating that Victorian ethics was a relatively unstable system—although it *has* too often been seen as the unbending moral code against which future generations rebelled—if not to show how ethical instabilities served various social struggles and strategies. Materialist critics of ethics, along with other genealogists of morals, have long been attuned to the ways moral order bolsters social hierarchies. The political use of moral *disorder*, however, is something that postmodern theories of symbolic dynamics have only recently allowed us to understand. As Eve Sedgwick has put it, in the context of a different kind of definitional incoherence: "Contests for discursive power can be specified as competitions for the material or rhetorical leverage required to set the terms of, and to profit in some way from, the operations of such an incoherence of definition."[2] It is my contention that the transgression of truth-telling norms had a political significance in Victorian culture which criticism has long overlooked, both because of its tendency to locate symbolic slippage outside normal social processes (whether as the sign of the literary or of liberatory ideological disruptions) and, even more fundamentally, because of its general embarrassment about ethical questions. This embarrassment has been the subject of an increasing number of theoretical critiques, although many of these seek to return political criticism to ethical philosophy, rather than to restore the political dimension to ethics.[3]

---

[1] Alasdair MacIntyre, *After Virtue: A Study in Moral Theory* (Notre Dame: University of Notre Dame Press, 1981), p. 22. My approach to texts throughout has been to use standard contemporary editions when they are widely available and otherwise to rely as much as possible on first editions. Citations in the form 1:11 are to volume and page numbers, while those in the form 2.22 are to chapter and page numbers.

[2] Eve Kosofsky Sedgwick, *Epistemology of the Closet* (Berkeley: University of California Press, 1990), p. 11. Sedgwick theorizes the incoherence in representations of homo/heterosexual identity.

[3] I am thinking, in particular, of such works as J. Hillis Miller, *The Ethics of Reading: Kant, de Man, Eliot, Trollope, James, and Benjamin* (New York: Columbia University Press, 1987); Geoffrey Galt Harpham, *Getting It Right: Language, Literature, and Ethics* (Chicago: University of Chicago Press, 1992); Tobin Siebers, *The Ethics of Criticism* (Ithaca: Cornell University Press, 1988); Charles Altieri, "From

In studying the ethical systems of individual writers, I have worked between two opposing goals. On the one hand, I have tried to develop a general model of transgression in nineteenth-century middle-class culture. My central claim is that middle-class culture, too often reduced to an ahistorical flatness and homogeneity, depended precisely on internal instability, incoherence, and stratification, instantiated by a symbolic logic of transgression, to produce and maintain its claims to cultural authority. This internal complexity, crucial to the resilience of middle-class culture, allowed it to incorporate energies whose dynamic power had everything to do with their "antibourgeois" character. Middle-class perversity, in other words, played an important role in middle-class privilege. Ethical inversions, particularly those involving truth-telling, were central to these processes. On the other hand, I have sought to apply the model of transgression flexibly, situating it in historically specific contexts, in order to recover the competing uses of this symbolic field by several middle-class Victorian subgroups. The differences I map out, then, represent various ideological permutations—and by no means the only possible ones—on a single cultural/symbolic dynamic. Another way to configure my dual goals would be to say that middle-class Victorian culture constituted a battleground of competing strategies of transgression, and that this book seeks to uncover some of the major sites of conflict. But the tension between these two forms of critical attention remains a crucial part of this book, because it shapes my response to the dual problems of ahistoricism and relativism that have plagued postmodern cultural theory, which tends either to formalize models of power or to overparticularize them.

The power of lies derives, paradoxically, from the centrality of truth-telling in Victorian culture and from the consequent seepage of honesty/dishonesty distinctions into all corners of the symbolic grid formed by Victorian social and sexual oppositions. Such power depends ultimately, however, on the reversibility of these ethical distinctions—which is what I have termed "transgression." Validat-

Expressivist Aesthetics to Expressivist Ethics," in *Literature and the Question of Philosophy*, ed. Anthony Cascardi (Baltimore: Johns Hopkins University Press, 1987), pp. 134–66; and Seyla Benhabib, *Situating the Self: Gender, Community, and Postmodernism in Contemporary Ethics* (London: Routledge, 1992).

ing the lie, or idealizing conduct that hybridizes honesty and dishonesty, gave novelists (among others) the opportunity to construct
potent new kinds of moral sophistication. Such sophistication, in
turn, justified writers in rearranging the symbolic social and sexual
oppositions that the discourse of truth-telling had seemed so securely
to order. In this way, forms of dissimulation always underpin Victorian writers' thinking about social and sexual change. The authority
to destabilize truth-telling norms came particularly to define the
antagonism between rising elements within the middle class and
traditional middle-class constituencies, as well as to define a struggle
for cultural status between these various rising factions themselves.
An "exceptional" moral authority, whose flexibility and freedom
signifies its antibourgeois moral progressiveness, was hotly contested
among competing middle-class elites.

Before I begin to explicate these mechanisms of transgression, I
want to outline, briefly, how central to Victorian culture its truth-
telling norms really were. To understand the power of Victorian
lying, we need to remember first how monumental and how extensively socially coded were the norms of truth-telling it violated. I
will begin with a quick sketch of the cultural prominence of Victorian truth-telling and then introduce theoretical frameworks for
understanding how useful it might have been to confuse the boundaries between honesty and dishonesty.

Victorian earnestness has long been a critical cliché—one of the
standard ways of defining the singularity of nineteenth-century
English culture. Our certainties about the rigors of Victorian truth-
telling have been so secure, in fact, that the topic has faded from
view, generating little recent discussion or debate. Even if criticism
had not shifted away from issues of moral character—issues it tends
to see, perhaps too precipitously, as the preoccupation of a falsely
universalizing, self-satisfied humanism—the Victorians' lofty regard
for honesty would still seem too obvious for comment. Convinced of
its self-evidence, historians of culture seem to forget that Victorian
honesty was never simply or entirely Victorian. That is to say,
up until the early twentieth century, Western culture had come
increasingly to value truth-telling over a very long period, at least

since the Renaissance. Lionel Trilling's well-known account traces the "invention" of sincerity to the Protestant Reformation, the beginnings of democratic movements, urbanization, and a variety of other forces that contributed to the storied rise of individualism.[4] Michael McKeon's more dialectical chronology gives the high moral status of honesty a history of similar length, although McKeon traces preoccupations with personal honor entirely to status inconsistencies at the advent of the capitalist period.[5] Nevertheless, it was perfectly clear even to nineteenth-century observers—as it is to us—that some momentous inflation of the cultural cachet of honesty took place in Victorian England. Trilling himself notes a new and widespread belief in the nineteenth century "that England produced a moral type which made it unique among nations. . . . This moral type which England was thought uniquely to have produced had as its chief qualities probity and candour."[6]

In taking this cultural fact for granted, however, it is easy to overlook just how curiously exaggerated Victorian truth-telling

[4] Lionel Trilling, *Sincerity and Authenticity* (London: Oxford University Press, 1972). Trilling notes that literary villainy has been synonymous with "dissembling" from the sixteenth century onward. J. Douglas Canfield identifies the rise of honesty as a dominant literary trope even earlier, and correlates it with the political ideology of feudal authority (*Word as Bond in English Literature from the Middle Ages to the Restoration* [Philadelphia: University of Pennsylvania Press, 1989]). Helpful as Canfield's book is as a topography of literary truth-telling before the Restoration, his ethical categories are so narrowly class-bound that he does not see the continuity between courtly or aristocratic literary ethics and those of the dominant bourgeois form, the novel. He asserts, astonishingly, that honesty was not a central literary concern after 1690 (pp. 313–14).

[5] Michael McKeon, *The Origins of the English Novel, 1600–1740* (Baltimore: Johns Hopkins University Press, 1987). McKeon finds a key role for the novel in the new eighteenth-century mapping of "stories of virtue" onto "stories of truth." See esp. pp. 265–70.

[6] Trilling, *Sincerity and Authenticity*, p. 110. In particular, Trilling discusses the prominence of this English moral type among heroic nineteenth-century literary figures: Alfred de Vigny's Admiral Collingwood, for example, and Melville's Captain Vere. See also Harold Perkin's comments on the "moral revolution" in English society during the period, in *Origins of Modern English Society* (New York: Routledge and Kegan Paul, 1969), p. 280. Alexander Welsh comments briefly on the centrality of nineteenth-century honesty (*The City of Dickens* [Oxford: Clarendon Press, 1971], p. 108). Walter E. Houghton cites the virulent self-policing of the Victorians when it came to "hypocrisy" as one symptom of their extraordinary pride in their own earnestness (*The Victorian Frame of Mind, 1830–1870* [New Haven: Yale University Press, 1957], pp. 395, 424–25).

seemed at the time and what this excessiveness might still have to tell us about the social implications of Victorian ethics, or of ethical reversals through lying. Ralph Waldo Emerson, no stranger to high standards of candor, was so struck by English hyper-honesty that he returned over and over in his "English Traits" to fascinated, if somewhat bemused, praise for the extravagances of English truth-telling, claiming that the imperial power of the English nation itself "rests on their national sincerity":

Emerson on English honesty(?)

> They are blunt in saying what they think, sparing of promises, and they require plain dealing of others. We will not have to do with a man in a mask. Let us know the truth. Draw a straight line, hit whom and where it will. . . . To be king of their word is their pride. When they unmask cant, they say, "The English of this is," etc.; and to give the lie is the extreme insult. The phrase of the lowest of the people is "honor-bright," and their vulgar praise, "His word is as good as his bond." . . . The English, of all classes, value themselves on this trait, as distinguishing them from the French, who, in the popular belief, are more polite than true. An Englishman understates, avoids the superlative, checks himself in compliments, alleging that in the French language one cannot speak without lying.[7]

As Emerson suggests, it was not just outsiders, but the English themselves who celebrated the uniqueness of their honesty, and their swollen moral pride played an important role in related domains of culture, like nationalist ideology. The popular moral philosopher W. E. H. Lecky adopted a complacent tone, for example, when he equated honesty with nineteenth-century England's superior economic and social development, finding honesty a fundamental justification of "Englishness": "Where the impositions of trade are very numerous, the supreme excellence of veracity is cordially admitted in theory, and it is one of the first virtues that every man aspiring to moral excellence endeavors to cultivate. This constitutes probably the chief moral superiority of nations pervaded by a strong

[7] Ralph Waldo Emerson, "English Traits," in *The Complete Works of Ralph Waldo Emerson*, Centenary Edition, 12 vols. (Boston: Houghton Mifflin, 1903), 5:117–18.

industrial spirit over nations like the Italians, the Spaniards, or the Irish, among whom that spirit is wanting."[8]

So powerful was the "Englishness" of high standards of honesty that such standards exerted an irresistible gravitational pull on nearly all phases of British culture. There is nothing peripheral about Victorian reverence for honesty, however unremarkable a part of the social text it may appear to twentieth-century eyes. Disparate and often uncongenial discourses had to be forced into compliance with it. The example of utilitarianism is an instructive one. Jeremy Bentham's notorious refusal to see falsehood as inherently evil, on the grounds that to do so would be to subvert the priority of utility as a first principle, was gradually and painstakingly transformed by his intellectual progeny in the face of constant criticism that utilitarianism was antipathetic to morality.[9] John Stuart Mill, for example, cleverly reconciled morality with utility by proclaiming truth-telling "a rule of . . . transcendent expediency." He went so far as to call such a rule "sacred" because of the paramount utility of upholding community standards of trust, even though he still invoked the logic of utility to justify violating it in the most extreme cases (e.g., lying to a murderer to protect an innocent life).[10] It has been pointed out that the development of "utilitarianism proper" depended in crucial ways on reconciling the notion of utility with basic moral imperatives like truth-telling.[11] Both Mill and Alexander

[8] W. E. H. Lecky, *History of European Morals from Augustus to Charlemagne*, 2 vols. (London: Longmans, Green, 1869), 1:144. Lecky goes on to observe, "The usual characteristic of the latter nations is a certain laxity or instability of character, a proneness to exaggeration, a want of truthfulness in little things, an infidelity to engagements from which an Englishman, educated in the habits of industrial life, readily infers a complete absence of moral principle."

[9] Jeremy Bentham, *An Introduction to the Principles of Morals and Legislation, Works of Jeremy Bentham*, 11 vols. (Edinburgh: William Tait, 1843), 1:105: "Falsehood, take it by itself, consider it as not being accompanied by any other material circumstances, nor therefore productive of any material effects, can never, upon the principle of utility, constitute any offense at all." A representative example of attacks on utilitarianism's indifference to truth-telling can be found in Lecky, *History of European Morals*, 1:52.

[10] John Stuart Mill, "Utilitarianism," in *Collected Works of John Stuart Mill*, ed. John M. Robson, 33 vols. (London: Routledge and Kegan Paul; Toronto: University of Toronto Press, 1963–91), 10:223.

[11] See, for example, Richard Wollheim, *The Thread of Life* (Cambridge: Harvard University Press, 1984), pp. 221–24. Symptomatically, in his essay on Bentham, Mill idealized the founder of utilitarianism primarily for the honesty of his methods,

Bain ultimately justified such a synthesis by introducing the "law of association" of feelings and ideas as a way to submit the notion of utility to certain sedimented human values. Although he strictly repudiated moral values based on sentiment rather than on rationally determined utility, Bain conceded that intellectual inconsistency produced such deep emotional pain that the "love of truth" would always be a more fundamental psychological motive than utility.[12] These kinds of reconciliation were so taken for granted by the 1870s that a devoted Millite such as John Morley—the liberal editor of the *Fortnightly Review*, which one critic has described as "an intellectual memorial to the dead master," with Morley the "chief incense-burner to the Saint of Rationalism"—was able to sound a strikingly anti-Benthamite chord when it came to standards of truth-telling.[13] In his influential treatise about political ethics, *On Compromise*, Morley argued that, although compromise is of great usefulness in the political process, there are no conceivable circumstances in which mere expediency might warrant compromising the "one commanding law" of morality: "that men should cling to truth and right."[14]

Similar adjustments were made in a variety of Victorian discourses,

---

seeing him as a demystifier of the verbal deceits of earlier writers: "During so many generations, in each of which thousands of educated young men were successively placed in Bentham's position and with Bentham's opportunities, he alone was found with sufficient moral sensibility and self-reliance to say to himself that these things, however profitable they might be, were frauds, and that between them and himself there should be a gulf fixed. To this rare union of self-reliance and moral sensibility we are indebted for all that Bentham has done. . . . Throughout life he never relaxed in his indignant denunciation of all laws which command such falsehoods, all institutions which attach rewards to them" (Mill, "Bentham," in *Collected Works*, 10:81). See W. David Shaw's discussion of Mill's own posture of exemplary candor in *Victorians and Mystery: Crises of Representation* (Ithaca: Cornell University Press, 1990), pp. 276–87. Doctrine and methodology aside, the Benthamites were famous as activists on account of their passion for moral reform—what Harold Perkin has called their "secular evangelicalism." Perkin points out that utilitarianism depended heavily on middle-class desires to "moralize" society—especially through such puritanical qualities as "seriousness of mind" (*Origins of Modern English Society*, pp. 287–88).

[12] Alexander Bain, *The Emotions and the Will* (London: John W. Parker and Son, 1859), p. 205.

[13] Paul Adelman, *Victorian Radicalism: The Middle-Class Experience, 1830–1914* (New York: Longman, 1984), p. 63.

[14] John Morley, *On Compromise* (London: Chapman and Hall, 1877), p. 3.

both intellectual and popular, to accommodate controlling standards
of honesty. Victorian scientific thought, for example, always attempted to connect itself to the moral value of truth-telling, even
while generally affirming (with the pointed exception of the positiv-
ists) that scientific law could not be conflated with moral law.[15] A
central trope of writers as different as Herbert Spencer, Charles
Darwin, and John Tyndall is the notion that scientific discourses are
"truthful" and can always be morally justified—if not in their
postulates themselves—on account of their ability to protect the
public from the duplicities of pseudoscience. At a more popular level,
that classic work of bourgeois instrumentalism, Samuel Smiles's *Self-
Help*, is shrill in defining honesty as the essence of gentlemanly
commercial conduct and idealizing such conduct as a prerequisite to
success—in sharp contrast to later success manuals, which typically
put a premium on gamesmanship.[16] It is a commonplace of cultural
criticism that evangelicalism strove to make moral values compatible
with business values, in much the same way that Smiles does.[17] It
may seem more surprising, though, that political conservatives also
attempted to appropriate standards of truth-telling for their own
ideological purposes, since Tory rhetoric had to veer far from traditional aristocratic ideals to find a place for more properly middle-class
norms of honesty.[18] The transformation of codes of "gentlemanly"

[15] See George Levine, *Darwin and the Novelists: Patterns of Science in Victorian
Fiction* (Cambridge: Harvard University Press, 1988), pp. 3, 36–37, 141.

[16] Smiles refuses to endorse deception of any kind as a means to financial reward,
arguing instead that "it is moral qualities in the main which rule the world." In his
anatomizing of moral character, he returns over and over, in particular, to truth-
telling: "The true gentleman has a keen sense of honour,—scrupulously avoiding
mean actions. His standard of probity in word and action is high. He does not
shuffle nor prevaricate, dodge nor skulk; but is honest, upright, and straightforward"
(Samuel Smiles, *Self-Help: With Illustrations of Character and Conduct* [London:
Ward, Lock, 1859], pp. 352, 366; see also pp. 242–47, 354–57).

[17] See, for example, G. M. Young, *Victorian England: Portrait of an Age* (London:
Oxford University Press, 1936), pp. 3–4.

[18] For a discussion of the distinction between middle-class honesty and aristocratic
ideas of honor, see Perkin, *Origins of Modern English Society*, pp. 273–78. The
coherence of the category "middle class" has been extensively debated recently, but
I am much in sympathy with the argument of Simon Gunn, who claims that for all
its internal variety, middle-class identity did coalesce in a number of fundamental
ways ("The 'Failure' of the Middle Class: A Critique," in *The Culture of Capital:
Art, Power, and the Nineteenth-Century Middle Class*, ed. Janet Wolff and John Seed

conduct to incorporate a new emphasis on sincerity—as opposed to eighteenth-century expectations about judicious performativeness (embodied notoriously in the advice of the man the Victorians most loved to hate, Lord Chesterfield)—was a fairly smooth one.[19] But in terms of political ideology, upper-class adaptation was often much more strained. A telling instance is Sir Robert Peel's disingenuous attempt, during a speech in 1835, to stigmatize middle-class entrepreneurship as dishonest, in contrast to the integrity of Tory paternalism:

> We disclaim any separation from the middling classes of society in this country. . . . If circumstances may appear to have elevated some of us above the rest, to what, I venture to ask, is that elevation owing? It is owing to nothing else but to the exercise, either on our own part or on the part of our immediate forefathers, of those qualities of diligence, of the love of order, of industry, of integrity in commercial dealings, which have hitherto secured to every member of every middle class of society the opportunities of elevation and distinction in this great community . . . . [I]t is because we owe our elevation in society to the exercise of those qualities . . . that we are resolved, with the blessing of God, to keep clear for others those same avenues that were opened to ourselves, that we will not allow their course to be obstructed by men who want to secure the same advantages by dishonest means—to reach by some shorter cut, that goal, which can be surely attained, but can be attained, only through industry, patient perseverance, and strict integrity.[20]

Cynical accommodations like Peel's raise serious questions about the deeper cultural conflicts fought out in the Victorians' rush to claim the high moral ground of honesty. Such conflicts were not simply

[Manchester: University of Manchester Press, 1988], pp. 17–44). Notably, Gunn argues that the Victorian middle class found a collective inheritance in the militant moral codes it saw as its puritan patrimony, in addition to its opposition to governmental restrictions on the pursuit of capital, its antagonism to the established church, and its antipathy to a powerful central state.

[19] See Robin Gilmour, *The Idea of the Gentleman in the Victorian Novel* (London: Allen and Unwin, 1981), pp. 16–36.

[20] Robert Peel, "At Tailors' Hall," in *Speeches by the Right Honourable Sir Robert Peel, Bart. During His Administration, 1834–1835* (London: Roarke and Varty, 1835), 11 May 1835, pp. 293–94.

concealed beneath a superficial veneer of ethical unanimity; they became embedded in moral discourse itself.

Further questions follow from the prominent absence of standards of honesty in a few areas of Victorian culture—particularly in conceptions of female virtue, whether in the domain of traditional sexual mythology or among feminist and protofeminist thinkers. It seems predictable enough that traditional images of female virtue, concentrating as they do on sexuality or on the most passive of moral ideals, should leave the flaunting of truth-telling largely to men. Indeed, Victorian ideas about "manliness" revolved absolutely around notions of candor—one of the chief features of Arnoldian reform in the public schools, for instance, was the prefectorial system, with its foundation in codes of manly trust.[21] Conversely, Mary Poovey has shown that a number of Victorian medical researchers tried to discover the physiological roots of a supposedly ingrained female mendacity.[22] It seems more surprising, however, that Victorian feminists were unwilling or unable to reappropriate this particular moral terrain. One might consider as symptomatic the absence of truth-telling among the lists of more "activist" Victorian female virtues catalogued by such feminist historians as Martha Vicinus and Philippa Levine.[23] Vicinus, in *Independent Women*, defines the "moral superiority" claimed by late-century

[21] See David Newsome, *Godliness and Good Learning: Four Studies on a Victorian Ideal* (London: John Murray, 1961), pp. 46–49, 195. See also the comments of Mark Girouard on the importance of "fair play" in the late-century cult of athleticism, *The Return to Camelot: Chivalry and the English Gentleman* (New Haven: Yale University Press, 1981), pp. 231–48. On questions of Victorian manliness I am also indebted to Gilmour, *The Idea of the Gentleman*, esp. pp. 18–23.

[22] In *Uneven Developments: The Ideological Work of Gender in Mid-Victorian England* (Chicago: University of Chicago Press, 1988), Mary Poovey cites the work of Thomas Laycock and Jules Falret (pp. 37, 46).

[23] Martha Vicinus, *Independent Women* (London: Virago, 1985), esp. pp. 288–90; Philippa Levine, *Feminist Lives in Victorian England: Private Roles and Public Commitment* (Cambridge: Basil Blackwell, 1990), p. 92. Welsh points out that Victorian heroines experience honesty mainly in terms of their loyalty to male figures of authority (*The City of Dickens*, pp. 168–69). One explanation for the great resilience of this gender-specific moral absence in the nineteenth century is suggested by Leonore Davidoff and Catherine Hall, "The Architecture of Public and Private Life: English Middle-Class Society in a Provincial Town, 1780–1850," in *The Pursuit of Urban History*, ed. Derek Fraser and Anthony Sutcliffe (London: Edward Arnold, 1983), esp. pp. 328–29. Davidoff and Hall demonstrate that because women were excluded from the demands of commercial and professional

feminists in terms of self-discipline, self-sacrifice, "freely chosen chastity," and powers of nurturance—but not honor. Carol Gilligan, in *In a Different Voice*, sustains this long-standing tradition by relegating principles of honesty to the periphery of female moral consciousness: she discusses such principles only when they come into conflict with what she sees as a more fundamental female moral code, revolving around notions of responsibility and protectiveness.[24] Adrienne Rich caught this kind of absence in the 1970s when she crusaded for new principles of feminist candor which she regarded as entirely neglected by the women's movement for largely historical reasons: "Honesty in women has not been considered important. We have been depicted as generically whimsical, deceitful, subtle, vacillating. And we have been rewarded for lying."[25]

The apparent male monopoly of honesty, and its absence in discussions of female virtue, should make us wary of arguments that Victorian women were monolithically identified with moral being. E. P. Thompson has recently documented similar absences both in working-class culture and in the works of its apologists.[26] Conflicts and absences like these form part of the subject of this book. Nevertheless, it is important to recognize that such cases do not usually involve any overt challenge to the sanctity of normative Victorian honesty, which seems impregnable to any frontal attack. Throughout the century, the canon of truthfulness is a fundamental, unarguable axiom of English ethico-philosophical writing. It is hard to imagine official disagreement with Carlyle's pronouncement that "sincerity . . . is better than grace," or with Huxley's claim, sixty years later, that "the foundation of morality is to have done, once and for all, with lying."[27] Even that deep reservoir of contrariness,

---

trust, they were also excluded from developing the "public virtues" so crucial to male economic relationships. Another explanation is that of Elaine S. Abelson, who argues that stereotypes of middle-class female dishonesty were linked to the construction of women as unstable sites of consumer passion (*When Ladies Go A-Thieving: Middle-Class Shoplifting in the Victorian Department Store* [New York: Oxford University Press, 1989]).

[24] Carol Gilligan, *In a Different Voice: Psychological Theory and Women's Development* (Cambridge: Harvard University Press, 1982).

[25] Adrienne Rich, "Women and Honor: Some Notes on Lying," in *On Lies, Secrets, and Silence: Selected Prose, 1966–1978* (New York: Norton, 1979), p. 186.

[26] E. P. Thompson, *Customs in Common* (London: Merlin Press, 1991).

[27] Thomas Carlyle, *On Heroes, Hero Worship, and the Heroic in History, The Works of Thomas Carlyle*, Centenary Edition, 30 vols. (New York: AMS Press, 1969),

Oscar Wilde, agreed that in Victorian culture lying had positively decayed out of existence.[28] As Joe Gargery puts it in *Great Expectations*, urging a characteristic Dickensian revulsion from untruth: "There's one thing you may be sure of, Pip . . . namely, that lies is lies."[29]

One of the most important nineteenth-century conflations wrought by preoccupations with honesty, from the perspective of literary criticism, is that the relatively clean separation of epistemological and ethical concerns that was taken for granted in preromantic aesthetic circles suffered a wholesale collapse—even though writers were painfully aware that claims for the honesty of art were on shaky ground, as J. Hillis Miller has recently shown.[30] Perhaps the most immediate legacy of romanticism was the aesthetic premium it placed on expressiveness over artifice, and there is always a latent moral exordium beneath the ardors of Wordsworth's "spontaneous overflow" and Mill's notion that "eloquence is *heard*, poetry is *overheard*."[31] Among Victorian novelists, formal questions about the truthfulness of fiction always shaded epistemological concerns into ethical ones. As George Levine puts it, for novelists, as for all Victorian intellectuals, "knowledge was an aspect of morality, so that the highest Victorian virtue was 'Truth.'"[32] When George Eliot's narrator, in *Adam Bede*, aspires "to give a faithful account of

---

5:30; T. H. Huxley, "Science and Morals," *Collected Essays*, 9 vols. (London: Macmillan, 1893–94), 9:146.

[28] Oscar Wilde, "The Decay of Lying," in *The Writings of Oscar Wilde*, ed. Isobel Murray (New York: Oxford University Press, 1989), pp. 215–40. Of course, Wilde reversed these values completely: "The first duty of life is to be as artificial as possible. What the second duty is no one has as yet discovered" ("Phrases and Philosophies for the Use of the Young," in *The Writings of Oscar Wilde*, p. 572).

[29] Charles Dickens, *Great Expectations* (Harmondsworth: Penguin, 1965), 9.100.

[30] See also McKeon, *The Origins of the English Novel*, p. 256, on the beginnings of this collapse in the mid-eighteenth century. The most important recent work on this conflation is Terry Eagleton, *The Ideology of the Aesthetic* (Cambridge: Basil Blackwell, 1990).

[31] William Wordsworth, "Preface to *Lyrical Ballads, with Pastoral and Other Poems*," in *William Wordsworth: The Poems*, ed. John O. Hayden, 2 vols. (New Haven: Yale University Press, 1977), 1:870–71; Mill, "Thoughts on Poetry and Its Varieties," in *Collected Works*, 1:348. On the convergence of literary emphases on unmediated truth, see Jonas Barish, "The Nineteenth Century," in *The Antitheatrical Prejudice* (Berkeley: University of California Press, 1981), pp. 295–349.

[32] Levine, *Darwin and the Novelists*, p. 3.

men and things as they have mirrored themselves in my mind," she does so primarily to produce, through her nonidealizing accuracy, a moral effect of "deep human sympathy."[33] Ruskin is one of the more intriguing figures in this regard. He strenuously denied, at the end of his career, that his work was the slightest bit inventive; he claimed, instead, that it was predicated on absolutely uncreative truth-telling. Ruskin's theories of composition are perhaps the most extreme example of Victorian attempts to disavow the disturbing connections between aesthetics and artifice. Trying to stress the unself-conscious, uncalculating nature of aesthetic production, Ruskin went so far as to claim that the best artists work with "involuntary power which approximates literally to the instincts of an animal."[34] One of the major difficulties for late Victorian critics with fin-de-siècle "decadence" was, in fact, the issue of its artificiality—even though late-century writers themselves, notably Pater and Wilde, developed surprising and convoluted ways of squaring their aesthetic theories with truth-telling, as James Eli Adams has recently shown.[35]

In the face of this extraordinary cultural consensus about the value of honesty, it may seem outrageous to argue that the Victorians were obsessed with lying. It would be strange, indeed, if I were denying the enormous cultural weight of Victorian earnestness, rather than simply telling the other half of the story. Of course, a moment's reflection must lead to the conclusion that the Victorians worried away at dishonesty, though perhaps in a very limited sense. That is, if the Victorians placed enormous cultural burdens on their own honesty, common sense tells us they must have expended much energy, conscious and unconscious, on warding off (or clandestinely thrilling to) what they construed as threats to it. Such is the contention of Nina Auerbach, who argues that "theatrical" impulses

[33] George Eliot, *Adam Bede* (Harmondsworth: Penguin, 1980), 17.221; 17.224.

[34] John Ruskin, *Sesame and Lilies, Works of John Ruskin*, 39 vols. (New York: John Wiley and Sons, 1885), 18:166–67. On Ruskin's difficulties with inventiveness, see Sheila Emerson, *Ruskin: The Genesis of Invention* (Cambridge: Cambridge University Press, 1993). Emerson points out that even though "imagination" remained an important category for Ruskin, his work is everywhere plagued with anxiety about the relationship between imagination and consciousness.

[35] James Eli Adams, "Gentleman, Dandy, Priest: Manliness and Social Authority in Pater's Aestheticism," *ELH* 59 (1992), 441–66.

were a repressed source of fascination and anxiety in a culture so committed to sincere self-presentation. Auerbach claims that "what the Victorians feared about theater was what they feared in life itself—the elusiveness of sincerity"—and that their indulgence of theatricality was emotionally charged but carefully guarded.[36] Auerbach thus typifies a critical tendency to read conceptual ambivalence solely as a symptom of anxiety or repressed desire.

The Victorians valued deceit much more positively than that, however. Victorian fiction is as interested in the qualities, the categories, and the productivity of lying as it is in celebrating honesty. In a culture so preoccupied with truth-telling, an affirmation of lying—or a blurring of this ethical distinction—could be a powerful symbolic gesture. Rather than being simply the dark underside of official ethics, lying came to have an enormous range of positive cultural values for the Victorians and was crucial to Victorian thinking about the nature of power in a number of different areas. Lying was seen, variously, as a fundamental form of resistance to social control, as a way to deepen norms of subjective development, as a way to recognize the presence and the force of desire, and—most important for purposes of this study—as a way to rethink the distribution of power across lines of social or sexual difference. That it could play so many productive roles resulted from the inevitable interdependence of oppositions between honesty and dishonesty in any symbolic system that reserves so prominent a place for issues of truthfulness. The social and historical forces that placed such an unusual premium on truth-telling forced Victorian culture to think about—and within—the structural interrelationships of honesty and dishonesty. Indeed, this book has its theoretical origin in my attempt to define the ways in which the honesty/dishonesty axis—taken as a binary, sometimes complementary, or reversible opposition—undergirded Victorian socio-symbolic systems.

Most accounts of the origins of Victorian truth-telling—and it is

[36] Nina Auerbach, *Private Theatricals: The Lives of the Victorians* (Cambridge: Harvard University Press, 1990), p. 114. Auerbach's wonderfully perceptive book nevertheless exaggerates Victorian fear of the performative, as if overcompensating for her earlier *Woman and the Demon: The Life of a Victorian Myth* (Cambridge: Harvard University Press, 1982), which catalogued the uses of "metamorphic" power in Victorian culture, if only among women.

significant that there is so little agreement about those origins—overlook the power of dishonesty which seems to emerge out of their very own logics, as a consequence of this structural interdependence. An overview of some general patterns of explaining the sources of Victorian hyper-honesty can demonstrate how attention to the countervailing role of dishonesty might supplement, rather than subvert, those accounts. I confess that working in this way forces me to develop my own model of transgression parasitically, by teasing it out of very differently oriented work. But such parasitism seems appropriate to a theory of symbolic reversibility. More incidentally, drawing on these various explanatory accounts will allow me to show how the power of lies results from an intersection of material and symbolic processes.

I look briefly, in the next section, at accounts of nineteenth-century truth-telling which attribute it to three principal causes: the structure of nineteenth-century social organization, the influence of postromantic models of subjectivity, and the increasing hegemony of official middle-class morality. The lack of proportion in my treatment of these three positions, and of the writers who have taken them, is deliberate. My purpose in looking at these patterns of explanation is not to exhaust the kinds of power a reversal of truth-telling norms made possible. Rather, I wish to show only how the multivalent power of dishonesty grows directly out of the various historical forces that overdetermined the centrality of Victorian truth-telling in the first place.

The accounts of truth-telling I trace in the next section implicitly suggest three particular kinds of power available through transgression: social, psychological, and libidinal. In subsequent chapters, I do not focus exclusively on one or another of these forms of power, though I cite all of them episodically. My project as a whole seeks to demonstrate how the transgression of truth-telling norms resonated against all these various domains of power in generalized symbolic terms. In Victorian fiction, transgressive lying provoked a multivalent cultural resonance as a centrifugal sign (if you will) of energies and forces that were, in fact, quite discrete. This kind of symbolic condensation worked to solidify the authority of groups that could express their exceptional moral and cultural power in very broad terms, through their affirmation and appropriation of transgressive codes of conduct which resisted reductive analysis and aspired instead to be irreducible, organic images of "natural" human vitality. This generalizing of transgressive power played an important role in the creation of large-scale shifts in categories of class and gender. Before I follow the novelists, though, in their generalizing of the symbolic power of transgression, I want to particularize these powers briefly in the following section, to stress the converging pressures of a number of distinct origins of nineteenth-century truth-telling, all of which contributed to make lying so potent an act.

First of all, neglect of the social function of dishonesty is a typical feature of analyses claiming that moral earnestness was coerced by changes in nineteenth-century social structure. This is evident, for example, in Foucauldian accounts of the nineteenth-century epiphany of confession. In Foucault's argument, compulsory Victorian honesty was the effect of a revolution in knowledge production, in which access to one's inner truth became crucially involved in the social production of the self by medical, juridical, and sociological discourses. In his account of the omnipresence in Victorian culture of confession, including its prominent role in professional discourses about the self, Foucault argues that the various branches of the human sciences depended for their power over the subject on a new emphasis on self-transparency. This power expressed itself, at the most unconscious level, in the nineteenth-century individual's primal incitement to "speak oneself"—to transform what were felt to be the secrets of inner nature into what were, in fact, highly conventionalized, disciplinary discourses.[37]

Foucault's treatment of confession is enormously valuable—not least for its anatomy of technologies of knowledge and its polemic about the privileged relation in Western culture between confession as a mode of self-knowledge and sexuality. But Foucault's account logically ought to feature a prominent place for lying, as a major

[37] See Michel Foucault, *The History of Sexuality*, Vol. 1: *An Introduction*, trans. Robert Hurley (New York: Random House, 1978), esp. pp. 57–65. D. A. Miller explores the Foucauldian paradoxes of confession thoroughly in "Secret Subjects, Open Secrets," in *The Novel and the Police* (Berkeley: University of California Press, 1988), pp. 192–220.

source of resistance—as, in fact, the most fundamental countermeasure—to social efforts to produce the self through confession. For all his interest in questions of subjection, Foucault is strangely silent on the construction of nineteenth-century lying as a reflex form of opposition to power. Instead, he completely collapses confession into the economies of power. He has little to say about the ways compulsory confession must have produced reflexive forms of evasion, except insofar as these hindrances ultimately worked to confirm the power of confessed "truth."[38] In the first volume of *The History of Sexuality*, his single mention of mendacity refers to obfuscations of the medical and psychiatric establishments, which are said to be merely a ruse of the production of truth, since they work to stress the danger of unmediated, nonprofessionalized disclosure.[39] He makes no mention at all of the confessing subject's capacities for deception; rather, Foucault's assumption is that the compulsion to confess fully constitutes the modern subject, producing unquestionable assumptions about the interior roots of self-knowledge. In the light of these assumptions, confession can never be critiqued or resisted from any standpoint that seeks to legitimate itself as a form of knowledge. Likewise, Foucault's later concept, "the care of the self," which purportedly unifies the entire Western tradition of sexual ethics, assumes that in cultures influenced by Christianity self-cultivation demands an authentic relation to interiority, in which the self must be fully deciphered—in order to be either affirmed or renounced.[40]

Foucault is notorious for underplaying possibilities for social and political resistance, and it should not at all surprise us that the missing piece in his account of confession is an examination of its inherent undependability: the new spaces for lying that it opens.

[38] Foucault, *The History of Sexuality, Vol. 1*, p. 62.

[39] Ibid., pp. 54–56.

[40] Foucault argues that modern, Christian-based practices of confession are founded in a hermeneutics of the self ("The Concern for Truth," in *Michel Foucault: Politics, Philosophy, Culture: Interviews and Other Writings, 1977–1984*, ed. Lawrence D. Kritzman [New York: Routledge, 1988], esp. pp. 260–61). This claim is the basis for what I believe is Charles Taylor's mistaken—but nevertheless illuminating—notion that Foucault intended to affirm deliberative Greek self-making as a palliative for our own confessional ills. See Taylor, "Foucault on Freedom and Truth," in *Foucault: A Critical Reader*, ed. David Couzens Hoy (New York: Basil Blackwell, 1986), esp. pp. 98–99.

Foucault has been routinely criticized for abstracting discourse from "everyday practices," and it is precisely within these kinds of practices that deception might be considered more normative.[41] What one tells one's doctor or lawyer may differ dramatically from what one tells one's neighbors or loved ones—as Victorian novels often demonstrate so well. Further, by collapsing all secular forms of confession into a Christian model very closely bound to notions of purgative self-disclosure, Foucault elides confessional situations that might make deception seem an enhancement, rather than a betrayal, of the self.[42] In general, because Foucault always sees resistance to confession as part of the economy of confession, he is unable to imagine lying—in terms of his own dramaturgy of power and knowledge—as an attempt to create and protect a counterdomain of knowledge, or as an attempt to refuse the legitimacy of institutional technologies of truth, or even as a repudiation of the political structures associated with "truth" production.

Sociological arguments that parallel Foucault's account of Victorian knowledge production often do make these kinds of claims for lying. The groundbreaking sociology of Georg Simmel, for instance, rests heavily on the perception that industrial nineteenth-century society came to depend in extraordinary ways on interpersonal trust—for reasons that conform strikingly to Foucault's thinking about technologies of knowledge. In Simmel's account, as in Foucault's, it is the explosion of information technology that compels nineteenth-century plain speaking, exacerbating an earlier premium on trust that Simmel, like many Marxists, sees as central to capitalist exchange.[43] "Our modern life," Simmel wrote, "is based to a much larger extent than is usually realized upon faith in the honesty of the other. Examples are our economy, which becomes more and more a credit economy, or our science, in which most scholars must use innumerable results of other scientists which they cannot examine. We base our gravest decisions on a complex system of conceptions,

---

[41] See Herbert L. Dreyfus and Paul Rabinow, *Michel Foucault: Beyond Structuralism and Hermeneutics* (Chicago: University of Chicago Press, 1982), pp. 51–78.

[42] This tendency has been thoroughly critiqued by Mark Cousins and Athar Hussain, *Michel Foucault* (New York: St. Martin's, 1984), pp. 210–15.

[43] Of the many Marxist commentaries on the rise of trust in relation to capitalism, see, for example, Christopher Hill, *Society and Puritanism in Pre-Revolutionary England* (London: Secker and Warburg, 1964), pp. 418–19.

most of which presuppose the confidence that we will not be betrayed."[44] For Simmel, this dependence rests ultimately on the indirectness of our access to information within the increasingly important information exchanges of a commercial and industrial society.

Alexander Welsh, who follows both Foucault and Simmel in his provocative study of blackmail in George Eliot, also stresses the importance of trust in advanced information cultures, but he points out that Simmel's account explains in addition why "secrecy" became simultaneously more important in Victorian culture. That is, in the light of the rise of nineteenth-century surveillance, which was an inevitable consequence of increased information and communication resources, Welsh claims that individuals necessarily took refuge to an increasing degree in various methods of secrecy.[45] These forms of concealment might very well be seen, in a Foucauldian sense, as a counteruse of knowledge. Simmel himself observed that in modern society, secrecy and deceit acquired crucial social roles as forms of distancing between individuals. He argued that lying might be seen as one element in a wide range of Victorian behaviors that concealed rather than revealed the self, in the interests of individuation or self-protection: nineteenth-century social relations "presuppose a certain ignorance and a measure of mutual concealment, even though this measure varies immensely, to be sure. The lie is merely a very crude and, ultimately, often a contradictory form in which this necessity shows itself. . . . The ethically negative value of the lie must not blind us to its sociologically quite positive significance in the formation of certain concrete relations."[46]

From this perspective, codes of honor themselves might be seen as distancing mechanisms, rather than simply as a capitulation to norms of confession. That is, to invoke one's honor could often be

---

[44] Georg Simmel, *The Sociology of Georg Simmel*, trans. and ed. Kurt H. Wolff (Glencoe, Ill.: Free Press, 1950), p. 313. W. J. Reader points out that the sheer scale of interdependence in industrial society makes conditions of trust imperative and that this increasing scale contributed to the rise of professional ethics (*Professional Men: The Rise of the Professional Classes in Nineteenth-Century England* [London: Weidenfeld and Nicolson, 1966], pp. 161–63).

[45] Alexander Welsh, *George Eliot and Blackmail* (Cambridge: Harvard University Press, 1985), pp. 55–56.

[46] Simmel, *Sociology*, pp. 315–16.

seen in Victorian culture as a prohibition against close questioning, a way of warding off trespassing against the self.[47] Fictional characters like Dickens's John Harmon and David Copperfield often invoke their gentlemanly honor as a way to forestall truth-telling. Claiming to be bound by one's honor, in these cases, could be seen as the most strategic of lies. To play on Foucault's famous formulation: why did the Victorians *say* so insistently that they repressed lying? In Simmel's view, the very social forces that created an increased interdependency in industrial society compelled unusual means of resisting the encroachment of others: "Social conditions of strong personal differentiation permit and require secrecy in a high degree; and, conversely, the secret embodies and intensifies such differentiation."[48] Welsh points out, further, that increased social mobility in the nineteenth century added to this dilemma by compelling individuals to conceal information about their pasts. He notes that Dickens, Thackeray, and Bulwer all commented that one of the more remarkable sensations of urban life was an awareness of being surrounded by others' secrets, while also being continually watched oneself by strange eyes.[49] The strategies of concealment compelled by such social pressures cannot entirely be reduced to Foucauldian notions of disciplinary self-production, nor should they blind us to the real creativity that Victorian writers celebrated in those who used discretion to defeat the prying of official eyes. It is also important to ask questions about the gendering of ethics in this context—something that neither Foucault nor Simmel does—since the opposition of public trust and private secrecy corresponds closely to the gendering of public and private spheres so characteristic of Victorian culture.[50]

Analyses of surveillance, information gathering, and technologies of confession are not the only discussions of structural social change which suggest, implicitly, the latent power of nineteenth-century lying. A similar point might be made about arguments that public

[47] Ibid., p. 321.
[48] Ibid., pp. 334–35.
[49] Welsh, *George Eliot and Blackmail*, pp. 72, 75.
[50] Of the many discussions of the gendering of public and private spheres in Victorian culture, perhaps the most extensive is Leonore Davidoff and Catherine Hall, *Family Fortunes: Men and Women of the English Middle Class, 1780–1850* (Chicago: University of Chicago Press, 1987).

honesty became more critical within an increasingly democratic society. John Stuart Mill was not alone in claiming that in a representative government, the primary requirement of politicians is moral accountability.[51] Calls for strict standards of candor from politicians were sounded regularly in Victorian culture, on a spectrum ranging from Herbert Spencer to George Eliot's Felix Holt. Welsh points out that in democracies, generally, "elected representatives are more often brought down for lying than for wrong policies."[52] This post-Enlightenment anxiety about democracy continues to fuel contemporary exhortations to public honesty, like Sissela Bok's philosophical plea for public candor.[53] Bok continues the tradition of democratic ethics by arguing that lies in public life become more devastating in a democratic society, since trust is the basis of democratic process. But, as F. G. Bailey points out in a provocative countertreatise, Bok and other liberal humanists do not seem to see the inevitable correlation—that precisely because of their enhanced power, lies are ineradicable from a democratic public sphere.[54] As Alasdair MacIntyre puts it, lying is only really possible in societies where people expect the truth to be told.[55] The underside of Victorian moral standards for political life, and for public life generally, was an increased sense of the power of the lie to dominate public affairs. Trollope's *The Way We Live Now* is a cynical (but nevertheless fascinated) estimation of the extent of Victorian political prevarication, fully matched in its open-eyed wonder by *Little Dorrit* and *Pendennis*. In a dramatic turnaround at the end of his life, Lecky blasted the degradation of English candor in public life—without recognizing the implications for his own smug theories about the correlation between industrial society and honesty.[56]

---

[51] See Mill, "Rationale of Representation," in *Collected Works*, 18:31–32. Charles Taylor comments on the relationship between democratic revolution and the replacement of feudal "honor" by ideals of authenticity in both public and private life (*The Ethics of Authenticity* [Cambridge: Harvard University Press, 1992], pp. 46–47).

[52] Welsh, *George Eliot and Blackmail*, p. 78.

[53] Sissela Bok, *Lying: Moral Choice in Public and Private Life* (New York: Pantheon, 1978).

[54] F. G. Bailey, *The Prevalence of Deceit* (Ithaca: Cornell University Press, 1991).

[55] Alasdair C. MacIntyre, *A Short History of Ethics* (New York: Macmillan, 1966), p. 77.

[56] W. E. H. Lecky, *The Map of Life: Conduct and Character* (London: Longmans, Green, 1899), pp. 83–87.

Arguments about structural social change have only been one general approach—and a comparatively recent one, at that—to Victorian honesty. According to a more long-standing set of explanations, an emphasis on honesty played a crucial role in the formation of postromantic subjectivity. This second approach has been taken by writers as diverse as Lionel Trilling, Erving Goffman, and Richard Sennett.[57] One of the more astute recent reformulators of this kind of thinking—though he would no doubt recoil at the company—is Terry Eagleton. In *The Ideology of the Aesthetic*, Eagleton argues that in the post-Kantian world, ethics has become conflated with aesthetics as an instrument of individual self-fashioning. I concentrate on Eagleton here because his account is, in my view, the most synthetic of these explanations precisely because it brings both politics and philosophy to bear on questions of subjectivity.

In Eagleton's account, traditional notions that ethics could be derived either from reason or from law were replaced after the Enlightenment by the concept of ethics as an irreducible and autotelic domain. This is a widely shared view, but Eagleton extends it by critiquing the relationship between this ethical domain and romantic aesthetics. According to Eagleton, romantic aesthetic philosophy sought to define autonomous objects valued for their own intrinsic sakes, not for their secondary effects and consequences. It also conceived aesthetic objects as structured by their own noncognitive, material "nature."[58] As Eagleton sees it, the invention of these aesthetic criteria in the eighteenth century was as much a political development as an epistemological one, for it fostered certain analogies between aesthetics and subjectivity, since the work of art had come to be thought of "as a kind of *subject*": "It is this notion of

---

[57] Trilling's *Sincerity and Authenticity* usefully traces parallels between the rise of romantic sensibility and sincerity. Erving Goffman, for all his psychological pragmatism, stresses that self-performing always involves some kind of capitulation to social control. Goffman's classic work is *The Presentation of Self in Everyday Life* (Garden City, N.Y.: Doubleday, 1959). Richard Sennett argues that postromantic models of subjectivity sacrifice the freedom of public role-playing for what he sees as the more dubious indulgences of intimacy (*The Fall of Public Man: On the Social Psychology of Capitalism* [New York: Random House, 1978]).

[58] Eagleton, *Ideology of the Aesthetic*, pp. 9–10, 13–14. My summary of Eagleton is primarily drawn from pp. 1–101.

autonomy or self-referentiality which the new discourse of aesthetics is centrally concerned to elaborate . . . [and] the idea of autonomy—of a mode of being which is entirely self-regulating and self-determining—provides the middle class with just the ideological model of subjectivity it requires for its material operations."[59] In the political struggles within which this analogy was hammered out, one price of conceiving subjectivity independently of social reason was the necessity of seeing it as internally rather than externally disciplined—in other words, the free individual becomes a law unto herself or himself. Bourgeois political rhetoric could negotiate its opposition to absolutism in no other way than by transforming "consent to the law" into a self-policing "consent to one's own inward being."[60] But such an exchange could have compensations in terms of personal liberty, Eagleton argues, if the controlling realm of morals was also granted the ungrounded, unpredictable "naturalness" of aesthetic self-realization. If ethical perfection could be conceived as the goal of individual self-development and if ethics were conceived as an organic aesthetic domain, then the righteous self, too, might be conceived in aestheticized terms as a self-governing, sovereign, but responsible entity. Ethical standards, in this framework, become a richly textured, limitless je ne sais quoi—not matters of dogmatic constraint, but matters of potentially expansive, fluid capacities for tact or know-how, whose very self-reflexivity defines the autonomous nature of the moral subject. In such an ideological system, Eagleton consistently implies, honesty is of paramount ethical importance, since the foundation of an aestheticized morality is its self-reflexive character.[61] What guarantees the truth of the ethical actor is, quite simply, truth to inner nature, properly apprehended. Only in this way can autonomy—which means conceiving oneself, in effect, as an artwork—be turned into a virtue.

Though Eagleton is more interested in the evolution of romantic and postromantic philosophy, his insights are confirmed by an influential strain of Victorian moral philosophy, typified by the

[59] Ibid., p. 9.
[60] Ibid., p. 19.
[61] Ibid., esp. pp. 20–24. Following MacIntyre in particular, Eagleton argues that such a formalized ethics represents the loss of a role-based morality modeled on class-bound conceptions of ethical behavior. See p. 80.

work of Lecky, whose opposition to utilitarianism revolved precisely around an intuitionist account of ethical principles. Invoking an eighteenth-century intuitionist tradition that included Joseph Butler, Richard Price, Thomas Reid, Samuel Clarke, and Francis Hutcheson, Lecky built an elaborately introspective moral system around the notion that there is an unselfish, disinterested moral center within human nature, even though this ethical sensibility can be realized only imperfectly over time through a series of "moral types."[62] As a Victorian, Lecky believed that his own culture honored truth-telling as the basis of its moral type: in industrial society, "veracity becomes the first virtue in the moral type, and no character is regarded with any kind of approbation in which it is wanting. It is made more than any other the test distinguishing a good from a bad man."[63] But Lecky was unwilling to close off the possibilities for future moral development in other directions, since "the superiority of the moral part of our nature, though unquestionable, is indefinite not infinite, and the prevailing stand is not at all times the same. The moralist can only lay down general principles. Individual feeling or the general sentiment of society must draw the application."[64] One of the central projects of nineteenth-century moralists was to prove that the moral sense was innate and emotional, rather than simply rational, and Lecky's system is paralleled by the more rigorous work of other intuitionists, such as Henry Sidgwick and James Martineau.[65] Among these Victorian intuitionists, ethics was conceived as an unformalizable domain of moral processes, resistant both to dogmatic codification and to historical closure.

Though the case would hardly have been made by Victorian intuitionists, claims for subjective freedom based on aesthetic conceptions of ethical truth necessarily imply a prominent place for dishonesty. If an aestheticized morality became a fundamental com-

---

[62] Lecky, *History of European Morals*, 1:163–68.

[63] Ibid., 1:144.

[64] Ibid., 1:120.

[65] For a good Victorian history of these positions, see Henry Sidgwick, *Outlines of the History of Ethics for English Readers* (1886; New York: St. Martin's, 1967); James Martineau, *Types of Ethical Theory* (Oxford: Clarendon Press, 1886); or Sidgwick's influential formulation of his own position, *The Methods of Ethics* (London: Macmillan, 1901).

ponent of the subject in postromantic culture, then a familiarity with deceit, conventionally understood, must have become indispensable to autonomous selfhood as well, for several different reasons. If individual freedom involves turning oneself into an intuitively guided moral sophisticate rather than observing moral rules, then subjective standards of truth and falsity necessarily come into conflict with social norms of truth and falsity. Aestheticized morality is inherently difficult to universalize—a lesson that might be seen as one of the legacies of nineteenth-century philosophy. Ethical iconoclasm, instead, would seem to be part of the baggage of subjective autonomy. Eagleton claims that just such an aestheticized—and, therefore, self-consciously transgressive—morality lies at the heart of compulsive postmodern resistance to mainstream values. The inherently transgressive qualities of that resistance help explain the difficulties that it encounters in trying to formulate its own principles positively.[66] Postromantic ethics leads inevitably to the proud consciousness of having broken the rules that bind others to convention, and, as such, it actively resists aligning itself with official morality.

Opposition to conventional morals is not the only destabilizing effect of an aestheticized morality. As Eagleton acknowledges, one of the crucial features of the postromantic aesthetic is that it perpetually undoes itself. That is, the aesthetic has become, by definition, a realm of experience that must never be completely known. To resist reason and law, the aesthetic must always incorporate into itself that which would release it from rational paradigms of understanding. This means that an aestheticized ethics must always verge toward unintelligibility in its willingness to undermine clear distinctions between good and evil. Welsh has concretely demonstrated this ethical self-resistance in one phase of Victorian culture, showing how a special kind of threat to tell the truth— blackmail—became, paradoxically, the centerpiece of Victorian conceptions of criminal injury. Welsh notes that in Victorian blackmail plots—like those in *Bleak House* and *Middlemarch*— reconcealing the truth becomes the paradoxical goal of moral

---

[66] Eagleton, *Ideology of the Aesthetic*, pp. 366–417. Eagleton also traces the complex struggles undergone by various philosophical traditions to universalize concepts of the aesthetic.

action.[67] Silencing the truth—even if that means covering it with discrete evasions—often becomes the route of moral refinement for Dickens's and Eliot's protagonists in these novels. But such paradoxes are inevitable in a morality that appeals to organic sentiment in order to circumvent or undo dogma. From a postromantic perspective, if ethics defines itself in opposition to reason and to law, then it necessarily has to explore those areas of experience that reason and law designate as transgressive, in order to differentiate itself from convention, as the sign of a more organically ethical "nature." It is no doubt partly for this reason that Victorian moralists were so ambivalent about the novel's ethical impact.[68]

Recent studies of Victorian secrecy or self-suppression, including my own work on the generative emotional values of Victorian repression, uncover the moral ambiguities of postromantic subjectivity in another way, by stressing the psychologically expansive possibilities of self-contradiction.[69] That is to say, depth models of subjectivity in Victorian culture can be seen to depend as much on deviation and evasion as on sincerity. The psychoanalytic model itself, for example, embedded as it is in Victorian views of the psyche, presupposes a "lying function" as the site of intersection between the unconscious and the conscious mind. Psychoanalytic sleuthing, in other words, presumes that the conscious mind has been deceived about its unconscious contents by such duplicitous forces as Freud's dream-censor. Along with other forms of evasion and displacement, lying can be seen as a sign of either primal or individualistic energies in a surface/depth psychic model that privileges depth over surface. As a form of "passionate repression," the

---

[67] Welsh, George Eliot and Blackmail, esp. pp. 13–15.

[68] The definitive work on this ambivalence is likely to be Patrick Brantlinger's book-in-progress, Culture as Anarchy.

[69] John Kucich, Repression in Victorian Fiction: Charlotte Brontë, George Eliot, and Charles Dickens (Berkeley: University of California Press, 1987). I am thinking of diverse works that explore the construction of Victorian subjectivity through various kinds of internal contradiction, for example, Audrey Jaffe, Vanishing Points: Dickens, Narrative, and the Subject of Omniscience (Berkeley: University of California Press, 1991); Laurie Langbauer, Women and Romance: The Consolations of Gender in the English Novel (Ithaca: Cornell University Press, 1990); Ronald Thomas, Dreams of Authority: Freud and the Fictions of the Unconscious (Ithaca: Cornell University Press, 1990); and Joseph Litvak, Caught in the Act: Theatricality in the Nineteenth-Century English Novel (Berkeley: University of California Press, 1992).

lie can be a potent sign of psychic depth. Such is the effect on our perception of Charlotte Brontë's narrator in *Villette*, to cite one famous example, when she finally admits having concealed from the reader the identity of Dr. John Bretton, who turns out to have been the object of her jealous childhood desire. As Eve Sedgwick has shown, one of the fundamental representational strategies of romantic art is the construction of psychic depth by means of veiling.[70]

Much of Victorian fiction, from this point of view, revolves around the kinds of multidimensional subjectivity that by definition cannot be presented directly, truthfully. Most antagonism to strict codes of sincerity—both Victorian and our own—originates in a defense of the psychological power of the mask. A willingness to defend the masked self conditions critical thinking about the constraints of nineteenth-century sincerity from Matthew Arnold, through Nietzsche, to contemporary writers such as Richard Sennett and Nina Auerbach, and it has recently made great inroads in our sense of the staged misrepresentations of the self in Victorian literature.[71] The Victorians themselves were well aware of the presence and even the desirability of theatricality in self-presentation, and characteristic Victorian debates about the tension between self-consciousness and unself-consciousness (much of the thought of Carlyle might stand as a meditation on this tension), or about the proper adjustment of forthrightness and reserve, verge on an uncomfortable recognition of the relationship between the staged self and deceit. In particular, this discomfort frequently involved a recognition of the disturbing ways in which Victorian manliness seemed compromised by tendencies toward reserve. Such tensions become overt in late-century writing, particularly in Pater's labyrinthine investigations of the relationship between earnestness and theatricality.[72]

I do not intend to add to these defenses of theatricality here,

[70] Eve Kosofsky Sedgwick, "The Character in the Veil: Imagery of the Surface in the Gothic Novel," *PMLA* 96 (1981), 255–70.

[71] See, for example, Shaw, *Victorians and Mystery*, esp. his concluding remarks, pp. 347–48.

[72] James Eli Adams's work-in-progress on Victorian masculinity explores these tensions in provocative ways. See also Carol Christ's influential essay on the instabilities of Victorian manliness, "Victorian Masculinity and the Angel in the House," in *A Widening Sphere: Changing Roles of Victorian Women*, ed. Martha Vicinus (Bloomington: Indiana University Press, 1977), pp. 146–62.

mostly because such defenses are often simply in pursuit of a higher standard of truth-telling—personal, psychological, metaphysical— rather than the counterstudy of deceit itself. There was clearly a hidden moral intent, for example, in Oscar Wilde's flaunted disdain for Victorian sincerity: "Man is least himself when he talks in his own person. Give him a mask, and he will tell you the truth."[73] But from the point of view of the present study, what these considerations demonstrate is that the same philosophical and psychological models that strained the relationship between knowledge and good faith also created the conditions by which dishonesty acquired new potentials, whether for good or ill, in the articulation of Victorian selfhood. Insofar as psychological depth is also a matter of personal power, these changes are related to the way Victorians negotiated power between subjectivities, or between the individual and the state. One of the focal points of this book is an examination of exactly how lying was imagined as a necessary means of private and public empowerment—both as an inwardly cherished sign of self-development and as a social sign of sophistication and privilege.

There is a much older account of the origins of Victorian honesty than either of these first two patterns of explanation, one that defines Victorian morality as the product of increasingly hegemonic middle-class puritanism. This third form of explanation encompasses several different sociological observations: the remarkable diffusion of evangelical morality in Victorian culture; the adversarial role of strict middle-class concepts of virtue, whose antiaristocratic bias came increasingly to dominate Victorian culture; and the growth of professional ethics, which depended on claims about the disinterest and, therefore, the moral integrity undergirding professional authority.[74] Cultural historians also point to the growing replacement of faith during the period with sincerity, as the next-best refuge of

[73] Oscar Wilde, "The Critic as Artist: A Dialogue, Part 2," in *The Writings of Oscar Wilde*, p. 282.

[74] On the first point, see Newsome, *Godliness and Good Learning*, pp. 6–8; on the last two points, see Perkin, *Origins of Modern English Society*, pp. 221–30, 273–90. An excellent account of the victory of middle-class morality in Victorian culture is Mark Girouard, *Life in the English Country House: A Social and Architectural History* (New Haven: Yale University Press, 1978), esp. pp. 268–72, which uses architectural evidence to demonstrate the incorporation of middle-class values into upper-class life.

secularized religious thought.[75] All of these observations document the rise of a deliberately, self-consciously monolithic middle-class ethics, which depends on the presentation of a militantly unified ethical front to define class identity.

There is no question that these various developments helped centralize middle-class honesty as an article of official morality. What I have been describing as Victorian truth-telling has indisputable middle-class roots, as I show more fully in Chapter 1. Nevertheless, the positive countercharge that these kinds of official moralities always generate in the realm of desire was not insignificant in the Victorian middle class. Mikhail Bakhtin and other writers who have theorized inversions of official and unofficial cultures have demonstrated that in any society "what is socially marginal may be symbolically central."[76] In *Rabelais and His World*, Bakhtin claims that, since the Renaissance, when hierarchical views of the cosmos were toppled, Western culture has tended to identify the most vital and dynamic of human drives with "the underworld" rather than with the heavens. Bakhtin argues that there has been a corresponding linkage of unofficial cultures with life forces thought to be lacking in the dominant culture.[77] Peter Stallybrass and Allon

---

[75] This is the primary claim of Houghton, *The Victorian Frame of Mind*, pp. 218–62; the point is also made by Auerbach, *Private Theatricals*, p. 3; and by Trilling, *Sincerity and Authenticity*, p. 117.

[76] Barbara Babcock, ed., *The Reversible World: Symbolic Inversion in Art and Society* (Ithaca: Cornell University Press, 1978), p. 32. Though Babcock does not explicitly invoke Bakhtin, her formulation is quoted by Peter Stallybrass and Allon White as an example of Bakhtinian logic (*The Politics and Poetics of Transgression* [Ithaca: Cornell University Press, 1986], p. 20).

[77] Mikhail Bakhtin, *Rabelais and His World*, trans. Hélène Iswolsky (Bloomington: Indiana University Press, 1984), pp. 368–69. See also pp. 412–14. Unlike many of his followers, Bakhtin attempted to historicize this shift, rather than simply to idealize underworld cultures as timelessly utopian. See especially his comments on the historicity of carnival laughter (pp. 134–35), and his extended history of laughter (pp. 102–36). Gary Saul Morson and Caryl Emerson argue that Marxist critics have misinterpreted Bakhtin's sense of "unofficial cultural forces" by seeing in them a certain ideological unity or a certain immutable social location (*Mikhail Bakhtin: Creation of a Prosaics* [Stanford: Stanford University Press, 1990], p. 30). Nevertheless, Bakhtin often does idealize these unofficial forces—especially in the Rabelais book—in ways that seem to essentialize cultural "subversion." An excellent critique of the formalist and intentionalist tendencies in Bakhtin is Ken Hirschkup, "Introduction: Bakhtin and Cultural Theory," in *Bakhtin and Cultural Theory*, ed. Ken Hirschkup and David Shepherd (Manchester: University of Manchester Press, 1989), esp. pp. 6–15.

White, more comprehensively than any other theorists, have demonstrated the close correlation between stigmatized models of behavior and a culture's thinking about primary physical and psychological representations of vitality.[78] In their view, all societies represent their most central libidinal desires from the repertoire of images they associate with socially excluded behaviors. The novel, given its traditional interest in sexual relations, seems to be especially sensitive to the way desire in Victorian culture was fundamentally affiliated with outcast behavior, including dishonesty.

It is crucial, in this Bakhtinian context, to see that what is at stake in the linkage of cultural prohibitions with desire is not some kind of return of the repressed. What is at stake is an arbitrary overcoding of one forbidden aspect of experience with psychic value—not a rediscovery of its real, repressed value. In this sense, there was a perfectly arbitrary overinvestment of lying with libidinal force in Victorian writing, an equation of lying with desire that is out of all proportion to any normative model of psychic functioning. One of the general claims of this book is that, precisely because of the centrality of honesty in "official" Victorian culture, writers were incapable of thinking about desire apart from dishonesty. This symbolic conjunction had tremendous repercussions on Victorian thinking about the prominence and function of deceit in sexual relations and in other forms of extreme emotional extension. In fact, the strongest evidence of the Victorian linkage between desire and dishonesty is the regularity of lovers' deceptions in the works of novelists as puritanical about both honesty and sex as Anthony Trollope and Elizabeth Gaskell.

Bakhtin's model of symbolic alignments between prohibition and desire can also reinforce my earlier claims about dishonesty's ability to structure relationships of social power. If Victorian honesty was meant to create a hegemonic norm for ethical subjects, then attention to the role of dishonesty can show how class and gender distinctions were remapped, as challenges to official social order, through transgressive conceptions of moral difference.[79] The argu-

---

[78] See Stallybrass and White, *The Politics and Poetics of Transgression*, esp. pp. 1–26.

[79] Joseph Litvak has argued, for example, that Oscar Wilde promoted the positive "classiness" of misrepresentation in a way that invoked fairly widespread late-Victorian expectations about social sophistication and deceit ("Class Acts: Theatri-

ment has, in fact, been made—by Pierre Bourdieu among others—that an anti-instrumental, "aesthetic" ethics is liable to become a status instrument simply because it is ungrounded, defining matters of moral "taste" rather than prescribing timeless codes of conduct.[80] In tracing the disruption of class and gender lines, as they are articulated by ethical oppositions, I have closely followed Bakhtin's ideas about symbolic reversal: the process of inversion by which the negative term in a symbolic opposition is invested with positive cultural value.[81] While I have profited as well from Bakhtin's work on symbolic displacement—the consequences for one symbolic domain of contradictions or transgressions in another—the conception of competitive power relations that I derive from Victorian ethical discourse is designed to avoid Bakhtin's politically simplistic tendencies toward either liberal pluralism or rigid oppressor/oppressed dichotomies.[82]

In all three areas of analysis I have sketched out—social structures, subjectivist psychology, and libidinal economies—dissimulation acquires enormous socio-symbolic power in Victorian culture through a series of inevitable structural reversals. Thanks to the conjunction of these several different kinds of reversal, Victorian lying took on an added symbolic potency as the general embodiment of forces that

---

cality, Vulgarity, and Aestheticism in *The Picture of Dorian Gray*," a talk delivered at the MLA convention in Washington, D.C., 28 December 1989).

[80] The most thorough analysis of this dynamic is Pierre Bourdieu, *Distinction: A Social Critique of the Judgement of Taste*, trans. Richard Nice (Cambridge: Harvard University Press, 1984). See also MacIntyre, *A Short History of Ethics*, p. 92.

[81] Bakhtin's most thorough—and least utopian—discussions of symbolic inversion are his analysis of Rabelais's reversal of medieval body/soul oppositions in "Forms of Time and of the Chronotope in the Novel," in *The Dialogic Imagination: Four Essays*, trans. Caryl Emerson and Michael Holquist (Austin: University of Texas Press, 1981), esp. pp. 169–70; and the sections on "hybrid construction" in his "Discourse in the Novel," in *The Dialogic Imagination*, esp. pp. 304–5.

[82] Bakhtin's most rigorous account of symbolic displacement is in "Discourse in the Novel," esp. pp. 358–66. See also the summary of these processes by Morson and Emerson, *Mikhail Bakhtin*, esp. pp. 38–62; or the account of Tzvetan Todorov, *Mikhail Bakhtin: The Dialogical Principle*, trans. Wlad Godzich (Minneapolis: University of Minnesota Press, 1984), pp. 17–28. By disavowing the liberal pluralist tendencies and the utopian victimology of Bakhtin's analysis, I wish to distance myself, specifically, from his reluctance to analyze issues of domination and control in the dialogic process, his essentializing of the grotesque body, and his aesthetic idealization of certain formal ideals (i.e., heteroglossia, polyphony, carnivalization, and the various features he identified monolithically with the novel as a genre).

could be linked, variously, to converging notions of social struggle, individual self-assertion, and instinctual gratification. In Victorian novels, lying often carries the force of individualist creativity placed in the service of class ideals, which are represented as the natural object of fundamental human passions. Any cultural discourse that could manage to harness this generalized vitality represented by the lie and to integrate it with official standards of moral uprightness—that is, any discourse of symbolic transgression—thus held out the potential for very broad socio-symbolic transformations. Among other things, such transgressive hybridity could represent a kind of wide-ranging, exceptional moral sophistication that, mapped onto social subgroups, distinguished progressive—even antibourgeois—elements of middle-class culture from more passive or reactive elements. It could also provide the symbolic volatility necessary to rearrange social and sexual boundaries upheld by honesty/dishonesty distinctions. These interrelated powers of Victorian lying, as they were harnessed by particular segments of middle-class society, are the central subject of my readings of Victorian novels.

My outline of the symbolic volatility of Victorian truth-telling suggests that the relationship between deceit and the distribution of social power must be understood in two basic, but reversible, ways. First, using codes of truth-telling as a means of simple exclusion, Victorian writers regularly characterized some social groups as outside the pale of honesty. Women, non-English races, and the working class were all obvious targets for scapegoating in terms of their dishonesty, as literary critics have long understood—though these exclusions could sometimes function in very subtle ways. Second, and more important to my own work, the distinctions could be reversed: that is, a certain convergence of Victorian social forces established the conditions for defining honesty as a sign of social victimization, psychological simplicity, or complicity with emotionally repressive official values. The reversal of truth-telling norms thus uses deceit to define "insider" identity rather than exclusionary differences. As I have suggested, the multiple powers that might be invoked by deceit—social resistance, subjective power, libidinal force—could also be unified as the sign of collective, and not just individual, empowerment. A central theme of my project is that various segments of the middle class sought to distinguish themselves precisely in this way, through an appeal to generalized forms of prestige associated with the lie. One hallmark of Victorian fiction is its exploration of the conditions in which finessing the truth could be regarded as a sign of collective social skill and authority. In fact, from one point of view, fiction could be seen as a kind of conduct literature defining exactly how one might achieve an aura of shared sophistication through deceit. Imitating privileged groups that could negotiate the gray areas between clear-cut truth and falsehood, sometimes even inverting them, was fundamental to the pursuit of cultural power. For professionals, social initiates, aesthetes, and others, dexterity with the truth became a sign of social privilege *within* the ranks of the middle class—a form of privilege that depended heavily on transient, tactful reversals of the honesty/ dishonesty axis, not on its complete overthrow.

The honesty/dishonesty axis was of such fundamental importance to Victorian thinking about social relations that Victorian writers were able to seize on the many distinct symbolic potentials of both honesty and dishonesty—sometimes as reversible parts of the same symbolic system—in order to think out the ways social relations might be transformed. These transformations were configured in contested, often contradictory, ways, and they do not lend them- selves to a single master narrative. I resist tendencies to define the more sensational instances of lying in Victorian fiction as either inherently subversive or inherently disciplinary, or as inherently both subversive and disciplinary at the same time. I am not interested in formalizing a model of dishonesty's relationship to authority. Rather, I am interested in evaluating the way the symbolic dynamics of honesty and dishonesty are embedded in complex negotiations of social power. To this end, I hope never to lose sight of the motivated nature of any appropriation of transgressive lying, which is some- times the case with the new historicist "thick description" from which I have, nevertheless, clearly benefited.

To help focus the competitive, historically situated nature of Victorian exploitations of the power of the lie, I have paired my readings of individual writers. In these pairings, I seek to uncover divergent social or sexual agendas that nevertheless make use of very similar symbolic strategies. I begin with a section on the phenomenon of middle-class cultural boundaries and the significance of locating oneself, as a writer, either "inside" or "outside" them. This section is centered on Anthony Trollope and Wilkie Collins, two figures who represent extreme poles of mid-Victorian writing—the one notoriously devoted to middle-class respectability, the other to protobohemian deviance. I attempt to show how very similar attempts to incorporate dishonesty into the realm of morally acceptable behavior led to two competing versions of middle-class cultural authority in Trollope and Collins. The differences revolve around a common semiotics of antibourgeois sophistication that depends on the boundary-crossing "exceptionality" of licensed lying, which Trollope claimed for the professional upper-middle class and Collins claimed for an emerging class of cultural intellectuals. What distinguishes Trollope and Collins in moral terms is not, finally, their flaunted positions either "inside" or "outside" bourgeois ethics, but, rather, the specific social location they claim for a logic of transgressive moral authority that they both actually shared.

In my second pairing of chapters, I investigate genderings of the honesty/dishonesty axis and the function of these genderings in a number of different contexts, including that of class. More particularly, I am interested in how two mid-century women writers conceived inversions of sexual roles as challenges to a conventionally gendered ethical axis. Both Elizabeth Gaskell and Ellen Wood invert a traditional moral axis of gender, and explore what happens when men begin to lie and when women tell the truth. Despite the similarities of their moral and sexual inversions, however, Gaskell and Wood made entirely different ideological uses of such inversions. Gaskell affirmed a liberal cross-fertilization of gender roles that might moderate sexual conflict without disrupting middle-class sexual norms. She hoped to achieve that result by appropriating for middle-class women the discourse of transgressive exceptionality so prominent in writers like Trollope and Collins, thus linking female empowerment to the wider project of middle-class elitism. Wood's inversions, by contrast, critique and reject the discourse of transgressive exceptionality. Wood attributes the symbolic logic of transgression entirely to changes in middle-class social identity at mid-century, which she sees as a threat to traditional forms of feminine moral authority. Even so, Wood was unable completely to resist the power of this logic. While bemoaning the drawbacks for women of ideals of transgressive sophistication, she nevertheless attempts to rewrite transgressive configurations of gender roles in ways more favorable to women. Both writers attempt to understand the position of women in relation to models of middle-class sophistication, though from perspectives that cause them either to embrace or to reject the dynamics of transgression and the cultural hierarchies of sophistication it defines.

Finally, with Thomas Hardy and Sarah Grand, I study the shift from Victorian ethics to more modernist conceptions of virtue and vice, in which questions about honesty are actively invalidated as a ground for moral distinctions. The 1880s and 1890s were the source of a number of self-consciously anti-Victorian intellectual postures that later became incorporated into modernism, and one crucial area of resistance to Victorian values was a rejection of sincerity. Although, in Hardy's case, that rejection is exploited partly in order to reformulate Victorian norms of gender in modernist terms, Grand shows how the deformation of Victorian ethics stranded late-century feminism by depriving it of an ethical foundation for new, public female roles. The erosion of Victorian discourses of truth-telling, along with the power of transgressive lying it made possible, becomes for Hardy an opportunity to develop a protomodernist aesthetics on the ruins of Victorian honesty. But for Grand it becomes a source of confusion, both activist and aesthetic, that prevents her from adapting Victorian truth-telling dynamics for feminism. In both the second and third parts of the book, then, my analysis reveals that transgressive power was much more difficult for women writers to appropriate. In the last part, I am concerned as well with the waning of transgressive sophistication as a form of cultural power available through deceit, a waning that results from the erosion of the Victorian norms for truth-telling upon which it depended.

While my decision to focus each chapter on a single novelist may keep me from a comprehensive account of the ideological permutations of Victorian transgression, I hope it has also freed me from the kinds of superficiality or irresolution that plague more wide-ranging formats. I have omitted many possible discussions—of obvious texts, such as *The Picture of Dorian Gray* and *Villette*, and of nonfictional discourses, such as Mill's analysis of ethics in *On Liberty*, Charles Kingsley's attack on John Henry Newman for lying, and Newman's elaborate defense. My "micronarratives" of Victorian thinking about honesty and dishonesty are meant to focus a number of specific conclusions, rather than to trail off in a sentimental affirmation of discursive pluralism and heterogeneity. One conclusion is—to be quite banal—that Victorian ethics is a much more intertextual domain than it is usually taken to be. Notions of Victorian earnestness, in particular, are desperately in need of revisionary study, and such study ought to resist naive assumptions that Victorian culture ascribed to some kind of monological or totalizing conception of "truth," in favor of a more structurally interdependent understanding of ethical difference. This kind of theoretical framework for studying moral disorder is essential to my chief cultural claim: that the transgression of distinctions between honesty and dishonesty was pivotal in struggles for middle-class cultural authority. The power of the lie is at the center, not on the margins, of middle-class writers' notions about their own social and sexual identity, and about the competitive potentials for moral leadership they sought to identify with particular middle-class factions.

Implicitly, my six critical narratives are meant to demonstrate a more general point: that thinking about ethics is always a way of thinking about social relationships. While the idea may seem obvious these days, reiteration is important, if only because this equation is often used to efface the complexities of ethical discourse. As a number of writers have also pointed out, our postmodern age has characteristically separated ethics from epistemology and focused attention on the latter. Thus, in most critical work on issues of "truth" in Victorian fiction, the metaphysics of truth has received all the attention, and the ethical axis has been taken for granted.[83] The result has been an oversimplified sense of how ethics is related to the kinds of political or ideological concerns that have preoccupied contemporary criticism. Hence, the bewilderment or indifference I have often encountered when telling colleagues that I am writing

---

[83] An exemplary exception, from which I have greatly benefited, is Julie Ellison, *Delicate Subjects: Romanticism, Gender, and the Ethics of Understanding* (Ithaca: Cornell University Press, 1990).

about Victorian ethics. What could be more self-evident or more irrelevant to the dynamics of power and desire so important to contemporary criticism? I hope to show that critical analysis— whether of the psyche or of social conflict—ignores the symbolic complexities of ethical thinking at its cost, for what is lost is a sense of how notions of power depend on a society's complex, competitive, and profoundly reversible distinctions between good and evil. It is out of this dependence that Victorian fiction is structured obsessively around the very real power of lies.

PART I

THE BOUNDARIES OF BOURGEOIS CULTURE

CHAPTER ONE

Trollope and the
Antibourgeois Elite

A nthony Trollope was long ago enshrined as the supreme
literary embodiment of middle-class stodginess. He has been
called, variously, "the apotheosis of normality," the last
"unalienated" English novelist, and the Victorian writer most "at
ease" with mechanisms of power and wealth. Mario Praz scorned
him as the quintessential "bourgeois" novelist, finding him to be
"the most typical representative . . . of the Biedermeier spirit."
D. A. Miller has added his voice to this already swollen chorus,
claiming (somewhat superciliously) that Trollope is in cahoots with
the police—that is, that he is a purveyor of mainstream disciplinary
norms.[1] It may seem strange, then, to talk about transgression
in Trollope, except in a very special sense—the sense in which
transgression is a fundamental part of nineteenth-century middle-

[1] Bradford A. Booth, *Anthony Trollope: Aspects of His Life and Art* (London:
Edward Hulton, 1958), p. 5; Walter Allen, *The English Novel: A Short Critical
History* (New York: Dutton, 1955), p. 309; Raymond Williams, *The English Novel:
From Dickens to Lawrence* (London: Chatto and Windus, 1970), p. 84; Mario Praz,
The Hero in Eclipse in Victorian Fiction, trans. Angus Davidson (Oxford: Oxford
University Press, 1956), p. 265; D. A. Miller, "The Novel as Usual: Trollope's
Barchester Towers," in *Sex, Politics, and Science in the Nineteenth-Century Novel:
Selected Papers from the English Institute, 1983–1984*, ed. Ruth Bernard Yeazell
(Baltimore: Johns Hopkins University Press, 1986), pp. 1–38.

class culture itself. The central argument of this book is that middle-class cultural power revolved around an affirmative staging of desires or behavior that had also been defined as illicit—a dynamic of reversibility that is either ignored or trivialized by smug condemnations of Trollope's one-dimensionality. In Trollope's work, and in middle-class culture generally, there is an energetic antibourgeois principle, dedicated to the reappropriation of transgressive categories of experience, which is as closely related to the way cultural authority is formulated as are the strict bourgeois moral standards that transgression appears to violate.

It has been easy to overlook the role of transgression in middle-class culture, and to concede that culture's ascetic standards too readily, because of middle-class revulsion from the immoral license of both popular and aristocratic culture. Whenever cultural historians do encounter violations of moral standards by bourgeois writers, they are often quick to isolate them as rare, forward-thinking challenges to social order, if not to trivialize them as nonserious exceptions that only confirm the norm.[2] But in overemphasizing the role of moral norms, which do, obviously, play a special role in middle-class culture, critics often overlook the extent to which that culture has needed to sanction images of desire that it has simultaneously marginalized or excluded. Such a mechanism is, in fact, crucial in Victorian middle-class culture, given its unique,

---

[2] In Trollope's case, I differ from Christopher Herbert, who claims that Trollope was "scandalous" in his approval of pleasure and gratification (*Trollope and Comic Pleasure* [Chicago: University of Chicago Press, 1987], pp. 21–31). I debate the usefulness of calling an emphasis on pleasure inherently "scandalous" or, for that matter, of defining the comic impulse as a synthesis of "rebellious" individual impulse and conservative social order, which is the liberal humanistic resolution that Herbert finds in Trollopian comedy. Herbert has largely revised the terms of this reading in *Culture and Anomie: Ethnographic Imagination in the Nineteenth Century* (Chicago: University of Chicago Press, 1991), where he argues that Trollope's power to "scandalize his contemporaries" (p. 286) derived instead from his ethnographic neutrality as an observer of social systems. It seems doubtful, however, that Trollope's neutrality was quite consistent or that his work was entirely "antagonistic to the taste of his public" (p. 284). James R. Kincaid rather perversely sees Trollope's novels as an attack on cultural norms, but only by generalizing that attack as the function of structural generic instabilities ("Anthony Trollope and the Unmannerly Novel," in *Reading and Writing Women's Lives: A Study of the Novel of Manners*, ed. Bege K. Bowers and Barbara Brothers [Ann Arbor, Mich.: UMI Research Press, 1990], pp. 87–104).

paradoxical needs to exalt at the same time both its morality and its desire. Social historians are increasingly coming to recognize that the middle class sought to base its cultural authority as much on its generalized vitality—its pure passions, its superior ardor, its unflagging energy—as on its moral circumspection.[3] The sanctity of its capacities for love, in particular—as expressed in the courtship plots of a novelist like Trollope—always includes both a fascination with the danger to social boundaries posed by romantic desire and a conviction that middle-class true love burns more brightly and more uncompromisingly than the eviscerated passions of other social groups. As Nancy Armstrong has argued, "The power of the middle classes had everything to do with that of middle-class love."[4] The tension between these two potentially conflicting sources of cultural authority—morality and desire—is often extreme in bourgeois culture. Although it is customary to assume that Victorian writers reconciled desire and morality in orderly ways, novelists such as Trollope needed, in fact, to avoid any complete domestication of passion and to maintain instead the transgressive associations of certain kinds of desire, if desire was to retain its force. As an expression of their general power, their difference from more moderate and economical energies, the images of desire employed by a novelist such as Trollope often draw on the same symbolic resources that his morality condemns.

These symbolic resources have a social dimension, for middle-class concepts of desire tend to draw on illicit behavior associated symbolically with excluded social groups. Having identified unruly desire with the classes it seeks to dominate, bourgeois culture is forced to develop its metaphors for desire precisely from those degraded social registers. Transgression thus involves the counte-

[3] Michel Foucault has made the most controversial statement of this principle in *The History of Sexuality, Vol. 1: An Introduction,* trans. Robert Hurley (New York: Random House, 1978). See esp. p. 125, where Foucault writes that "bourgeois hegemony" depended on "what the 'cultivation' of its own body could represent politically." But there are many less tendentious studies of bourgeois pride in its emotional and physical vigor. See, for example, Bruce Haley, *The Healthy Body and Victorian Culture* (Cambridge: Harvard University Press, 1978). The more traditional form of this argument focuses on middle-class justifications of individualist enterprise.
[4] Nancy Armstrong, *Desire and Domestic Fiction: A Political History of the Novel* (New York: Oxford University Press, 1987), p. 4.

nancing of desires that are structured at once along both moral and class lines. That is to say, the middle class is perpetually redis-covering the class-coded energies it has excluded from its behavioral norms and reformulating them in partially disguised ways, so that they might appear as its own fundamental images of vitality. Peter Stallybrass and Allon White have argued that such transformation, which sublimates the borrowing of images of desire that have been projected onto other social groups, is "perhaps the most characteris-tic manoeuvre of bourgeois identity."[5] Moreover, the recuperation of these transgressive energies is one of the hallmarks of middle-class sophistication, and writers such as Trollope used it as an instrument of intraclass warfare, defining a middle-class elite largely through its facility with the various powers, both public and private, that it might activate through transgression.

If we focus our attention on such high-profile issues as Victorian sexual conventions and political attitudes, it is easy to overlook the antibourgeois elements in novelists such as Trollope. But if we focus instead on his treatment of principles that typify a middle-class moral consensus, the simultaneous expulsion and recuperation of transgression in his novels can more easily be revealed. In relation to the commonly shared ethical ideal of truth-telling, even a relatively conservative Victorian writer such as Trollope projects illicit energies outside the middle class, stigmatizes them as the moral defects of the enemies of bourgeois culture, and then reappropriates these same antibourgeois energies for his more privileged protagonists. To locate this symbolic process in Trollope's work, and his consequent produc-tion of a sophisticated middle-class elite, I will be looking mostly, though not exclusively, at the earlier novels—chiefly those of the Barsetshire series, including *Framley Parsonage* and *Barchester Towers*, in detail. These works were written in secure and confident terms, with few traces of the embitterments, political and otherwise, that Trollope suffered in the 1870s. But before I turn to the novels, I will sketch out the specific class boundaries marked by Trollope's legend-ary concern with the truth and the way these boundaries define a particular position of authority within middle-class ranks.

[5] Peter Stallybrass and Allon White, *The Politics and Poetics of Transgression* (Ithaca: Cornell University Press, 1986), pp. 200–201.

Critics who want to define the fundamental moral norms in Trollope frequently cite his reverence for honesty.[6] While Trollope often convicts his readers or his characters of oversimplifying moral questions, he is hardly a moral relativist himself.[7] Quite the contrary, he claims that he "ever thought of myself as a preacher of sermons," and these "sermons" revolve relentlessly, almost obsessively, around honesty.[8] "Does it not come home to the mind of every man as a first principle in morals that harm cannot come of the truth?" he wrote in *The New Zealander*.[9] This basic creed is expressed everywhere in his writings. His concern with honesty reaches obsessive and diffuse proportions in the *Autobiography*, which begins with the extraordinary assertion that "nothing that I say shall be untrue" (1.1–2). But the novels are also didactically centered on promises broken or kept, on lies and their exposure, and on acts of constancy or betrayal. Even more so than most Victorian novels, they manage to reward truthful characters and to punish deceivers such as Adolphus Crosbie in *The Small House at Allington* and Alaric Tudor in *The Three Clerks*. An aversion to lying is also one of the fundamental qualities of a Trollopian gentleman.[10] In *The Way We*

[6] See, for example, Roger L. Slakey, "Trollope's Case for Moral Imperative," *Nineteenth-Century Fiction* 28 (1973), 305–20. R. D. McMaster writes that "the central virtue to which virtually all of his novels and estimates of character return is truth-telling" (*Trollope and the Law* [London: Macmillan, 1986], pp. 6–7).

[7] Ruth apRoberts first used this term to describe Trollope's ethical tendencies (*The Moral Trollope* [Athens: Ohio University Press, 1971]). As instances of the brief popularity of this line of thought, see also James Gindin, *Harvest of a Quiet Eye: The Novel of Compassion* (Bloomington: Indiana University Press, 1971); and Robert Polhemus, *The Changing World of Anthony Trollope* (Berkeley: University of California Press, 1968).

[8] Anthony Trollope, *An Autobiography*, World's Classics (Oxford: Oxford University Press, 1980), 8.146. Unless otherwise noted, further references to Trollope's works are to chapter and page numbers in this edition. In the case of *The Way We Live Now*, references in the form 1.11.111 are to volume, chapter, and page numbers in this edition (which preserves the original volume numbering of the novel within a single bound text).

[9] Anthony Trollope, *The New Zealander* (Oxford: Clarendon, 1972), 4.56. The book's epigraph is "It's gude to be honest and true."

[10] James R. Kincaid comments usefully on this idea in *The Novels of Anthony Trollope* (Oxford: Oxford University Press, 1977), p. 14. Shirley Robin Letwin includes honesty as one of the four cardinal virtues of Trollope's gentlemen

Live Now, Roger Carbury "is a gentleman all round and every inch," says Paul Montague, because "he never lies" (1.38.362). To a greater degree than most Victorian writers, Trollope even extended his rule of honesty—though in qualified ways—to women: in *Dr. Thorne*, Mary Thorne recognizes that "honour, honesty, and truth, outspoken truth, self-denying truth, and fealty from man to man, are worth more than maiden delicacy" (36.435).[11] Trollope claims that a reverence for honesty is the chief object that his novelistic "sermons" seek to cultivate in both public and private spheres: that is, he means to "teach politicians that they can do their business better by truth than by falsehood" and to "make young men and women believe that truth in love will make them happy" (*Autobiography*, 12.225).

Conversely, when Trollope apologizes for the moral deviations of characters like Lady Mason, the forger of *Orley Farm*, and Mr. and Mrs. Peacock, the well-meaning cohabitors of *Dr. Wortle's School*, he still convicts them unequivocally on their dishonesty. The often-noted excess of scorn heaped on Lizzie Eustace in *The Eustace Diamonds*—a degree of scorn unusual in a novelist noted for his tolerance—is targeted on her compulsive dishonesty: "She liked lies," the narrator says in his final, condemnatory judgement, "thinking them to be more beautiful than truth" (79.719). Accusations of dishonesty are, for Trollope, the most powerful of ideological weapons. His bias against the Irish, for example, often took the form of slurs on Irish honor: as a people, he says, the Irish are "little bound by the love of truth" (*Autobiography*, 4.65). In the novels, charges of dishonesty prop up Trollope's anti-Semitic, anti-American, and generally xenophobic tendencies, most evident in the virulent stereotypes of foreigners in *The Way We Live Now*.

(*The Gentleman in Trollope: Individuality and Moral Courage* [Cambridge: Harvard University Press, 1982], pp. 68–71).

[11] Deborah Denenholz Morse notes that Trollope was unconventional in embodying the moral ideal of the gentleman, with its stress on honor, in women (*Women in Trollope's Palliser Novels* [Ann Arbor, Mich.: UMI Research Press, 1987], p. 19). On the shared honesty of Trollope's men and women, see also George Levine, "Can You Forgive Him? Trollope's *Can You Forgive Her?* and the Myth of Realism," *Victorian Studies* 18 (1974), 15. Jane Nardin, however, argues strongly that Trollope affirmed traditional feminine moral ideals in the Barsetshire novels (*He Knew She Was Right: The Independent Woman in the Novels of Anthony Trollope* [Carbondale: Southern Illinois University Press, 1989], esp. pp. 31–88).

Trollope conceives honesty in specifically middle-class terms. That is to say, he rejects traditional aristocratic codes of honesty, which were based on combative, chivalrous values and revolved around the paramilitary idealization of valor. Chivalrous honesty reinforced the solidarity of the aristocracy (a gentleman's word was sacred among gentlemen, not necessarily when extended to social inferiors, especially tradesmen); the public nature of gentlemanly virtue; and the aggressive need among aristocrats to defend their honor from imputations of cowardice. While English aristocrats were slightly more detached than other European ruling classes from this chivalric code—Eric Hobsbawm attributes the irregular character of British chivalry to England's "open aristocracy"—it is significant that a half-dozen eighteenth- and early nineteenth-century prime ministers (Shelburne, Pitt, Fox, Canning, Wellington, and Peel) all defended their honor in the traditional way by fighting duels.[12] Middle-class honesty, on the other hand, as it evolved out of Puritanism, is a much more absolute and subjective concept. It is a universal psychological imperative, not a class-bound, public one. Middle-class honesty signifies, not the aggressive assertion of one's honor, but peacefulness, humility, and self-denial. It is a correlative of equanimity and conscientiousness, not valor.[13] Thus, when Septimus Harding humbly resigns his position in *The Warden* to have "truth on his side" (17.218), he must resist Archdeacon Grantly's pleas that he do his duty to his class and his political faction; that he rise publicly to combat enemies like the *Jupiter*; and—above all—that he not give in to "weakness" (19.241). In *Phineas Finn*, Phineas fights a duel only because he is forced to by Lord Chiltern, who considers himself dishonored by Phineas's candid, perfectly voluntary confession of his love for the woman who has already rejected Chiltern. Ignoring Phineas's amicable motives and his scrupulous sincerity, Chiltern sees only what he interprets as rivalry and competition, an insult to honor. In this blatant confrontation between middle-class and aristocratic ideals, Phineas clearly has the

[12] E. J. Hobsbawm, *Industry and Empire: From 1750 to the Present Day* (Harmondsworth: Penguin, 1968), p. 32. On dueling politicians, see Octavius Christie, *The Transition from Aristocracy, 1832–67* (New York: G. P. Putnam's Sons, 1928), p. 23.
[13] For an excellent discussion of the history of honesty, see Harold Perkin, *Origins of Modern English Society* (London: Routledge and Kegan Paul, 1969), pp. 274–78.

narrative's sympathy. With heroic pacifism, he takes a bullet in his shoulder while refusing to aim his pistol at his adversary, after trying to prevent the duel through an extended explanation of his motives, which is, as the narrator puts it (in an attempt to appropriate aristocratic codes), "even chivalrous in its absolute honesty" (37.431). Above all else, though, middle-class honesty pertains to private life and statements about emotional being or intimate relationships, often conceiving standards of public behavior simply as an extension of private demands for sincerity. Trollope's ideal politician, Plantagenet Palliser, is remarkable for applying to public life (with mixed results) a pure and uncompromising subjective integrity: "His honesty is not like the honesty of other men. It is more downright;—more absolutely honest; less capable of bearing even the shadow which the stain from another's dishonesty might throw upon it" (*The Prime Minister*, 28.323). As a standard of "public" values, Palliser represents nothing so much as the moralization of politics and the reduction of public life to moral values that unify private integrity with political stands.

The absolute, radically subjective character of middle-class honesty guarantees it a broad range of significance for Trollope. Honesty means absence of pretense, lack of prejudice against others, and forthright declaration of one's ideas or feelings.[14] It also means constancy in love: faithful lovers are "true," and unfaithful lovers "false." Other correlations are more ideologically loaded. Honesty, for Trollope, often means "disinterest." The most exemplary gentlemen in Trollope—like Roger Carbury—are also the most self-denying, the most "disinterested." As we will see later in more detail, it is not enough, in Trollope, to be candid about one's desires; one must be able to renounce desire itself to be truly honest, as if ambitious or competitive desires are themselves a form of subterfuge. Honesty is further associated with labor and work, as opposed to idleness or commercial fraud. Moreover, the aesthetic of the novel is itself imbued with honesty, over and above the novel's function as a "pulpit" (*Autobiography*, 8.146). Trollope's conception of honesty completely shapes his attitudes toward narrative realism, which always revolve around moral conceptions of truthfulness.

[14] Slakey catalogues these characteristics of Trollopian honesty in "Trollope's Case for Moral Imperative," pp. 314–15.

In a famous passage from *Barchester Towers*, for example, Trollope declared his dislike for sensation fiction by claiming that he disdained to keep secrets from his readers: "Have not often the profoundest efforts of genius been used to baffle the aspirations of the reader . . . ? And is there not a species of deceit in this to which the honesty of the present age should lend no countenance? . . . Our doctrine is, that the author and the reader should move along together in full confidence with each other" (15.130). In relation to his own subject matter, of course, Trollope was able, he believed, "to produce even some not untrue resemblance" of the real (20.168). Roger Slakey notes that there is an "impulse toward manifestation" in the events of Trollope's novels.[15] Important information never remains hidden, as it might in the novels of Balzac or James, but always becomes a matter of unrestricted knowledge. This manifestation of the truth in events is symptomatic of a much larger convergence of aesthetics with moral and social symbolic structures. As Walter Kendrick puts it, "the dream of a language in which no lies can be told . . . is dreamt everywhere in Trollope's writing, theory and practice alike."[16]

Trollope's realism is fully embedded in a symbolic exchange between codes of social class, morality, and aesthetics. His banishment of poetic exaggeration, "romance," and riddling detective plots—all of which he sees as aesthetic "lies"—parallels the social strategies of domination adopted by the middle class. Because of this interrelationship between the domains of class, morality, and art, Trollopian realism borrows some of the specific attributes of middle-class honesty—disinterest, constancy, labor—as aesthetic self-definitions. So it is, for example, that the production of realistic "truth" for Trollope becomes associated with the moral value of hard work, rather than with some other class-coded aesthetic principle (like "the sublime," for instance). In *Barchester Towers*, the narrator speaks of realism as a "burden" or "work" (20.168), and claims that it is only through hard work that faithful, realistic portraiture is achieved, not through technical wizardry: "*Labor omnia vincit improbus*. Such should be the chosen motto of every laborer." To the

[15] Ibid., p. 315.
[16] Walter M. Kendrick, *The Novel-Machine: The Theory and Fiction of Anthony Trollope* (Baltimore: Johns Hopkins University Press, 1980), p. 98.

extent that labor vindicates realism, then, realism is dependent for its own credibility on inscribing the signs of its labor within itself. Unlike poetry, which compresses or conceals the traces of its production, realistic fiction proclaims its labor self-righteously. Trollope asserts in the *Autobiography* that every word of his novels represents a certain fraction of labor-time and that his value as a writer lies, finally, not in the vicissitudes of "quality," to which he makes no claim, but in his "constancy in labour" (20.365). Similar arguments can be made for the "constancy" of tone or design in Trollope's novels and for the various ways in which "disinterest" is inscribed in the novels—in Trollope's narrative detachment, in his rejection of satire (which he stigmatized for its espousal of a single, interested view), and in his strained, almost formulaic impartiality.[17] Needless to say, all of these tendencies are characteristic of much Victorian realism, and Trollope simply supplies the moral rationale, in its crudest terms, for widely shared middle-class aesthetic practices.[18]

Despite the middle-class roots of Trollope's conception of honesty, however, his aristocratic subject matter sometimes seems to blur the class affiliations of his moral norms. After all, Trollope wrote about, envied, and idealized the squirearchy, and he showed obvious Tory leanings in his dislike of both middle-class trade and Whig parvenus.[19] Barsetshire is a world that has completely excluded middle-class commercial prosperity. Nevertheless, Trollope's aristocrats and their moral conflicts are largely projections of fundamentally middle-

[17] Trollope even considered revision to be a form of dishonesty. See N. John Hall, *Trollope: A Biography* (Oxford: Clarendon Press, 1991), p. 92.

[18] John P. McGowan makes a similar argument, in somewhat different terms: "the Victorians' penchant to locate spiritual or moral truths as the most fundamental reality marks their distance from the realism found in France during the same period" (*Representation and Revelation: Victorian Realism from Carlyle to Yeats* [Columbia: University of Missouri Press, 1986], p. 1).

[19] Juliet McMaster shows convincingly how land and its proprietors have a "transcendent" value for Trollope ("Trollope's Country Estates," in *Trollope Centenary Essays*, ed. John Halperin [London: Macmillan, 1982], pp. 70–85). apRoberts traces his ideals of tolerance to the influence of Anglican permissiveness (*Moral Trollope*, pp. 90–124). Richard Faber is particularly acute about Trollope's upper-class bias (*Proper Stations: Class in Victorian Fiction* [London: Faber and Faber, 1971]). But contemporary reviewers were just as sure of it. A long review in the *National Review* 7 (1858), 416–35, unequivocally equates Trollope with traditional Toryism.

class concerns. The centrality of moral debate in his fiction reflects middle-class, not upper-class, preoccupations. More important, Trollope used his moral norms to separate out approved forms of what I call "middling" (if not empirically middle-class) behavior against both "high" and "low" corruption. In this symbolic drama, upper middle-class professionals and the marginalized gentry are usually defended in middle-class moral terms, while immoral behavior is generally attributed to those either above or below this group in social rank. In other words, middle-class moral norms are rotated slightly upward in the social scale. The exact social identity of Trollope's characters was in this way transformed by his ability to rank their moral behavior in a symbolic hierarchy clearly divided into low, middle, and high registers. His primarily aristocratic subject matter thus forms a fluid social background on which a middle-class moral hierarchy is clearly superimposed. This projection of a middle-class symbolic logic on social territory apparently alien to it is symptomatic of several things. It is an attempt to conceive the goals of social-climbing in terms acceptable to middle-class readers. It is also an aggressive attempt to transform social codes of gentility themselves by filtering them through middle-class values. But most important, it reflects the historical victory of middle-class ideology over upper-class life and institutions, and the degree to which, after mid-century, aristocratic life had been emptied of its more traditional values.

Trollope's rotation of middle-class norms upward reflects this ideological transformation in his handling of the Barsetshire clergy, for example. His ability to treat the clergy with nostalgia, and his middle-class readers' ability to respond, is symptomatic of the diminishment of the clergy during the 1860s as both a symbol and an effective instrument of class conflict. During the 1830s, the tremendous upsurge of reform activism in the church had been a self-conscious attempt to consolidate upper-class opposition to middle-class intrusions. Both the Oxford high church movement and the evangelical low church movement strove to insulate church power from the state, the one by professionalizing the clergy and stressing their corporate, institutional power, the other by appealing to the sanctity of the clerical vocation and its disciplinary mission to all classes of English society (its duty to "the souls of the people," as

Mrs. Proudie would put it). But the failure, by the 1850s, of both movements to do anything but reinforce lay impressions of the church's irrelevance is reflected in Trollope's trivialization of these clerical doctrines, and of the antagonism between them. While Archdeacon Grantly valiantly (and comically) resists an increasingly non-Anglican Parliament's control over the church, his fellow churchmen are more realistic: "The cigar has been smoked out, and we are the ashes," says one of them. "The government is to find us all in everything, and the press is to find the government" (*Barchester Towers*, 34.330).

This implicit political and ideological victory is much more important to the savoring of the Barsetshire novels by middle-class readers than is the nostalgia for so-called "old English values" that Trollope critics often extol. Middle-class Dissent had been violently opposed to the church in the 1830s and 1840s, viewing its power as a galling reminder of aristocratic privilege and as a reactionary political influence. The Anti–Corn Law League was rabidly anti-church, and there were various other movements for the abolition of church rates and the disestablishment of the church during this period.[20] A Barsetshire series would have been unthinkable in 1840, as would Margaret Oliphant's Carlingford series and George Eliot's *Scenes of Clerical Life*. But after mid-century, the decrease in the number of strictly separatist middle-class radicals in Parliament suggests that upper-class institutions like the church had already been captured. Palmerston's evangelical bishops—like the fictional Dr. Proudie—were shrewdly chosen in order to divide the church against itself and thus to neutralize it. Palmerston hoped to appeal to middle-class Dissenters, as well as to the Scottish vote, by advancing the interests of the evangelical wing. More deviously, he chose weak, nonactivist evangelical bishops who had little interest in crusading for theological or political dogmas of any kind.[21] From roughly 1855 to 1865, Palmerston's appointments transformed the

[20] See Perkin, *Origins of Modern English Society*, esp. pp. 349–62.

[21] Owen Chadwick, *The Victorian Church*, 2 vols. (London: Adam and Charles Black, 1966), 1:468–76. An excellent documentary account of the losing battle for independence of the early Victorian clergy is Owen Chadwick, *Victorian Miniature* (London: Hodder and Stoughton, 1960). In the case Chadwick describes, the vicar of Ketteringham loses his battle with the local squire as the result of an alliance between squire and bishop.

clergy's desire for independence from the state to the more pathetic goal of independence from its own bishops, and he helped erase the causes of middle-class hostility. The comic trivialization of the struggle between high and low church in Trollope's novels underlines the fact that middle-class questions about moral choice have become much more central in his characters' lives than doctrine and the upper-class authority that doctrine once embodied.[22] This shift greatly transforms the symbolic social identity of the clergyman, regardless of Trollope's claim that a cleric is "a gentleman as it were by Act of Parliament."[23]

The "capture" of the church by middle-class interests is only one phase of a general mid-Victorian phenomenon in which aristocrats continued to hold certain forms of power only by remodeling institutions and values on bourgeois terms. Aristocratic portraits of the period, for example, tend to represent family groups occupied in domestic activities, rather than solitary, formally dressed figures. The country houses built after mid-century organize domestic space around moral considerations—by providing architecturally for a newly efficient, nonsociable regimentation of the workspace and a rigid separation, both in activities and living quarters, between male and female servants.[24] In politics, the situation is even clearer. The failure of the middle class to form its own political party after enfranchisement is attributable primarily to the gravitation of both the Liberal and Conservative parties toward middle-class political stands. Strictly middle-class political institutions like the Anti–Corn Law League were far more active before than after mid-century. Mid-Victorian culture shows many symptoms—like the Barsetshire chronicles themselves—of middle-class retention of the ornaments of aristocratic cultural authority, but on middle-class ideological terms.[25] The strange emergence of British nostalgia for chivalry

[22] A related development is the fall in social status experienced by clergymen after mid-century, which made them more palatable to the middle-class imagination. See Alan Haig, The Victorian Clergy (London: Croom Helm, 1984), esp. pp. 7–12; and Brian Heeney, A Different Kind of Gentleman (Hamden: Archon, 1976), p. 94.

[23] Anthony Trollope, Clergymen of the Church of England (Leicester: Leicester University Press, 1974), p. 99.

[24] See Mark Girouard, Life in the English Country House: A Social and Architectural History (New Haven: Yale University Press, 1978), esp. pp. 268–72.

[25] Asa Briggs explains the decline of open class conflict after mid-century in this

after mid-century—from the monumental (and disastrous) Eglinton tournament, to aspects of pre-Raphaelite painting, to the invention of the Boy Scouts—can also be explained in these terms.[26]

The Barsetshire series, then, ought to be seen not as a study of old-fashioned aristocratic culture but as an example of its appropriation by the middle class. Trollope was an extremely likely candidate for such a task, having reacquired the social standing he was repeatedly denied as a young man through that eminently middle-class instrument, hard work. An argument can, of course, be made that this appropriation of cultural authority worked the other way as well, and that Trollope's middle-class aristocrats are in some cases more co-opting than co-opted, having adopted middle-class ideological positions to defend their own social and political authority.[27] The squirearchy had long sought to appropriate middle-class moral norms, both as an attempt to domesticate middle-class opposition and as a rebuke to Regency values. Examples of this kind of appropriation are evident in Henry Fielding's Tories, in Samuel Richardson's transformation of Squire B, and in Frances Burney's genteel women. But the point remains that upper-class individuals, at mid-century, managed quite broadly to conceive of themselves as the "middling" point in an ideologically bourgeois moral and social hierarchy.

Keeping in mind Trollope's rotation of middle-class norms upward in the social scale, we can begin to map his hierarchy of high, low, and middling conceptions of honesty across both social and moral symbolic domains. These linked hierarchies can be traced clearly through a close look at *Framley Parsonage*, Trollope's first great financial and popular success. The novel itself is, perhaps, one of the most thorough meditations on honesty in the Barsetshire series. Discussing its composition, Trollope was moved to say that it exemplified his lifelong efforts to illustrate the simple principle that

---

way ("The Language of Class," in *Essays in Labor History*, ed. Asa Briggs and John Saville [London: Macmillan, 1960], pp. 69–73).

[26] For a general account, see Mark Girouard, *The Return to Camelot: Chivalry and the English Gentleman* (New Haven: Yale University Press, 1981).

[27] This is essentially Hobsbawm's position. See his *Industry and Empire*, esp. pp. 18–19. On the persistence of aristocratic political control into the 1880s, see David Cannadine, *The Decline and Fall of the British Aristocracy* (New Haven: Yale University Press, 1990), p. 14.

"honesty is the best policy" (*Autobiography*, 8.145). He found the
two lovers of *Framley Parsonage* to be a particularly good illustration
of that policy: "it was downright honest love,—in which there was
no pretence on the part of the lady that she was too ethereal to be
fond of a man, no half-and-half inclination on the part of the man
to pay a certain price and no more for a pretty toy. Each of them
longed for the other, and they were not ashamed to say so" (8.143).
Lucy Robarts he found to be "perhaps the most natural English girl
that I ever drew." Trollope's retrospective insistence on Lucy's
forthrightness is oddly compromised by her conduct in the novel,
and *Framley Parsonage* thus provides an excellent place to uncover
Trollope's clandestine recuperation of dishonesty and the bourgeois
sophistication it signifies. For the middle-class aristocracy he sought
to define depended not simply on traditional truth-telling norms,
but on the authority to transgress them as well. The symbolic logic
Trollope rotates upward, for all its middle-class emphasis on candor,
is a decidedly reversible one.

In *Framley Parsonage*, Trollope seems, on the surface, to draw
clear equations between the norm of honesty and his "middling"
characters. The novel places a premium on the truthfulness of
characters with upper middle-class or professional roots, in particular
on that of Miss Dunstable and Lucy Robarts—the daughters of,
respectively, a successful marketer of ointment and a physician—and
on Fanny Robarts, whose background is kept vague, aside from the
fact that she has "no home" (1.5) and that she has been adopted
into the Framley circle as a dependent of Lady Lufton's. Miss
Dunstable, whose rough, frank speech and boisterous vitality are
singularly out of place in fashionable circles, is especially distinguished as being "fond of truth, and prone to honesty" (24.260).
Recognizing that scrupulousness, Mrs. Harold Smith advises her
brother, Mr. Sowerby, that in any proposal of marriage to Miss
Dunstable, the only strategy with any prospect of success is one with
"a semblance of honesty"—advice that leads to Mrs. Smith's bizarre
declaration to Miss Dunstable that her brother wants to marry her
for her money. Thanking her for "the truth, the whole truth, and
nothing but the truth," Miss Dunstable observes that "one's first

efforts in any line are apt to be a little uncouth" (24.266). Similarly, the physician's daughter, Lucy Robarts, is told by her lover, Lord Lufton: "You, I know, will tell me nothing but the truth" (16.177). Lucy characteristically announces that she "won't tell a lie" (21.232) on any subject and that she "does not care to have any secrets" (35.379) from her friends. Fanny Robarts, too, is so compulsively honest that she quarrels with Lady Lufton rather than disguise her sympathy with her husband—especially when she must argue that Mark "is no hypocrite" (5.49) and that "he has done nothing to deceive" (5.50). In other novels, these equations between honesty and socially "middling" characters are sometimes drawn even more clearly. In *The Eustace Diamonds*, it is Lucy Morris, the governess, who represents the novel's extreme of truth-telling and to whom Frank Greystock says, "You are truth itself" (13.120).

What finally places these characters as "middling," though, more than their social origins, is that their general commitment to the value of honesty makes them, in some sense, indifferent to higher kinds of social ambition. In obsessive and repetitive ways, Trollope, like many other Victorian novelists, specifically associates the moral value of disinterest with the apparent renunciation of social desire. Mr. Harding, in *The Warden*, defines this choice quite clearly, and the abdication from social struggle that he exemplifies is always correlated with principles of "middling" honesty, whether configured as the Tory traditionalism of Lady Lufton, the evangelical asceticism of Josiah Crawley, the high-church intellectualism of Mr. Arabin, or the romantic idealism of Frank Gresham. One antonym of honesty in Trollope could be said to be an ambition for high rank, which is always associated with unscrupulous behavior, if only in the constant temptations it presents to such characters as Archdeacon Grantly and Plantagenet Palliser (who redeem themselves by resisting most of those temptations). Trollope certainly never indicates that high rank itself, or the acceptance of advancement, absolutely excludes honesty: the tenuousness of the opposition is proved by the number of characters who are exempted from it entirely, who never have to choose between honesty and "the good things of the world" (*Barchester Towers*, 38.369) at all. But the choice for honesty in Trollope, when it does have to be made, is always pitted—as in Mark Robarts's case—against the allure of higher rank. "In these times,"

Trollope wrote in the *Autobiography*, "the desire to be honest is pressed so hard, is so violently assaulted, by the ambition to be great" (12.220). Trollope's moral categories thus intersect his symbolic adjustment of class categories by conceiving social identity partly in terms of desire rather than official rank.

Because he takes social disinterest as a correlative of moral disin-terest, Trollope can include figures such as Lady Lufton as a spiritual ally of his "middling" group of characters. As a general rule, Tories like Lady Lufton—who are out of the mainstream of mid-Victorian social power and therefore easy to idealize as contented with their station—come close to the middle-class moral/social disinterest Trol-lope assigns to his empirically middle-class protagonists. Fiercely dedicated to honesty, Lady Lufton "was essentially a true woman, and not even with the object of carrying out her views in so important a matter [as her son's marriage] would she be guilty of such deception as she might have practiced by simply holding her tongue" (43.467). But Lady Lufton's honesty is made possible precisely by her retreat from higher aristocratic social circles (she is always uncomfortable in London during the season), and it is exercised instead chiefly in her private dealings with Fanny, Mark, Lucy, and her son. Only when she is drawn away from this domestic circle into London society and tempted by the competitive marriage market does her honesty begin to waver. When she schemes to bring her son and Griselda Grantly together, for example, she is guilty of telling a "tarradiddle" (16.172), and the narrator rebukes her for succumbing to fashionable deceptions, despite the fact that the world would view her lie as "excusable." In these ways, certain aristocratic characters in Trollope's novels become figures for middle-class symbolic distinctions that link honesty to a kind of social neu-trality.

The danger of unambiguously "high" social circles for Trollope's protagonists is always the danger of deceit. In *Framley Parsonage*, Mark Robarts finds the lack of earnestness of the fashionable set at Gatherum Castle to be seductive at first, so seductive that he, too, joins in their mockery of Harold Smith's lecture about "civilizing" New Guinea—mockery that contrasts pointedly with the stolid respect and attention of the tradespeople in the Barchester audience. But Mark finds himself sadly at odds with his profession and with his own values the next day, when he must give a charity sermon on the exact same theme. This early conflict between insincerity and earnestness signals the basic crisis of Mark's social-climbing, in which he is ultimately subjected to public gossip that he had won preferment in the church through dishonest means. His reputation suffers from the "dishonesty" (44.477) of Mr. Sowerby and also from the "low" character of Tom Tozer—a "thorough liar in his heart" (32.354)—who executes his bills. Sowerby, in particular, is "a great liar" with an enormous "depth of fraud," who takes a positive "pleasure in cheating" (44.482). Like Collins, Thackeray, and other chroniclers of Victorian high society, Trollope tends to see aristocratic life in traditional puritanical terms as a theater of deceptions—so much so that the very personalities of his fashionable aristocrats often revolve around fraud. Griselda Grantly's "statu-esque" (11.119) inscrutability is one form this artifice takes. A more interesting form is the multiple personalities or "masks" that aristocrats manipulate. Mr. Fothergill "enacted two altogether differ-ent persons on occasions which were altogether different" (27.294). And "nothing could be more different than Mr. Sowerby's tone about money at different times" (21.227–28). Trollope's novels constantly dwell on the postures, deceptions, and insincere behavior of his "high" characters. This stigmatization of the "high" as dishon-est betrays a class resentment that also underlies Trollope's often-misunderstood emphasis on the plodding mechanicalness of his own literary work. Trollope's literary ressentiment is plainly evident when he scolds those writers striving to achieve "authorship . . . of the highest class known," and he advises them to abandon their pre-tences and "to seat themselves at their desks day by day as though they were lawyers' clerks;—and so let them sit till the allotted task shall be accomplished" (*Autobiography*, 7.122).

Although Trollope avoids writing about lower-class subjects, never-theless he does formulate an ideological "lowness" that he imposes on certain well-to-do figures, again projecting a bourgeois ideological hierarchy on a nominatively upper-class social spectrum. While low behavior in Trollope can be distinguished in any number of conventional ways—vulgarity, lack of taste or refinement, lack of physical or emotional control—the low and the high meet most often in their affinity for dishonesty. In *Barchester Towers*, Mr. Slope is denied genteel status partly because he is a liar: a "low-bred hypocrite" (6.40), a "sly *tartuffe*" (18.155). Possessing "neither honesty nor truth" (13.106) and guilty of multiple misrepresentations—to Harding, to Quiverful, to the bishop, to Signora Neroni, and to Eleanor—Slope is reviled, variously, as "bad company" (18.152) and "vulgar" (17.147). But he is also seen as ungenteel because of his ambition: he is "greedy" (17.147), one of those "lowly-born pretenders to high station" (33.321). What low and high have in common, in this symbolic drama, is ambition and a lack of honesty—precisely the linked moral and social qualities that "middlingness" excludes. To this same end, *The Way We Live Now* was conceived as an attack on commercial "dishonesty magnificent in its proportions, and climbing into high places" (*Autobiography*, 20.354). At the other end of the social scale, Sowerby, the gentleman, brings Mark Robarts into connection with the "dirt" of "the lowest dregs of mankind," a conjunction of high and low in which Mark is "sickened . . . with all these lies" (33.361). "Middlingness" in both moral and social domains is defined, by Trollope, as the capability of rejecting desires for hierarchical advancement—a gesture toward the democratic values so central to bourgeois self-understanding. Ambition and dishonor are projected as the linked sins of both high and low social standing.

This equation of dishonesty with social desire creates a problem, however, for the countervailing expression of genuine bourgeois vitality, as well as bourgeois social competition. To avoid lapsing into the insipid passivity and the noble poverty of figures such as Mr. Harding, "middling" characters need to formulate the repressed underside of disinterest—that is, desire—transgressively. If this formulation is to avoid the direct, vulgar expression of social desire, it must adopt its closely linked moral correlative: dishonesty. The firm associations Trollope makes, not simply between dishonesty and class, but between dishonesty, class, and social desire, help explain the appeal of those characters who find acceptable ways to lie, as a means of asserting various kinds of personal or social power that they must also deny. *Framley Parsonage* forcefully expels lying as illicit, morally and socially, but the novel also exalts lying as the form necessarily taken by healthy "middling" passions, including those passions linked indirectly to a rise in social status. It is as obsessed with its protagonists' rare but monumentally significant lies as with their characteristic honesty, as fascinated with transgressive dishonesty as it is scrupulous about norms of truthfulness.

In *Framley Parsonage*, strangely enough, we are asked to approve of a "middling" heroine who is gifted in deception. The pivotal act of Lucy Robarts's story, the act that paradoxically defines her moral strength, is her telling of a "falsehood" (26.288) to Lord Lufton—a falsehood about the most important subject of all in the Victorian novel, the state of her affections. Pressed by Lufton to admit her love for him, but suffering from a fear that she will be seen as ambitious ("scheming" and "artful" [21.229]), Lucy sends him away by swearing her indifference. In her case, the lie about ambitious desire is shifted away from the realm of social power toward that of romantic love, where it can more easily be countenanced. Nevertheless, Lucy's lie is not taken lightly. It is highlighted thematically by the forceful opposition of honesty and dishonesty in the Mark Robarts plot. Lucy herself repeatedly asks Fanny and Mark, "was I wicked to tell that falsehood?" (26.288). At the end of the novel, the fact of her lie makes her uncomfortably coy with her husband: "We'll let bygones be bygones, if you please" (48.524), she tells him when he pressures her to admit that she had lied. Yet this is clearly a lie for which he admires her, a point of friction, secrecy, and potential tragedy that eroticizes their otherwise more or less cordial relationship.

Lucy's lie to her lover might be taken as a mere romantic device if it were her only lie in the novel. But Lucy is consistently distinguished by her ability to play with the truth. She falsifies her feelings about Lord Lufton from her very first encounter with him, earning the comic charge from the narrator that she is "a hypocrite" (11.119). Lucy also routinely deceives Josiah Crawley by smuggling sweets to his children in defiance of his orders. "Was she not deceiving the good man—nay, teaching his own children to deceive him?" (22.239). She also kidnaps and quarantines his children, circumventing Crawley's proud refusals of neighborly help, to prevent their exposure to their mother's fever. The narrator always seems to forgive such deceptions ("There are men made of such stuff that an angel could hardly live with them without some deceit," he says of Crawley), but Trollope also reinforces their exceptional quality by contrasting them to the rigid demands for honesty he makes of other characters, including Lucy's brother Mark.

Of course, Lucy's lies always have an ostensibly moral goal. They are presented as forms of selfless behavior rather than as acts of dishonest ambition. Lucy's actions seem to separate dishonesty from ambition, breaking the usual Trollopian conjunction. In doing so, they place her among a large, select group of transgressive characters in the Barset chronicles, including Dr. Thorne (who conceals the illegitimate birth of his niece, Mary, and also Mary's relation to the vulgar parvenu Scatcherd); Mary Thorne herself (who is a "false, black traitor" [*FP*, 39.428] for breaking Miss Dunstable's confidence in regard to her uncle, thus facilitating their marriage); matchmaking conspirators such as the Earl and Julia De Guest; and many others who are valued precisely for their skill at what appear to be innocent—that is, socially neutral—deceptions. The approved, "disinterested" dishonesty of these characters has much in common with that of such men as John Eames and Paul Montague, who are excused by Trollope's narrators for breaking promises of marriage—in sharp contrast to the harsh treatment of Adolphus Crosbie and Gustavus Moffat, who are singled out as paragons of treachery after breaking their engagements for transparently ambitious purposes. The female version of this authorially forgiven "noble jilting" is, of course, Alice Vavasor in *Can You Forgive Her?* What is problematic in all these cases, however, is that legitimately "false" characters all ultimately do benefit from their deceptions, however indirectly or belatedly—usually through advantageous marriages. The lies of disinterest become expressions of innocent but powerful vitality precisely because they always help these characters negotiate economic or marital dilemmas. Such lies never entirely break the general Trollopian connection between dishonesty and the transgression of social desire: "It was his title that killed me. I had never spoken to a lord before" (26.283), Lucy says, only half in jest, trying to account for her own love. Without this continued but carefully distanced association with the social desire Trollope has embedded in dishonesty, these "innocent" lies would lose the power of their ambivalence.

In its transgressive appropriation of ambitious energies, supposedly disinterested lying sometimes reveals the social desire of Trollope's protagonists by psychologizing ambition as a personality strength more allied to moral qualities like courage than to simple social-climbing. Lucy's victory over Lady Lufton in the matter of her engagement, which is made possible entirely by the lie she has told her lover, is far from socially neutral, since it permits the incursion of a socially undistinguished character into the ranks of the gentry. But it is the psychological power Lucy exercises in getting Lady Lufton actually to ask Lucy to marry her son that undermines Lady Lufton's initial objection to the match, which had to do with Lucy's "missish want of importance—that lack of social weight" (35.381). "If I were forced to put my objection into one word," says Lady Lufton, "She is—insignificant" (43.469). Lady Lufton quickly learns that Lucy has personal resources of boldness and strength when Lucy, empowered by her lie, courageously confronts Lady Lufton over the engagement. Moreover, during the very passages in the novel when Lady Lufton meditates on Lucy's lack of social power, Lucy proves her personal prowess in the reader's eyes by dominating Mr. Crawley through various acts of duplicity at Hogglestock Parsonage. Crawley himself, the man who rules over his own wife with conventional patriarchal authority, finds Lucy "ruthless" in "her new power" (34.375), the "absolute mistress of the house" (43.463). Significantly, when Lady Lufton relents toward Lucy, she neither acknowledges nor denies the relation between Lucy's redeeming personal courage and her own earlier concerns about Lucy's social bearing. The proof of the power of Lucy's personality ultimately comes to rest on her ability to play with the truth, but this power is explicitly affiliated with the power of personal leadership and only implicitly related to her capacities for upholding the authority of rank itself.

The realistic writer, like the honest bourgeois, is also symbolically dependent on and confusedly haunted by dishonesty—specifically, by imaginative deviation from the real, which often seems to return problematically as the source of realism's power, its vitality, and even its pretensions to respectability. Lucy's transgressive energies thus articulate the mechanisms of literary authority which Trollope himself depended on more surreptitiously. In the *Autobiography*, though he banishes romantic ideas about inspiration, Trollope is nevertheless troubled by his admissions that his work "improves" reality in its misrepresentations of the worldly fates of virtue and vice, or in its hope to alter the world for the better by so misrepresenting reality.[28] He argues that the novelist must "make virtue alluring and vice ugly, while he charms his reader instead of wearying him" (12.222) and must censor his knowledge of reality for moral purposes, rather than "sacrifice something for effect" (12.221). But he also struggles to deny that didactic improvement has distorted reality: "I have always desired . . . to make men and women walk upon [the earth] just as they do walk here among us,—with not more of excellence, nor with exaggerated baseness,—so that my readers might recognize human beings like to themselves, and not feel themselves to be carried away among gods or demons" (8.145). The tension between distortion and disinterest pervades all of Trollope's discussions of didacticism in art. His comparison of imaginative creation to daydreaming—the invention of another world in compensation for the injustice and the disappointments of this world, a youthful habit he later "regarded with dismay" (3.42)—is even more disturbing. "There can, I imagine, hardly be a more dangerous mental practice; but I have often doubted whether, had it not been my practice, I should ever have written a novel" (3.43).

Many of Trollope's assertions about his own honesty, literary or otherwise, are notoriously unreliable. We know that he borrowed heavily, despite his denials, from other writers, and his claims about his methods of production and such things as the inspiration for the death of Mrs. Proudie are highly suspect.[29] Obviously, Trollope also keeps secrets from his readers in the manner of "deceitful" sensation novelists, even though he denies that he does so—as Henry James mercilessly pointed out in his famous essay on *Barchester Towers*.[30]

[28] Sarah Gilead traces the oscillation between documentary realism and mythic self-projection in the *Autobiography* ("Trollope's *Autobiography*: The Strategies of Self-Production," *Modern Language Quarterly* 47 [1986], 272–90).

[29] On his borrowings from sensation fiction, see Henry J. W. Milley, "*The Eustace Diamonds* and *The Moonstone*," *Studies in Philology* 36 (1939), 651–63; and Bradford A. Booth, "*Orley Farm*: Artistry *Manqué*," in *From Jane Austen to Joseph Conrad: Essays Collected in Honor of James T. Hillhouse* (Minneapolis: University of Minnesota Press, 1958), pp. 146–59. John Sutherland has exposed the unreliability of Trollope's statements about his publishers ("Trollope, Publishers, and the Truth," *Prose Studies* 10 [1987], 239–49).

[30] Henry James, "Anthony Trollope," in *Partial Portraits* (London: Macmillan, 1888), pp. 97–136. James is "startled and shocked" that Trollope would even dream of "admitting to the reader that he was deceiving him" (p. 117).

The perverse attractions of dishonesty are, in fact, a constant subcurrent of the *Autobiography*, where Trollope often tries to redeem the transgressive value of lying even in the face of his excessively pedestrian version of realism. When discussing his travel writings, for example, Trollope strains to defend his impressionistic accounts as both "inaccurate" and "true" at the same time, in order to distinguish himself from the plodding researcher: "There are two kinds of confidence which a reader may have in his author. . . . There is a confidence in facts and a confidence in vision. The one man tells you accurately what has been. The other suggests to you what may, or perhaps what must have been, or what ought to have been. . . . The former does not pretend to be prescient, nor the latter accurate. . . . I have written very much as I have travelled about; and though I have been very inaccurate, I have always written the exact truth as I saw it" (7.129–30).[31] Trollope's literary "distortions" are in service of the essential truth beyond the literal truth—to paraphrase the dilemma of all realist writing. Yet the affinity of realist indirection with dishonesty is an anxious and an obsessive one for Trollope as for other Victorian realists, especially those concerned with their literary and social respectability.

Through characters like Lucy Robarts, then, Trollope was able to articulate a moral doubleness closely allied to his own, less easily acknowledged, form of cultural sophistication. The apparent moral inconsistency evident in the charm of Lucy's lying is actually a symbolic dynamic of expulsion and recuperation crucial to many phases of middle-class cultural authority, and it compresses a number of different kinds of vitality into a kind of generalized power. The power of "innocent" lying heals the social, psychological, and moral contradictions embedded in Victorian writing, as it defines the uncanny, nearly irresistible symbolic power of bourgeois culture itself.

[31] In his letters, Trollope repeatedly reiterates his proud but anxious defense of descriptive inaccuracy. See, for example, *The Letters of Anthony Trollope*, ed. N. John Hall, 2 vols. (Stanford: Stanford University Press, 1983), 2:595–96, 625, 791–92.

In many Trollope novels, the seductive, generalized power of lying is disturbing enough that it must be presented only in terms of a confusion of symbolic categories—a transgression of ethical differences—rather than as a direct appropriation of falsehood. In *Barchester Towers*, lying is subjected to a series of subtle parallels and contrasts between Slope and the novel's two lovers, Arabin and Eleanor, in which the difference between truth and falsehood becomes enchantingly confused. In contrast to Slope, Arabin is described as a man "panting for the truth" (21.186), a man "debarred as it would seem from man's usual privilege of lying" (38.374–75) and "unable to falsify his thoughts when questioned." Eleanor, too, is remarkable for the innocent truthfulness with which she takes all her suitors—Bertie Stanhope and Mr. Slope included—at their word. Yet the courtship of Arabin and Eleanor consists of a series of concealments and withholdings that sustains their mutual affection. At the moment when he means to declare his love, Arabin "could not find a word wherewith to express the plain wish of his heart" (30.290). Eleanor, during this same scene, lets Arabin's misconception about her involvement with Slope stand uncontradicted by not declaring herself honestly. "Why had she been so stiffnecked when asked a plain question?" (38.365), she wonders later. These lies, like many of Slope's lies, are lies of omission—not boldfaced lies. The narrator trivializes them in Arabin and Eleanor's case by joking, "How easily would she have forgiven and forgotten the archdeacon's suspicions had she but heard the whole truth from Mr. Arabin. But then where would have been my novel?" (30.285). These untruths are crucial to the plot in more than one sense, however, for the lovers' feelings about each other flourish in the midst of the jealousy, frustration, and anger spawned by misconception. Of Arabin, we learn that "as soon as he heard that she loved someone else," which, of course, is untrue, "he began to be very fond of her himself" (30.279). And when Eleanor angrily responds to his suspicions, but without forthrightly denying them, allowing Arabin to draw the wrong conclusions, Arabin "had never seen her so excited, he had never seen her look half so beautiful" (30.286). In another kind of linkage of deceit and desire, Eleanor becomes preoccupied with Arabin when she recognizes that she might have repelled him through her pretensions to indifference. Her inability to express her thoughts honestly is the manner in which she begins to experience her love.

The entire courtship of Arabin and Eleanor consists of miscommunications in which "they were as unable to tell their own minds to each other as any Damon and Phillis" (41.401). Ironically, Slope, too, is so aroused by Eleanor's indirectness (which he misinterprets as encouragement) during the Ullathorne fête that he literally throws himself at her, only to get his ears boxed. Deception and eroticism in this novel come to seem inextricably linked. As Signora Neroni proves when she brings Eleanor and Arabin together, their deceptive indifference toward each other is clearly legible to others as the true sign of their love. This principle of romantic interpretation suggests that, in Slope's case, Eleanor's displays of indifference are not morally sufficient and can be read as irresponsible deception. During Eleanor's "boxing" scene with Slope, the narrator first seriously considers the weight of wrongdoing on Eleanor's part: "she cannot altogether be defended" (40.389), he tells us, for having passively encouraged three lovers. By denying the facts to herself and to others, Eleanor has unwittingly produced a contagion of love.

It is crucial, finally, that the two lovers are brought together by Signora Neroni, who is both a proficient liar and a disturbingly blunt, honest character, able to decipher and to speak the truths that other characters avoid or conceal. Neroni is most dangerous, in fact, because she confusedly mixes lying and honesty. She astounds others by speaking "home truths" (27.256), and yet she uses every artifice at her command to manipulate her many lovers. Her honesty itself is actually threatening, a tool of her dishonest purposes: Eleanor is pained at being "so searched and riddled by a comparative stranger" (45.447), as well as by Neroni's demonstration that Arabin "should have concealed his love from her and shown it to another." Yet it is only through contact with such dangerous mixtures of honesty and dishonesty, a disruption of categories personified in the physically deformed signora, that Eleanor and Arabin can remove the barriers to romance and discover the truth of their love. Eleanor surely does "stoop to conquer" (45.446) when she discusses Arabin with Neroni. This kind of confusion of honesty with dishonesty is rampant in the love plot of *Barchester Towers*: the "lies" people appear to be telling Eleanor about Slope turn out to be true;

constitutional liars such as Neroni and Bertie Stanhope turn out to tell important truths; and moments of candor between Eleanor and Grantly, or between Slope and Bishop Proudie for that matter, only produce misunderstandings and distortions of the truth. "What lies people tell" (48.474), Mrs. Grantly thinks, when one aspect of the story is unraveled—yet at this point the narrator stresses an even deeper confusion: "But people in this matter had told no lies at all."

Trollope's authorial fascination with stories about lying is an even stronger but more subtle symptom of his dependence on transgressive dishonesty. Having officially excluded dishonesty from the moral domain of his "middling" classes, Trollope as a novelist is then free to observe it without contamination in the social circles he has rejected. The object of bourgeois voyeurism or spectatorship (the underside of its social neutrality) in Trollope's novels is precisely the amazing, outrageous lies attributed to the private lives of aristocrats. In *Framley Parsonage*, Mark Robarts finds himself "half fascinated . . . and half afraid" (8.92) of Sowerby, for "it made one almost in love with ruin to be in his company" (12.132). The novels themselves are both fascinated and appalled by Sowerby, by Slope, by Signora Neroni, by Adolphus Crosbie, by Augustus Melmotte (whose word or *mot* is bad, *mal*), and by other chronic liars whose strategies are dissected in all their shameless arrogance and greed. Since lying has come to seem the epitome of uncontrolled desire, it must be distanced through the narrator's serene detachment from his characters' follies. But through such distance, the novels also teach how desire may be approached without loss of respectability—that is, through a guarded appreciation of socially promiscuous lying that withholds any direct approval. Such cool spectatorship—like the gaze of the respectable outsider on the rabble—is the source of the ability to make moral distinctions and to classify the acceptable and the unacceptable, the honest and the dishonest. But it is also the safe distance that admits either a vicarious identification with liars or the flirtation with a loss of moral distinctions which Trollope indulges in *Barchester Towers*. It is the sign of what Stallybrass and White call a "phobic enchantment."[32] Enacting this ambivalence, Trollope's narrator often apologizes for the dishonesty of his more

[32] Stallybrass and White, *Politics and Poetics of Transgression*, p. 124.

disreputable characters, drawing near in sympathy to sources of contamination and confusion, only to draw back again, reflexively, and to insist that morality is not relative, that differences remain firm. In our last view of Sowerby, the narrator compassionately and at some length admits to having "some tender feeling" (44.482) for him, but then staunchly draws himself up and confesses: "I cannot acquit him from the great accusation" that "it is roguish to lie, and he had been a great liar." In Eleanor's case, on the other hand, after admitting that she "cannot altogether be defended" (40.389), the narrator proclaims categorically, "yet it may be averred that she is not a hoyden." These vacillations usually have been understood as the expression of an enlightened, liberal moral sensibility, whose rules cannot be determinedly written because they acknowledge moral complexity.[33] They ought to be understood, however, as the effects of a dynamic ambivalence, a simultaneous attraction to and repulsion from transgressive dishonesty. They represent a class-coded exclusion of dishonesty, but yet a willingness to identify remotely with it, that motivates the transformation of dishonesty into acceptable forms—the deceitful innocence of love, for example, or the personality strength demonstrated by fooling others for their own good.

It is important to remember that, despite the comic handling of many dissembling protagonists and the fragile "disinterest" attributed to them, their actions are nevertheless constantly referred to as transgressive. Early in *Framley Parsonage*, Lucy is described as a "poison" (13.146) and "dangerous" (11.125). Lady Lufton's first reaction when she hears of her son's proposal is that Lucy is a "horrid, sly, detestable, underhand girl" (34.368). In the last chapter, Lucy herself considers her love "all but illicit" (48.522). These references are, of course, meant as comic hyperbole. Certainly, it would be foolish to attach any great shock value to Lucy's transgressions themselves. Contemporary readers were hardly shocked; one reviewer remarked that "there is something ludicrous in the iteration with which [Lucy's] precious case of conscience is discussed by all

[33] See, for example, Kincaid, *The Novels of Anthony Trollope*, pp. 11–15; and Herbert, who speaks of Trollope's antipuritanical striving after "moral amplitude" (*Trollope and Comic Pleasure*, esp. pp. 52–53).

the *dramatis personae*."[34] What is more crucial than the immediate shock value of particular transgressions, however, is their structure. There is an unmistakable element of fear in Trollope's attitude toward transgressive dissembling, however much it is rationalized, affirmed, or domesticated through comic irony or melodrama. In later novels, he expresses this fear more directly in the troubling emotional blackmail exercised by a dissembling "good" character like Lily Dale, who self-destructively conceals her love from John Eames in *The Small House at Allington*, or Josiah Crawley, who histrionically plays the martyr in *The Last Chronicle of Barset*. In the later novels, Trollope's exploration of this transgressive ground between honesty and dishonesty is much more self-consciously problematic. Paul Montague, in *The Way We Live Now*, is consistently but uncomfortably defended for trying to prove "that a man may break a promise and yet not tell a lie" (1.26.250), both when he terminates his engagement to Mrs. Hurtle and in his breach of trust with Roger Carbury. Carbury persists to the end in regarding Paul as "treacherous" (2.93.404), but the narrator is guardedly tolerant about Paul's constant affinities with lying. Mildly, somewhat cynically ironic about Paul's ability to cover his deceit with personal charm, the narrator observes at one point, "The soft falsehoods which would be sweet as the scent of violets in a personal interview, would stand in danger of being denounced as deceit added to deceit, if sent in a letter. I think therefore that Paul Montague did quite right in hurrying up to London" (2.76.243).[35] Trollope's ambivalence combines social and moral fears inextricably: characters such as Paul manage to penetrate the gentlemanly precincts of Carbury's world through their "treachery"; characters such as Crawley and Lily Dale threaten, perversely, to drop off the social scale through theirs. In any case, it is important to see that the structure of this fearful ambivalence is fully present in *Framley Parsonage* and, even earlier, in the comic half-truths told by Eleanor Harding to John Bold in *The Warden*.

To ameliorate dangerous associations with dishonesty, Trollope often transforms lying into seemingly more innocent forms. The

---

[34] *Westminster Review* 76 (1861), p. 283.

[35] In a letter to Mary Holmes, Trollope says point-blank, "Paul Montague is all right" (*Letters*, 2:631, 7 October 1874).

characteristic "badinage" of both Miss Dunstable and Lucy Robarts, for example, functions as a licensed violation of earnestness—an excess of playfulness that distinguishes them from aristocrats, whose deceptions and pretences are deadly serious, and from more puritanical characters at the same time.[36] Such badinage is a trait Trollope was increasingly fond of giving to his female protagonists, notably to Lily Dale. Whatever its charm, though, Trollope makes it difficult to overlook the transgression implicit in this kind of flippancy. All of these women dare to joke about their love and their lovers. The degree of irony they direct at their own affections is not trivial and is often found disconcerting by other, more earnest characters. Fanny is deeply troubled, for example, when Lucy wonders whether it is Lord Lufton's title or his legs that she has fallen in love with. And Mary Gresham—whose earnest and straitlaced principles were put approvingly to the test in *Dr. Thorne*—is so puzzled by the worldliness in Miss Dunstable's "aptitude" for "frolic" (*Framley Parsonage*, 7.100) that she thinks "she was as it were two persons" (38.408). This multiplication of personality is often condemned in the novels, as we have seen.

These tensions and ambiguities are themselves devices of social ambition, however. Traditional analyses of middle-class ideology tend to overlook not simply the role of transgression, but also the ways in which symbolic violations of bourgeois norms reflect internal tensions within bourgeois society itself. For in assuming middle-class hegemony about most behavioral norms and by taking for granted the middle-class presentation of a united moral front against the Victorian upper and lower classes, critics tend to overlook the rabid struggle for cultural authority within the ranks of the middle class itself. This struggle was especially acute, in the nineteenth century, between the professional and nonprofessional factions of the middle class and appears to have become more intense from the 1860s on (that is, during Trollope's most productive years), after threats from above and below had largely been warded off.[37] The mid-Victorian

[36] On occasional self-conscious performativeness in Trollope as a sign of creative moral dexterity, see Sarah Gilead, "Trollope's Orphans and the 'Power of Adequate Performance,' " *Texas Studies in Literature and Language* 27 (1985), 86–105.

[37] Marxist historians have greatly complicated our understanding of the gradations of Victorian status conflict. See esp. Perkin, *Origins of Modern English Society*; and

novel, in its use of transgression to define a certain exceptional area of experience, works to widen these middle-class differences by representing transgression as a sign of bourgeois elitism. It was crucial to this project that transgression not be made to seem the province of the "ordinary" bourgeois—even as it formed the desires of a broadly based but always upward-looking middle-class reader-ship—nor that it be understood simply as the privileged attitude of a group that had escaped its roots and become upper class. Through their distribution of legitimated transgression and abilities to indulge antibourgeois energies, Trollope's novels construct a special category of cultural authority within the broadened ranks of the "middling" class, along with the important fantasy that certain transgressions against bourgeois values do not ultimately threaten one's "middling" respectability.

The intraclass elitism implicit in various forms of transgression against honesty—outright lying, withheld love, devious disinterest, social aspiration, badinage—is most apparent in Trollope's steady critique of "middling" characters who have an unambiguous commit-ment to truth-telling. However gently, Trollope always mocks those middle-class characters who believe too simply in the truthfulness of others or who limit their own personalities to simplistic standards of honesty. In *Framley Parsonage*, Trollope has Mark commit a doltish financial suicide by retreating to a position of honest self-reliance so severe that he refuses to accept discreet financial arrangements that might save him. Mark's obstinacy here—in sharp contrast to Lucy's flexible behavior—prefigures Crawley's inflexibility in *The Last Chronicle of Barset*. It resembles the nightmarish constancy of Lily Dale or Marie Melmotte, or the compulsive forthrightness that nearly ruins Lucy Morris. Rigidly honest characters in Trollope often turn out to be victims, either willingly or unwillingly, their honesty a weapon used against them. Alternatively, their honesty is associ-ated with the obstinacy of old-fashioned values, as in the case of

R. S. Neale, *Class and Ideology in the Nineteenth Century* (London: Routledge and Kegan Paul, 1972). On struggles within the middle class after mid-century, see Darko Suvin, "The Social Addressees of Victorian Fiction: A Preliminary Inquiry," *Literature and History* 8 (1982), 16–17.

Squire Dale and Roger Carbury, values that are often presented as a danger to genuine friendship or sympathy. By contrast, transgressive characters such as Miss Dunstable—altogether unlike Mark Robarts—are able "to touch pitch and not to be defiled" (*Framley Parsonage*, 42.458). For if the lesson of Mark's story is that dishonest companions contaminate irrevocably, Miss Dunstable strangely violates that lesson with impunity, living in the world of honesty and dishonesty at the same time, having both "real friends" and fashionable "mock friends" (38.414). Her sensibility is enlarged, not jeopardized, by the transgressive experience, by her exemption from the consequences of touching pitch: "She smiled with equal sweetness on treacle and on brimstone" (17.181), much as Trollope's narrator affects to do himself. In Miss Dunstable's case, in particular, we are made to feel the vitality and the appeal of her fast-paced life as well as the positive danger to sincerity that it represents. Her marriage, with its two houses, in which she retains her semidecadent gatherings in London but submits to her husband's puritanical discipline in the country, demonstrates the privileges of moral and social ambivalence available to those with superior means, intelligence, and moral creativity. It is crucial for Trollope to distinguish as well between an exceptional, dissembling Lucy Robarts and her middling, honest relatives, Mark and Fanny, and between honest Mr. Harding and his more creative daughter, Eleanor, in *The Warden*. The novels regularly contrast characters who toy with temptation but ultimately refuse it, with characters like Lucy Robarts who do successfully transgress, who "get out of old-fashioned grooves" (16.176), as Lord Lufton puts it. In Trollope's novels, we are presented both with inadequate yet respectable "middling" honesty, and with strikingly contrasted exceptional characters, who define a certain area of moral and cultural privilege through their capacities for transgression. Social mobility itself is largely reserved for these exceptional characters. Material rewards in Trollope are correlated, not simply to virtue, but to the transgressive coupling of virtue and its diametrical opposites—dishonesty and desire.

Trollope's attempt to "except" transgression in certain individuals creates a lexicon of elite behavior which is both honest and dishonest, bourgeois and antibourgeois at the same time. The analogical plots of his novels, which compare parallel models of behavior in differing circumstances, produce these patterns of exceptionality by creating an elaborate network of symbolic echoes and contrasts between disinterest and desire. The result is a narrative formula for transgression which seems, paradoxically, to base moral authority in the exercise of transgressive desire itself, and vice versa. At the heart of nineteenth-century bourgeois liberalism is a dynamics of elite transgression meant to separate the sophisticated bourgeois from the dullard. A novelist such as Trollope ought to be understood not as the enemy of the antibourgeois impulse, but as a significant example of its fundamental processes and paradoxes. If he leaves his readers with a general sense of complacency, it is not necessarily by describing the world as a safe and comfortable place, but by showing them how to acquire cultural sophistication—that is, how to include certain kinds of transgression within their own notions of cultural wisdom and their presentation of themselves to others.

The transgression of class boundaries essential to middle-class self-consciousness is not always a sublimated displacement of disturbing energies and desires (which is often how it is conventionally trivialized). This internal tension is part of a general phenomenon of conscious bourgeois self-resistance, evident throughout the history of the novel and in every other phase of middle-class culture. For middle-class culture, in addition to militantly opposing the classes above and below it, has always been strangely oppositional to itself, as a direct result of its need to serve the cultural and social mobility of its vanguard elements. The antibourgeois impulse, to the extent that it is present in a novelist like Trollope, helps form the kind of middle-class elite that depends on a conviction, however liminally expressed, of the transcendent fluidity of its social and moral identity. A recognition of this elite component of transgression can ultimately help us understand the continuity between Victorian writing and the more urgent kinds of antibourgeois stands in modernist and contemporary culture. Readers have always attempted to place such Victorian writers as Trollope either "inside" or "outside" middle-class norms—labels that have always been a symptomatic temptation for modern criticism, which very often seeks to validate "scandalous" literary postures in morally righteous terms. But it is more important to understand the way in which symbolic structures that oppose middle-class values to what they exclude allowed the

Victorian novelist to create a space of cultural exceptionality. This transgressive exceptionality aspires to be neither wholly outside of bourgeois culture nor wholly reconciled to it. In this way, self-conscious transgression becomes one aspect of the wise apartness and moral detachment that is so oddly congruent, in elite bourgeois culture, with convictions of one's sophisticated initiation into the mysteries and enchantments of vice.

CHAPTER TWO

Competitive Elites in Wilkie Collins: Cultural Intellectuals and Their Professional Others

Contemporary literary criticism, in its political nervousness, has hurried to demystify the oppositional postures of even the most virulent Victorian rebels. But up until at least the mid-1980s, critics routinely perceived certain Victorian writers—Charles Reade, M. E. Braddon, Wilkie Collins—to be essentially deviant. Their works were seen as a challenge to mainstream bourgeois culture so fundamental that it promised a radical break from that culture. "Deviant" Victorian fiction used to be linked, proleptically, to the modernist's strident rebellion against middle-class culture, and this historical narrative of liberation lent urgency to critical explorations of the Victorian underground.[1] It is easy to hear the thrill of rediscovered origins in U. C. Knoepflmacher's praise for

[1] Winifred Hughes claims that certain sensation novelists openly flouted bourgeois moral conventions in a way that prepared for the radical subversions of the modernists (*The Maniac in the Cellar: Sensation Novels of the 1860s* [Princeton: Princeton University Press, 1980], pp. 71–72). U. C. Knoepflmacher, in his well-known "The Counterworld of Victorian Fiction and *The Woman in White*," in *The Worlds of Victorian Fiction*, ed. Jerome H. Buckley, Harvard English Studies no. 6 (Cambridge: Harvard University Press, 1975), pp. 351–69, describes these and more "serious" writers such as Meredith and Thackeray as part of a gathering underground movement that sought to question official bourgeois values. Richard Altick studies the proliferation, during the 1860s, of crime novels about middle-class lawbreakers, which he finds to be harbingers of the middle-class rejection of

Wilkie Collins's *The Woman in White*, which Knoepflmacher called "a unique instance of a mid-Victorian novel in which the author openly acknowledges an anarchic and asocial counterworld as a powerfully attractive alternative to the ordered, civilized world of conventional belief."[2]

Such claims now seem politically and culturally naive. Nancy Armstrong, D. A. Miller, and Mary Poovey, among other critics, have detailed the ideological economies of Victorian fiction.[3] Scrupulous historical scholarship has also shown that the Victorian novel was an unusually well-regulated and insular art form, thanks to marketplace mechanisms that shaped quality fiction to the needs of a narrow middle-class readership.[4] These critical reorientations are welcome ones—the preceding chapter draws on them to demonstrate how transgression in Trollope serves the interests of a bourgeois elite. Nevertheless, critics are in danger of forgetting an important symbolic dynamic of Victorian culture by overlooking the way images of deviance anchored the symbolic repertoire of Victorian self-representation. The "inside" and the "outside" of Victorian culture were quite deliberately staked out by Victorian writers in ways that are yet to be fully understood. If Anthony Trollope represented himself as the consummate insider (despite the transgressive sophistication we have seen him incorporate into the social identity of the

---

its own traditional values later in the century; see his *Deadly Encounters: Two Victorian Sensations* (Philadelphia: University of Pennsylvania Press, 1986).

[2] Knoepflmacher, "Counterworld of Victorian Fiction," p. 353.

[3] For a reading of the disciplinary dynamics of sensation fiction, see Ann Cvetkovich, *Mixed Feelings: Feminism, Mass Culture, and Victorian Sensationalism* (New Brunswick, N.J.: Rutgers University Press, 1992). Cvetkovich's argument is complex, but her critical attitude toward the nineteenth-century politics of affect inclines her to see "figures of resistance" in sensation fiction as ultimately "a covert form of domination" (p. 8).

[4] J. A. Sutherland shows in great detail how the publishing industry deliberately restricted the availability of fiction to middle-class budgets, partly to preserve the growing respectability of the novel (*Victorian Novelists and Publishers* [London: Athlone Press, 1976]). Darko Suvin shows that until the 1890s the reading audience for fiction was a startlingly small proportion of the general public, perhaps no more than 5 percent to 7 percent of the population, and that it was overwhelmingly middle-class in composition ("The Social Addressees of Victorian Fiction: A Preliminary Inquiry," *Literature and History* 8 [1982], 11–40). The most clinical of these accounts is N. N. Feltes, *Modes of Production of Victorian Novels* (Chicago: University of Chicago Press, 1986). See also Terry Lovell, *Consuming Fiction* (London: Verso, 1987).

insider), Wilkie Collins clearly styled himself as the prototypical outsider. When Collins satirized muscular Christianity in *Man and Wife*, for example, he reveled in the knowledge that he was running against the grain of popular opinion. Reviewers in England, nearly unanimous in denouncing the novel's attack on British athletics, gratified Collins's desire to write "an *un*-popular book," and to savor the "oddity of a modern writer running full tilt against the popular sentiment instead of cringing to it."[5] Collins's flippancy on the subject suggests a histrionic cultivation of the role of the outsider that we tend to reserve for turn-of-the-century rebellions.

However we evaluate Victorian deviance, it is impossible to deny that very different postures toward the writer's social position— either within or without mainstream bourgeois culture—were self-consciously adopted by mid-Victorian novelists themselves. It is no critical misprision that inspired Hawthorne to find Trollope "as English as a beef-steak" or that tempted others to stress Collins's francophilia.[6] Any repression of these social postures can risk their return, often despite strenuous critical efforts to the contrary. Even a careful and rigorous reader such as D. A. Miller, whose Foucauldian principles incline him to regard all Victorian novels as captive to disciplinary norms, tends to see Trollope as the most unself-critical advocate of mechanisms of social control, while he finds that Collins at least revealed the norm to be "monstrous."[7] In any case, the polar extremes represented by Trollope and Collins in the Victorian imagination seem to be clearly marked by the two writers' attitudes— both explicit and implicit—toward social authority. Although Trollope relished the way his profession had gained him access to the

[5] Letter to Messrs. Cassell, 25 September 1869, held by the Humanities Research Center, University of Texas at Austin. See Kenneth Robinson's summary of the novel's reception in *Wilkie Collins: A Biography* (London: Bodley Head, 1951), p. 239. See also Nuel Pharr Davis, *The Life of Wilkie Collins* (Urbana: University of Illinois Press, 1956), pp. 263–65.

[6] Trollope quoted Hawthorne's remark approvingly in *An Autobiography*, World's Classics (New York: Oxford University Press, 1980), 8.144. On Collins's francophilia, see Robinson, *Wilkie Collins*, p. 250.

[7] D. A. Miller, "The Novel as Usual: Trollope's *Barchester Towers*," in *Sex, Politics, and Science in the Nineteenth-Century Novel: Selected Papers from the English Institute, 1983–1984*, ed. Ruth Bernard Yeazell (Baltimore: Johns Hopkins University Press, 1986), pp. 1–38; D. A. Miller, "*Cage aux folles*: Sensation and Gender in Wilkie Collins's *The Woman in White*," *Representations* 14 (1986), 119.

society of lords, Collins developed—or at least affected—a distaste for "that lamentable commonplace about the 'making of aristocratic connections.'"[8] Legendary diatribes against sensation fiction by the Archbishop of York and others identified the genre popularly by its social provocations. As Henry James put it, the sensation novelist "interprets the illegitimate world to the legitimate world."[9]

Some of Collins's oppositional postures were rooted in genuine political extremism, and his political differences with Trollope were quite concrete. Trollope (a self-described "Advanced Conservative-Liberal") professed a belief in moderate social reform, but novels like *The Warden* make it clear he had more sympathy for the victims of social change than for the victims of established order.[10] Collins, however, was a maverick reformer. Beginning with *No Name*, his novels launched a series of assaults on problems of social injustice, and he was widely regarded at the time to have gone into decline as his novels became too stridently propagandistic. In an essay on Collins, Swinburne parodied a well-known rhyme of Pope's:

> What brought good Wilkie's genius nigh perdition?
> Some demon whispered—"Wilkie! Have a mission."[11]

Collins's late novel, *The Fallen Leaves*, features a socialist hero and expresses considerable sympathy with American utopian socialist communities.[12] In *No Name*, an attack on the legal standing of bastards, he came disturbingly close to sanctioning a string of crimes—including forgery, burglary, and imposture—perpetrated by an illegitimate heroine outraged at the hypocrisy of the law. Review-

---

[8] William Wilkie Collins, "A Rogue's Life," *Household Words* 13 (1856), 158. On Collins's "conscious decision to be not quite a gentleman," see Catherine Peters, *The King of Inventors: A Life of Wilkie Collins* (London: Secker and Warburg, 1991), p. 101.

[9] Henry James, "Miss Braddon," *Nation* 1 (1865), 594.

[10] For a good discussion of his political views, see N. John Hall, *Trollope: A Biography* (Oxford: Clarendon Press, 1991), pp. 112–13, 138; and Jane Nardin, "The Social Critic in Anthony Trollope's Novels," *SEL* 30 (1990), 679–96.

[11] A. C. Swinburne, "Wilkie Collins," *Fortnightly Review* 52 (1889), 598. Peters explains Collins's decline in much more complicated terms, in *King of Inventors*, pp. 313–14.

[12] On Collins and socialism, see Peters, *King of Inventors*, pp. 107, 386.

ers barely had time to complain about the heroine, however, in their rush to chastise Collins for his depiction of her parents, the Vanstones—a couple living in sin without shame (mirroring Collins's own irregular unions with Caroline Graves and Martha Rudd).

Nevertheless, it is often difficult, in Collins's case, to distinguish ideological substance from cultural mythmaking. Collins's fondness for scandalizing middle-class sensibilities was felt to be gratuitous even by his close friend Dickens. In 1858, Dickens wrote to W. H. Wills, the assistant editor of *Household Words,* "I particularly wish you to look well to Wilkie's article . . . and not to leave anything in it that may be sweeping, and unnecessarily offensive to the middle class. He always has a tendency to overdo that."[13] During his occasionally tense trip to Italy with Collins and Augustus Egg, Dickens boasted with double-edged irony, "He occasionally expounds a code of morals, taken from modern French novels, which I instantly and with becoming gravity smash."[14] Reviewers jumped at Collins's bait with less self-detachment, calling *Basil* "absolutely disgusting," a work aspiring to the "aesthetics of the Old Bailey."[15] An American critic claimed of *The New Magdalen* that "a play so utterly vicious . . . has never before been produced at a New York theatre."[16] Evidently, Collins took great delight in this atmosphere of scandal. Having witnessed a young girl on a railway car furtively reading *The New Magdalen,* only daring to pull the book out of her bag after her father had fallen asleep, Collins told an interviewer, "Alas for my art! . . . it was stuff . . . which raised the famous Blush, stuff registered on the Expurgatory Index of the national cant. Who will praise *The New Magdalen* when I am dead and gone? Not one humbug—thank God!"[17] It is a short step from this kind of posturing

[13] *The Letters of Charles Dickens,* ed. Walter Dexter, 3 vols. (London: Nonesuch, 1938), 3:58. See also Knoepflmacher, "Counterworld of Victorian Fiction," p. 360.

[14] Walter Dexter, ed., *Mr. and Mrs. Charles Dickens: His Letters to Her* (London: Constable, 1935), Fall 1853, p. 188.

[15] *Westminster Review* 69 (1853), 372; *Athenaeum,* no. 1310 (4 December 1852), 1323.

[16] Quoted by Robert P. Ashley, "Wilkie Collins and the American Theater," *Nineteenth-Century Fiction* 8 (1954), 250.

[17] William Wilkie Collins, "Reminiscences of a Story Teller," *Universal Review* 1 (1888), 191.

to literary commonplaces that associate Trollope with fox hunting and Collins with opium.[18] Or to the more cunning backlash that sees such distinctions as simply two sides of the same hegemonic coin.[19]

I am interested neither in erasing nor in reifying the opposition between Trollope and Collins, nor am I proposing a comprehensive materialist analysis of all its discrete origins (though this last project would certainly be worth doing). Rather, I believe that taking the insider/outsider dynamic seriously as a cultural logic, and reading it as a generative one within the works of *both* these writers, can demonstrate a fundamental political difference between them: that is, a difference in the ways this shared cultural logic exalted the particular subclasses with which Trollope and Collins identified themselves. These two writers can thus show us that recognition of the difference between bourgeois and antibourgeois energies in the Victorian novel must also attend to the interdependent nature of these energies. The fluid opposition between the two general camps of Victorian fiction that Trollope and Collins emblematize so well is, in one sense, the large-scale projection of an interdependent opposition between bourgeois and antibourgeois energies that is embedded more subtly in all Victorian writing. Neither an absolute break, nor an insignificant one, the Trollope/Collins opposition can be interpreted as one phase of a fundamentally middle-class symbolic process, a process best explained through reference to shared structural principles in the works themselves. At the same time, though,

[18] See Davis, *Life of Wilkie Collins*, p. 295; and Robinson, *Wilkie Collins*, p. 281. Collins took opium not for recreational purposes but for his mysterious "rheumatic gout."

[19] Collins and Trollope both published in *The Cornhill*, for example, and were both read by the same general class of readers. Though Collins seems to have attracted the hostility of many reviewers, he was praised warmly by such diverse paragons of Victorian taste as Prince Albert, Thackeray, William Gladstone, Edward Fitzgerald, and A. C. Swinburne. See Amy Cruse, *The Victorians and Their Reading* (Boston: Houghton Mifflin, 1935), p. 322. When Collins spoke of writing an "*un*-popular book," he also expected to "make a hit" out of it (Letter to Messrs. Cassel), and *Man and Wife* actually turned out to be the most remunerative of all Collins's novels. Sue Lonoff shows quite clearly that Collins's greatest ambition was to be a popular novelist, "selling widely and appealing to middle-brow, middle-class readers" (*Wilkie Collins and his Victorian Readers: A Study in the Rhetoric of Authorship* [New York: AMS Press, 1982], p. 1). One could reverberate endlessly between Collins's difference from or identity with Victorian literary norms, if one chose to view such questions in absolute terms.

I want to make it clear that Trollope's and Collins's divergent uses of this process demonstrate the very different political interests served by transgressing the symbolic boundaries of inside and outside.

Victorian fiction routinely exploits an opposition between specifically bourgeois and specifically antibourgeois energies, between official and deviant values—an opposition that was just as important to novelists like Trollope as it was to novelists like Collins. The crucial symbolic product of this opposition is transgression itself, which always depends on metaphors of inside and outside. For both Trollope and Collins, the symbolic production of transgression is crucial to a number of generalized powers, but it is fundamental, most of all, to their construction of a domain of bourgeois sophistication. In this chapter, I compare Collins's handling of antibourgeois energies to those I have already outlined in Trollope, in order to show how, in both "official" and "deviant" fiction, transgression retains the same symbolic structure, particularly in its dependence on categories of class for the projection of a sophisticated middle-class elite.

As we have seen in the case of Trollope, the existence of an exceptional middle-class identity—what Nancy Armstrong has called a "middle-class aristocracy"—depends on the tensions between bourgeois norms and antibourgeois resistance to those norms.[20] Collins, too, sought to affirm an exceptional middle-class identity, and he participated in the general Victorian strategy of defining the elite through an *upward* form of transgression, a crossing of inside/outside boundaries that testified to the acquisition of more cultural power by one subgroup than by the rest of the middle class. But instead of endorsing the genteel, largely professional upper-middle class that Trollope rendered sublime through transgression, Collins wrote about and for an entirely different middle-class elite—that of what I call "cultural intellectuals." Though they are surrounded by a large supporting cast of doctors and lawyers, Collins's protagonists tend to be drawing masters, writers, actresses, amateur painters and philosophers—especially in his major novels of the

[20] Nancy Armstrong, *Desire and Domestic Fiction: A Political History of the Novel* (New York: Oxford University Press, 1987), p. 160.

1860s, when he was consolidating his literary success. In his identification with this cultural fringe, and in his attempt to produce their
identity through an ambiguous antiprofessionalism, Collins's general
posture of outsiderhood had a culturally specific foundation that its
flamboyant individualism, as well as its flamboyant slumming, often
conceals. Rather than wholly taking on an outlaw identity, Collins
exploited his outsiderhood to support a particular kind of collective
middle-class authority.

Collins's protobohemian class, with the eagerness to define itself
through vilification that characterizes all cultural fringes, took professional figures as their negative role models—guides to social
mobility through rationalized standards of expertise, on the one
hand, but serious threats to the legitimacy of a nonscientific elite,
on the other. Collins's novels tried to associate the sophisticated
enchantments of transgression with cultural intellectuals by opposing
them, not simply to more elevated and more degraded social figures
(as was the case in Trollope), but also to their more securely
established professional brethren, who had recently carried out their
own successful assault on the status hierarchy—particularly (but not
exclusively) on those in the law.[21] Though we have heard a great
deal, recently, about the new professional self-consciousness of
mid-Victorian writers, the ambivalence and even hostility toward
professional culture of a certain kind of Victorian literary authority
has received considerably less attention.[22] The presence of such
intraclass antagonism ought to qualify analyses of social hegemony,
such as D. A. Miller's, that take the law (or any other specific social

---

[21] By contrast, Trollope tended to view the law as "not only a machinery for the
practical functioning of society but an expression of spiritual principles" (R. D.
McMaster, *Trollope and the Law* [London: Macmillan, 1986], p. x). Coral Lansbury
shares this view; see her *The Reasonable Man: Trollope's Legal Fiction* (Princeton:
Princeton University Press, 1981).

[22] See, for example, Mary Poovey, "The Man-of-Letters Hero: *David Copperfield*
and the Professional Writer," in *Uneven Developments: The Ideological Work of
Gender in Mid-Victorian England* (Chicago: University of Chicago Press, 1988),
pp. 89–125; Feltes, *Modes of Production*; and Gaye Tuchman, *Edging Women Out:
Victorian Novelists, Publishers, and Social Change* (New Haven: Yale University Press,
1989). Tamar Heller traces the professionalization of Walter Hartright in *The
Woman in White*, but she neglects the novel's simultaneous antipathy to professionalism (*Dead Secrets: Wilkie Collins and the Female Gothic* [New Haven: Yale University
Press, 1992]).

practice) to be a model of undifferentiated disciplinary normalization.[23]

Largely because of the greater social insecurity of the cultural intellectual, Collins subjects the dynamic of insider and outsider to a more corrosive scrutiny than does Trollope. One reason why Collins has always occupied the niche of the literary deviant, in fact, is that he attempted to make conventional social boundaries between inside and outside seem extremely volatile—though only in terms of familiar institutional markers. His ultimate goal was not anarchic liberation from class categories, but expression of the convoluted social claims to insiderhood, relative to social institutions of legitimacy, of the "outcast" cultural intellectual. Collins has often been slighted by later, more radical writers for presenting his rebellious protagonists as victims and for reconciling them, eventually, to what he clearly sees as an oppressive society. Collins's outsiders have often been regarded as slaves to their desire to recover a legitimate place as insiders.[24] But Collins actually sought to suspend institutional distinctions between inside and outside, largely by confusing the legal principles distinguishing legitimacy and illegitimacy as social metaphors. The paradigmatic Collins protagonist has been abruptly and "unfairly" deprived of legitimate social position, inheritance, and identity. But the reasserted claims to legitimacy of this figure are often impossible to reconcile—which is not always a bad thing—with available standards of social rationalization, of which the law is the chief embodiment. Magdalen Vanstone is the classic example. By manipulating our sympathy in her favor, *No Name* seems to support Magdalen's claim that she has "natural rights" to the inheritance she lost due to her father's legal incompetence.[25] Yet her violent assertion of those rights is also contrasted unfavorably with her sister Norah's acceptance of legal inevitabilities

[23] See Miller, "*Cage aux folles*," p. 113.

[24] George Bernard Shaw wrote of Collins that "what has happened since is that we have changed sides to a great extent; and though we may not all care to say so, yet it is the rebel against society who interests us; and we want to see the rebel triumphant rather than crushed or reconciled" ("The New Magdalen and the Old," in *Dramatic Opinions and Essays* [New York: Brentano's, 1907], p. 223).

[25] William Wilkie Collins, *No Name*, World's Classics (New York: Oxford University Press, 1986), p. 437. Unless otherwise noted, references to Collins's novels will be to page numbers in this edition.

that serendipitously restore both sisters' inheritances anyway.[26] Collins's plots tend to revolve around attempts to reassert the legitimacy of disenfranchised figures, but these attempts must always circumvent legal methods and principles that the novels question without entirely overthrowing. Collins's lifelong fascination with legal quirks, loopholes, and labyrinths defines both the indispensability and the tragic unreliability of legal systems, which can never make social justice conform to intuitive human sympathies. He reveals the legal grounds of social legitimacy to be precariously adventitious, even as they offer necessary safeguards against the vindictive excesses of the disenfranchised.

Ambiguities about the distinction between legitimacy and illegitimacy, juridically defined, allowed Collins to evoke very different emotional responses to characters whose legal dilemmas are strikingly similar. For instance, his victims of belatedly discovered bastardy—Sir Percival Glyde in *The Woman in White*, Magdalen Vanstone in *No Name*, Rosamond Treverton in *The Dead Secret*—are viewed with extraordinarily different degrees of sympathy and revulsion (or combinations of the two). These instabilities tend to explode legal "unfairness" as an index of narrative sympathy. Once everyone's social status has become equally vulnerable to legal caprice, disastrous encounters with the law are no guarantee of sainthood. In fact, the grudges of disenfranchised outsiders are sometimes cast in ominously underdetermined forms—as in the curse of the moonstone and the obscure sense of fatality that haunts *Armadale*. In one sense, increasing the legal friction along the insider/outsider boundary without supplying any way to reduce it in institutional terms provided Collins with a way to express the tortured desire of cultural intellectuals to both identify with and distance themselves from arbitrarily enfranchised insiders. It also allowed him to make legally grounded distinctions between the social inside and outside seem hopelessly porous.

Appropriating an age-old strategy of middle-class English fiction,

[26] Helena Michie demonstrates that the novel undermines the moral distinctions between the two sisters, preventing a reductive moral reading (" 'There Is No Friend Like a Sister': Sisterhood as Sexual Difference," *ELH* 56 [1989], 401–21). See also Lewis Horne, "Magdalen's Peril," *Dickens Studies Annual: Essays on Victorian Fiction* 20 (1991), 281–94.

Collins destabilized prevailing standards of legitimacy in order to correct legal fallibility in meritocratic terms. The *moral* axis of legitimacy, which is articulated in Collins's novels (as in Trollope's) primarily in terms of truth-telling, turns out to be much more reliable than institutional markers of legitimacy. But such merits depend in fundamental ways on ethical reversibility. That is to say, like Trollope, Collins tried to distinguish the special social deserts of those who could negotiate the moral gap between honesty and lying in ways that seem to advance the administration of social justice. Legitimate claims to insiderhood come to rest, not simply on moral grounds, but on the logic of *transgressive* moral authority. Critical analyses of the traditional moralizing mission of English fiction often overlook the role of such sophistication, which uses transgressive means to (supposedly) moral ends. The differences in our sympathies for characters like Sir Percival, Magdalen, and Rosamond are made to depend, finally, on their skill and discretion in making exceptional forays across the honesty/dishonesty distinction, rather than on either the legal circumstances of their claims or on their simple moral purity. Destabilizing legal markers of legitimacy thus paves the way for Collins's reorganization of social boundaries on morally transgressive terrain, and particularly for his creation of a space of middle-class elitism reserved for cultural intellectuals—and explicitly opposed to the authority of the law—in which moral issues of honesty and dishonesty are histrionically finessed.

Though Trollope tried to stigmatize sensation fiction in its entirety as "a species of deceit" (*Barchester Towers*, 15.130), Collins's novels are similarly centered on the moral authority of truth-telling.[27] The last pages of *The Dead Secret*, for example, could have been written by Trollope himself. Rosamond's frank, unforced confession of illegitimacy overwhelms her husband's prejudices about rank and teaches him a "lesson" about social position that he, in turn, articulates for his exemplary wife: "The highest honours, Rosamond, are those which no accident can take away—the honours that are conferred by LOVE and TRUTH."[28] As in Trollope, the greatest of all

[27] See the comments of Alexander Welsh on the conventionalism of Collins's moral framework (*Strong Representations: Narrative and Circumstantial Evidence in England* [Baltimore: Johns Hopkins University Press, 1992], pp. 217–18).

[28] William Wilkie Collins, *The Dead Secret*, 2 vols. (London: Bradbury and Evans, 1857), 2:331.

crimes in Collins is falsehood. The most magnificent viper in Collins's work, Lydia Gwilt, is characterized primarily by her false-hoods: "No creature more innately deceitful and more innately pitiless ever walked this earth" (*Armadale*, 27). But—again, as in Trollope—this entirely conventional moral framework allowed Col-lins to explore the possibilities of moral transgression through con-junctions of honesty and dishonesty in his independent, resourceful, "insider/outsider" protagonists. Collins's heroic figures are always those who nimbly cross this moral divide, and their transgressions are presented as a linked mastery of both moral and social difference. Collins's chief difficulty, however, lay in distinguishing the trans-gressive sophistication of cultural intellectuals from that of the more socially secure professional models—like those celebrated by Trollope, for example—on which it seems to be based.

A close look at *The Woman in White*—which was serialized at the same time as Trollope's *Framley Parsonage*, in 1860—reinforces the claims of the last chapter, that a strong antibourgeois principle flourished at the heart of the bourgeois Victorian novel through transgressions of the distinction between honesty and dishonesty. It also reinforces my argument that the antibourgeois principle defines a space of cultural privilege not entirely independent of middle-class norms, as a region of morally fluid middle-class sophistication. Writers as solidly "establishment" as Trollope and as seemingly antiestablishment as Collins depended on this dialectic equally, and attempts to place these figures on either side of a great cultural boundary neglect the similar symbolic role of antibourgeois energies in both. Yet the very different terms in which this symbolic logic was mapped across class terrain can provide a new way of charting the political differences of Victorian writers. It can also suggest how the battle over "insider" and "outsider" positions among Victorian writers expressed (and also disguised) more subtle social tensions, in which the social mapping of symbolic processes served the needs of a number of distinct constituencies. In the next two sections, I trace the dynamics of transgression in *The Woman in White* and show how, in Collins, the antibourgeois sophistication of cultural intellectuals depends on an uneasy antiprofessionalism that distinguishes it from Trollope's much more comfortable identification with professional enfranchisement.

❦

Whatever the overt differences in their attitudes toward sex, art, and politics, both Collins and Trollope define honesty as one of the most important moral and psychological norms to which their protagonists must adhere. In *The Woman in White*, Collins makes honesty not just a central moral value but a necessary erotic condition. Despite the intermittent romance of the sensational, honesty and its vehicle—rational understanding—constantly shape the protagonists' desires. To begin with, the attraction between Walter Hartright and Laura Fairlie depends on their reverence for each other's extraordinary candor. Laura, in particular, is desirable because of her exemplary sincerity. During his first glimpse of her, Walter returns over and over to adjectives like "plain," "natural," and "simple" (40–41). He quickly concludes that "the key to her whole character" is that "generous trust in others which, in her nature, grew innocently out of the sense of her own truth" (44). Laura's bizarre declaration to her fiancé, Sir Percival Glyde—her voluntary confession that she is in love with someone else, yet willing to submit to the marriage she promised her late father—is only the most extreme instance of a systematic equation the novel makes between honesty and the heroine as love object. "She never broke a promise in her life" (123), Marian claims, and Sir Percival himself acknowledges sarcastically that Laura is "famous for telling the truth" (221).

Walter is equally distinguished for his honesty, from his opening encounter with the woman in white, who resolves eventually to trust him, through his nightlong confrontation with Count Fosco, in which he stakes his life on a strategy of telling and demanding the truth. During his pursuit of Fosco and Sir Percival, Walter pointedly disdains the use of disguise, which would be "something so meanly like the common herd of spies and informers" (445). In these ways, Walter answers Marian Halcombe's heartfelt yearning, shared throughout the novel by her sister, to discover a "clear-headed, trustworthy man acting for [our] good" (281). Marian explains that "the delicacy and forbearance and sense of honour which drew me to poor Hartright . . . were just the qualities to appeal most irresistibly to Laura's natural sensitiveness and natural generosity of nature" (145). Appropriately, Walter and Laura are altogether incapable of concealing the first blooming of their love from each other. In telling us that Laura easily "surprised my secret" (56), Walter acknowledges also that her "true face owned all." Moreover, as the active male counterpart to Laura's embodied feminine truthfulness, Walter defines the social goal of all three protagonists as a quest, not for financial restitution, but for simple recognition of the truth of their story. Walter's collection of multiple narratives, while it calls attention to ambiguities of interpretation, is explicitly compared at the beginning to the testimony of witnesses before a court of law—"with the same object, in both cases, to present the truth always in its most direct and intelligible aspect" (1). At this stage, Walter invokes the example of the law to claim that his narrative can model itself on professional standards of probity.

As does Trollope, Collins conceives the boundary between honesty and dishonesty in strict class terms, and he defines transgressions against honesty as problems of moral ideology. As a drawing master from a modest family in financial difficulties, Walter is essentially middle-class in his social origins and attitudes—as his attraction to the passive, dependent, and truthful Laura (rather than the independent and strong-willed Marian) makes clear. Laura and Marian may initially confuse class categories, but this confusion only helps prepare for their later rectification. Laura is of high birth on her father's side, but her mother's social background, as well as fidelity and charity, are decidedly nonaristocratic. In her conduct, Laura seems to exemplify her mother's values: she is a model of middle-class female self-denial, as her deliberately modest dress and faithfulness to her father's wishes demonstrate. Marian, on the other hand, is of lower birth and lacks both wealth and beauty. Yet she displays the "unaffected self-reliance of a highly-bred woman" (26), and she dresses to her high social station. This initial inversion is important in establishing the exceptional class character of the three protagonists and their transcendence of strict class limits—aspects of their general exceptionality I will explore later. But despite their lingering class liminality, all three undergo an unmistakable realignment with middle-class social identities in the last third of the novel. Marian's assumption of the duties of housewife in the threesome's London hideaway and her increasing dependence on Walter, as well

as Walter's discovery of a profession free of upper-class patronage—
journalistic illustration—signify a clarified distance from aristocratic
privilege (certified, ironically, by Count Fosco's scorn for Walter's
love-marriage).

This class-coding of honesty as a "middling" (if not inflexibly
middle-class) virtue is further reinforced by the social location of
dishonesty in the novel. Like Trollope, Collins associates deception
and falsehood with "low" characters such as Mrs. Catherick, and
also with foreigners (even Pesca fakes being English), in a virtual
paranoia about the deceitfulness of disenfranchised figures. But, like
Trollope, he identifies dishonesty most of all with his aristocratic
villains. In Sir Percival, deception and aristocratic privilege are
closely linked in what Walter calls "armed Deceit," which makes
Walter's own quest a "struggle against Rank and Power" (381). Sir
Percival's deceit in marriage is, perhaps, his most unforgivable sin
against middle-class standards of honesty, but all his many crimes
amount to "a series of atrocious falsehoods" (359), as Mrs. Michelson puts it. As for Count Fosco—whose wife claims, "his life was
one long assertion of the rights of the aristocracy" (582)—the very
essence of his character is performative deception.

In the teeth of this clear-cut opposition between the bourgeois
sincerity of his protagonists and the limitless extent of aristocratic
deception, Collins's novel sets up a moral gray area—an area of
exceptionality—in which his protagonists appropriate the devious
energies of Percival and Fosco without abandoning their basic commitments to truthfulness. Marian's jokes about the way her sketches
"misrepresent nature" (28) early in the novel, for example, signal an
ambivalence in her conduct that becomes gradually more and more
significant. Marian is the first to "descend to deceit" (63) when she
instructs Walter how to deceive Mr. Fairlie about Walter's reasons
for leaving Limmeridge. Later, in her direct confrontations with
Fosco and Sir Percival, she begins to employ some of the same
strategies as the villains—eavesdropping, secret correspondence,
misleading accounts of her actions, fraudulent conciliation of the
enemy. By the end of the novel, she is capable of bribing a nurse in
order to get Laura out of the London asylum. Yet Marian is never
comfortable with her descent into deceit. She worries constantly
about her "unworthy suspicion" (156) of Sir Percival. And just

before the climactic action of her narrative—her spying on Sir Percival and Fosco from the verandah—she thinks, "I, who once mercilessly despised deceit in other women, was as false as the worst of them, as false as the Judas whose lips had touched my hand" (278). This "Judas"—that is, Count Fosco himself—is more than eager to point out the special affinity between himself and Marian, an affinity that he declares ominously to signal "a Profound Truth" (308). Fosco's great attraction to Marian, ascribed by many readers to Collins's attempt to humanize his villain with a weakness (following the Count's own self-description), actually stems from Fosco's recognition of their similar skills in deception. Immediately after declaring his "Profound Truth," Fosco dwells on "the excellence of the stratagem" in which Marian spies from the verandah. He fantasizes about her, not as a paragon of domestic virtue, but as a possible accomplice in crime: "With that woman for my friend, I would snap these fingers of mine at the world" (296). Collins explored precisely this kind of affinity in his next novel, *No Name*, through the conspiratorial friendship of Magdalen Vanstone and Captain Wragge—the wayward ingenue and the confirmed rogue—who both grow fond of each other's powers of deception. It is not simply due to a chill that at the height of Marian's recognition of her own deceit and at the very point when Fosco articulates in her hearing the affinity between them, Marian falls ill—her narrative place taken over by the more straightforward Hartright. Marian's delirium coincides with a slippage of her middle-class moral identity, and she resembles a number of heroines in Collins who suffer broken mental health after practicing deception.

The significance of Walter's narrative supplanting Marian's, however, lies partly in Walter's superior dexterity in joining honor together with cunning. Throughout Collins's novels, it is usually men—usually male cultural intellectuals such as Walter—who model a moral balance unrealized by either excessively bold or excessively tentative women.[29] This kind of sexual competition in the realm of

[29] Welsh recognizes this gender difference in standards for truth-telling (*Strong Representations*, p. 229), though I believe he turns a relative difference into an absolute one. Contrary to Welsh's claim, the veracity of male protagonists in Victorian fiction is always an issue—if only as the springboard for transgressive possibilities. Welsh mistakes the greater flexibility of male moral sophistication for the absence of any symbolic tension in masculine moral identity.

transgression produces the backlash by women writers against moral sophistication that I explore in Chapter 4. On his return from Central America (a marginal social space in which the British male colonialist learns the kind of "stratagem" [418] necessary for dealing with his enemies), Walter begins his vindication of Laura by compelling all three protagonists to live under "assumed names" in an "assumed relationship"—"we are numbered no longer with the people whose lives are open and known" (379). Not only must Walter resort to stratagems in his duel with Percival and Fosco—"there was no choice but to oppose cunning by cunning" (411)—he also manipulates crucial information out of Mrs. Catherick and Mrs. Clements, frequently asking them whether "our interest in the matter . . . was not the same" (423), a strategy that echoes Fosco's approach to Anne, Marian, and Sir Percival himself. Perhaps Walter's most disturbing lie is his "innocent deception" (442) about Laura's sketches, which he only pretends to sell in order to appease her anxiety about being usefully employed. Sir Percival is not Laura's only deceitful husband. But it is perhaps more significant that, after Walter models his narrative on the law, it is from the law itself that he withholds the biggest "Secret" (254) of all—Sir Percival's forgery—in order to protect Laura's reputation.

Many critics have also commented on Walter's "rhetorical lying" as a narrator and on the now commonplace connections between crime and detection that it reinforces.[30] Both criminals and detectives in this novel are centrally concerned with the manipulation of texts—letters, diaries, registries, epitaphs, account books, tattoos—and their mutual engagement in the play of textual deception points to a common contagion. Count Fosco philosophizes, "The hiding of a crime, or the detection of a crime, what is it? A trial of skill between the police on one side, and the individual on the other" (210–11). Despite Walter's claim in the "Preamble" to present his material "in its most direct and most intelligible aspect" (1), the very existence of mystery and suspense depends on Walter's (and Collins's) crafting of secrets, gaps, and false leads—the narrative's own "hiding of the crime." The presence of such narrative deceit

---

[30] Walter Kendrick's discussion of these connections, in "The Sensationalism of *The Woman in White*," *Nineteenth-Century Fiction* 32 (1977), 18–35, is especially illuminating.

was a common complaint raised against sensation fiction by Victorian critics. Sir James Stephen wrote, in 1864, "All these stories are open to the same criticism. Those that hide can find. The person who invented the riddle and knows the explanation is of course able to pretend to discover it by almost any steps . . . and thus he can easily convey the impression of the exercise of any amount of sagacity."[31]

Walter's assumption of the authority to reveal or conceal information at his own discretion, however, is implicitly represented as exceptional, especially since his possession of the narratives of others—at least one of which is frankly extorted—furthers a parallel between himself and Fosco, the invasive possessor of others' letters and diaries. In a novel so concerned with the distinction between honesty and deception, truth and mystification, respect for and invasion of privacy, these parallels call attention to Walter's assumption of a special license to bend the rules of honor under circumstances that he judges might warrant exceptional conduct. Fosco himself points out that Walter's exploitation of information about the Brotherhood constitutes "treachery" (548) against some friend. Walter's antibourgeois assumption of the authority to be dishonest flirts with Fosco's philosophy of moral relativism and Fosco's thesis that the "wise man" is not he who commits no sin, but he who is not "found out" (209). Walter's moments of dishonesty may mark him as exceptional in the most general ways, since the novel resists examining these moral enigmas too closely, but they clearly signify his claim to a special moral status that sanctions his deviations— much as Lucy Robarts's deviations are sanctioned in *Framley Parsonage*.

These deviations remain anxious ones for Collins, and Marian's loss of faith in her own moral status suggests the difficulty of occupying the transgressive ground of deceit. Nevertheless, Collins was always tempted to reward those who transgress against honesty as a sign of their own moral and psychological sophistication. Mercy Merrick, the reformed prostitute of *The New Magdalen*, fraudulently

[31] Sir James Stephen, "Detectives in Fiction and in Real Life," *Saturday Review* 17 (1864), 713. This is also the thesis of Patrick Brantlinger, in "What is 'Sensational' about the Sensation Novel?" *Nineteenth-Century Fiction* 37 (1982), 1–28; see esp. pp. 15–20.

poses as Grace Roseberry and wins the love of the clergyman Julian Gray as a result (though, like other women in Collins, Mercy's deviousness does not win her social respectability). Sometimes, Collins indulged in the thrill of moral transgression by having his characters lie without knowing it—as do both Franklin Blake and Rachel Verinder in *The Moonstone*. His fascination with conjunctions of honesty and dishonesty produced many bizarre narrative permutations, including patterns in which characters pretend to names that are, in fact, legally their own—as when Magdalen "Bygrave" marries Noel Vanstone—and in which such characters as Ozias Midwinter and Sarah Leeson are placed in moral double binds, their loyalty to one party requiring deception of another.

Closely allied to the morally transgressive play of truth and falsehood in Collins's protagonists is *The Woman in White*'s suggestion that psychological maturity depends on exceptional conduct. On the one hand, the protagonists' earnestness is constantly qualified by their discretion. The great "Secret" of Sir Percival and the general secrecy of the Count—signs of aristocratic villainy—are paralleled by a series of secrets the protagonists keep from, or confide in, each other: the secret of Walter's love for Laura, the secret of the resemblance between Laura and Anne Catherick, the secret of Walter's doings in the country. On numerous occasions, the protagonists withhold information from each other when secrecy seems a measure of subjective competence. Confession of secrets to one's enemies in this novel may lead to enslavement, but confession to one's friends may disrupt equilibrium in even more serious ways—as Walter discovers when his face betrays his "unprofessional" love for his pupil. Marian's biggest "lie" is her suppression of her feelings about Walter's marriage, a suppression in which he seems to acquiesce, as he ignores her "sad, hesitating interest" (510) in him. However much romantic renunciation is honored in Victorian fiction, Marian's self-suppression calls attention to her dexterity with certain kinds of silent lying.

On the other hand, the protagonists are strangely allied to the opposite form of class-coded deceit: extravagant self-display. Bourgeois ideology has always contrasted its own "natural" reserve—a sign of inner depth or value—to the ostentatious self-display of the lower or the upper classes, which is labeled either vulgarity or theatricality. In *The Woman in White*, Laura's honesty is signaled by her avoidance of performance—her shyness about her sketches, her refusal to play the piano on demand, her simple clothes. Symptomatically, Walter's narration, in marked contrast to that of Count Fosco, is extremely straightforward and unembellished. Nevertheless, when Fosco brags about his facility for performance through "the grand faculty" of narration, he says suggestively to Walter, "I possess it. Do you?" (552). The novel's hypersensitivity to unexpected resemblances should draw our attention to the oddity of Walter's decision to piece together a narrative at all, especially since his explanation of the conspiracy to the tenants and villagers of Limmeridge has already accomplished his only stated goal—the recovery of Laura's standing in her family home. The "Preamble" thus proves a duplicitous introduction to the novel, preparing us to judge evidence that, as it turns out, has already been judged. Even though Walter claims to have condensed material and to have hidden the clues that would allow readers to trace out the identity of the participants, the fact of the narrative itself points to his exceptional capacity for performance. The "grand faculty" of narration is a talent he consciously prides himself on possessing, in contrast to several of the characters he interviews. Only by "watchful questioning," for example, can Walter carry Mrs. Clements on "from point to point" (423), and his observations on Mrs. Clements's disordered mind parallel Fosco's boast that his own narrative power comes from facility at "arranging [his] ideas" (552). If nothing else, Walter's stoical performance of disinterest systematically disguises his own personal stake in solving the crime, as a number of readers have pointed out.[32]

As a sign of psychological power, the authority to transgress norms of honesty is more than just a means to combat crime in *The Woman in White*. Anne Catherick's psychological emptiness, her possession of the shell of a secret without its kernel, is a metaphor for the "lie" of all understanding about identity, all possibilities for honesty about the self. Thus, Walter's recognition that what was "wanting" (42) in Laura was actually "wanting" in his own memory (i.e., his

---

[32] This is the argument of Pamela Perkins and Mary Donaghy, "A Man's Resolution: Narrative Strategies in Wilkie Collins' *The Woman in White*," *Studies in the Novel* 22 (1990), 392–402. See also Cvetkovich, *Mixed Feelings*, pp. 74–75.

recognition of her resemblance to Anne) parallels the novel's repeated reminders about the distance between word and sensation,
understanding and desire. The loss-of-identity theme in the novel
further reinforces this doubt about the possibility of truth about
the self. Laura is not the only character who loses track of her
identity—whether through delirium, madness, or disorientation.
"Was I Walter Hartright?" (18), the question we hear in the opening
pages, announces a symptomatic problem in a novel that repeatedly
shows how knowledge about the self can prove to be deceptive.
Dreams, suppressed desires, doubles, and premonitions regularly
haunt the subjective solidity of Collins's characters.[33] In this sense,
the capacity to keep secrets—a necessary condition of selfhood in
Collins, as in many Victorian writers—does not imply that such
secrets must be true.

It is perhaps even more obvious in Collins's case than in Trollope's
that unequivocally middle-class characters are critiqued for believing
too simply in the truthfulness of others and for limiting their own
behavior to simplistic standards of honesty. The housekeeper at
Blackwater Park, Eliza Michelson, parodies the middle-class norm
by declaring, "I have been taught to place the claims of truth above
all other considerations" (327), while failing, at the same time, to
see the truth about Count Fosco. Only experience with deceit can
prepare others for a more accurate understanding.[34] Mr. Gilmore,
who is too ready to accept the word of a gentleman as honorable,
and Mr. Kyrle, who will not take Marian's "shocking suspicion"
(383) seriously, suggest how lawyers, too, can suffer from middle-
class blind faith. Laura herself is too trusting to be able to apprehend
the motives of others, as a slavish promise to her unworthy father
and a lack of suspicion about Sir Percival—the fatal errors that drive
the entire novel—make clear. "Her own noble conduct had been
the hidden enemy, throughout, of all the hopes she had trusted to
it" (153), admits Marian. Though Marian is far more suspicious

[33] The most comprehensive study of subjective instability in Collins is Jenny
Bourne Taylor, *In the Secret Theatre of Home: Wilkie Collins, Sensation Narrative, and
Nineteenth-Century Psychology* (London: Routledge, 1988). See also Albert D.
Hutter, "Dreams, Transformations, and Literature: The Implications of Detective
Fiction," *Victorian Studies* 19 (1975), 181–209.

[34] See Jerome Meckier, "Wilkie Collins's *The Woman in White*: Providence against
the Ethics of Propriety," *Journal of British Studies* 22 (1982), 104–20.

than her sister, she, too, fails to free herself of middle-class scruples about suspicion: she fears she will be "distorted by the suspicion which had now become a part of myself" (276), and she repeatedly fights off doubts about Sir Percival and Fosco that turn out to have been justified. The novel's tendency to embarrass those who do not suspect is among its most potent antibourgeois weapons.

One of the characteristic pleasures sensation fiction offered its middle-class readers—a "classy" thrill, it turns out—was the indulgence of suspicion without fear of losing respectability. Quite the contrary: suspicion turns out to be an indispensable instrument of social and psychological empowerment. Echoing the conventional distancing of suspicion, however, the novels sometimes identify it as the special professional climate of the lawyer. The narrator of *No Name*, for example, notes in Mr. Pendril "the latent distrust which is a lawyer's second nature" (114). No doubt, the affinities between either law or medicine and detection ought to have made professionalism a safe reservoir of methods for negotiating transgressive moral space. Professionals in Victorian fiction often prove that an ethos of suspicion—including both a mistrust of others and a willingness to respond with counterstrategies of deceit—can be compatible with middle-class norms of conduct. But in Collins's novels, the antibourgeois pleasures (as well as the necessary subjective skills) of secrecy, deception, and disguise, turn out to be even more deftly wielded by cultural intellectuals like Walter Hartright than by certified professionals. I now look at the competition between these two cultural elites in the general context of Collins's novels of the 1860s, before returning in the last section to examine the cultural intellectual's role in *The Woman in White*.

Almost as a matter of course, Collins stigmatized the two extremes of "lumpenbourgeois" honesty (like Mrs. Michelson's) and aristocratic dishonor, in order to map the transgressive area between them as the socio-symbolic terrain of a new elite. In this respect, he was Trollope's partner in the production of an emergent Victorian self-consciousness, articulated largely in terms of moral discourse, about upper-middle-class sophistication. But rather than being preoccupied with the relatively uncomplicated terms of this project that we have seen in Trollope, Collins spent a good deal more time distinguishing the transgressive moral and psychological skills of a certain micro-elite from the very similar transgressive models found in upper-middle-class professional practices, particularly legal ones (which Collins, having flirted briefly with a legal career as a student of Lincoln's Inn, had both personal and class reasons for wanting to keep at a distance).

One of the ways Collins articulated the symbolic boundaries to be crossed by sophisticated insider/outsiders, in fact, was by projecting moral ambivalence onto the legal institution itself, making legal unreliability seem the result of its moral incoherence. The law, according to Collins, turns out to be a victim of its disorganized commitment to the moral extremes of both honor and deceit. Collins represents the law either as inherently fraudulent—the "pre-engaged servant of the long purse" (*Woman in White*, 1)—or as too credulous to administer justice in any but the most nearsighted and gullible ways. The law's affinity with deception in Collins's novels is often an occasion for cynicism. Repeating a time-honored joke, the novels frequently remark of deceitful women—Lydia Gwilt, Miss Clack—that they would have made good lawyers. In *The Moonstone*, when the three Indian conspirators are incarcerated for a week on a trumped-up charge, we learn that "Justice . . . will stretch a little, if you only pull it the right way" (93). Throughout *The Woman in White*, Sir Percival is aided and abetted by legal devices, most of them designed by his unscrupulous solicitor, Mr. Merriman.

But Collins is just as intent on demonstrating how obtuse the law can be, as a result of its tendency to take supposedly "factual" evidence at face value—that is, without suspicion. The narrative premise of *The Woman in White* underscores the law's limitations when it comes to penetrating deceptive appearances: "If the machinery of the Law could be depended on to fathom every case of suspicion . . . the events which fill these pages might have claimed their share of the public attention in a Court of Justice" (1). This failure to fathom is not entirely attributable to the "oil of gold" that perverts legal "machinery." The excessive faith of Mr. Gilmore and Mr. Kyrle in appearances and gentlemanly honor, in and of themselves, make Walter and Marian more effective instruments of detection than their lawyers. Kyrle generalizes this obtuseness to

English juries, telling Walter he must prove conclusions—which every reader of the novel readily accepts—to a legal system that credits only what is put beyond the reach of all speculation: "When an English jury is to choose between a plain fact, *on* the surface, and a long explanation *under* the surface, it always takes the fact, in preference to the explanation" (408). Readers of the novel's own "long explanation," conditioned by the detective plot to appraise themselves on their interpretive abilities to penetrate surfaces, can only conclude that the law is an ass. In its moral schizophrenia, the law parallels very closely Collins's treatment of the feminine—for womanhood is also represented in the novels as either excessively puritanical or diabolically clever. Thus feminized, the law's moral incoherence reinforces the notion that the law is an erratic institution, when it comes to truth-telling, susceptible to the kinds of accidents and manipulation that render it an unreliable index to social legitimacy.

Mr. Gilmore himself tries to differentiate the two moral extremes of the law by separating legal functions and judicial ones:

> It is the great beauty of the Law that it can dispute any human statement, made under any circumstances, and reduced to any form. If I had felt professionally called upon to set up a case against Sir Percival Glyde, on the strength of his own explanation, I could have done so beyond all doubt. But my duty did not lie in this direction: my function was of the purely judicial kind. I was to weigh the explanation we had just heard; to allow all due force to the high reputation of the gentleman who offered it; and to decide honestly whether the probabilities, on Sir Percival's own showing, were plainly with him, or plainly against him. My own conviction was that they were plainly with him. (117)

Gilmore's professional distinctions do not necessarily hold throughout Collins's novels, though they do show how we, too, are constructed as gullible whenever the reader is compared to "A Judge on the bench" (*Moonstone*, 213). Sensationalism depends, to some degree, on our acceptance of occasional failures to anticipate the novels' reversals of appearances as evidence of our own lagging sophistication. In general, the double-faced moral extremism of the law is a telltale sign of its clumsiness in the areas of transgressive sophistication that Collins sought to affirm as the grounds for social authority.

It is not that Collins never admires professional moral sophistication—far from it. The novels are full of charismatic figures, legal and otherwise, who model moral transgression in their professional methods and are more canny practitioners as a result. Sergeant Cuff, the notoriously brilliant detective of *The Moonstone*, outrages Gabriel Betteredge because his methods make him a "snake in the grass" (127) who can "mystify an honest woman by wrapping her round in a network of lies" (140). But Cuff also awes Betteredge with his ability to work with "a horrid clearness that obliged you to understand him; with an abominable justice that favoured nobody" (184). The Pedgifts, both Senior and Junior, demonstrate a competence in the legal "art of diplomacy" (*Armadale*, 348) that captivates even the reluctant Allan Armadale (Pedgift Sr.'s skill in dealing with Lydia Gwilt comes from having "learnt his profession at the Old Bailey" [346]). Yet they are both paragons of loyalty and good faith to Allan himself. Collins always modeled his protagonists on the moral dexterity exercised by these and other professional crime-solvers. In his admiration for professional sophistication, Collins also tended to conform to general class topographies, favoring the transgressive skills of professionals from the middle branches—such as the Pedgifts—but casting suspicion on upper-class solicitors—such as Merriman—and on "the common herd of spies and informers"— such as the Bashwoods. In this sense, Collins perversely exploited the early nineteenth-century hierarchy of professional "branches" which the professions themselves were combatting, at mid-century, as an obstacle to the consolidation of their unified social authority.[35]

Yet it is striking how often even Collins's favored professionals fail to get to the bottom of the mysteries in the novels, and how often their failures are a consequence either of their excessive distrust or of their excessive honor. Cuff and Bruff, in *The Moonstone*, fall short of solving the novel's mystery by throwing the moral scales out of balance in opposite directions: Cuff, by offending the entire Verinder

[35] On the consolidation of professional branches, see W. J. Reader, *Professional Men: The Rise of the Professional Classes in Nineteenth-Century England* (London: Weidenfeld and Nicolson, 1966); and Philip Elliott, *The Sociology of the Professions* (London: Macmillan, 1972), esp. pp. 32–43.

household with his suspicions of Rachel; Bruff, by holding himself aloof from what he sees as the quackery of Ezra Jennings. The symmetry of their names and failures is not always maintained so perfectly in other novels, but excesses of these two opposed kinds always lead professionals to investigative dead-ends. Mr. Pedgift, Sr., for example, ruins his own efforts in Allan Armadale's behalf by encouraging him to set a spy on Lydia Gwilt, which precipitates Allan's rupture with Midwinter—who calls this act "the vilest of all means," the idea of "some low fellow" (*Armadale*, 387)—and, in consequence, with Pedgift himself. Meanwhile, Pedgift's son gives Allan equally disastrous advice when he recommends that Allan drop the pursuit of Lydia's criminal history out of a sense of honorable, gentlemanly reserve.

The more successful heroes of Collins's novels tend to come, not from the professional world, but from its aestheticized fringes. *The Moonstone*, for example, graphs these social configurations quite clearly. Ezra Jennings, the unlikely solver of the novel's riddle, operates, in his decoding of Dr. Candy's delirious babblings, on the experimental fringes of medical science. His final "exhibition" (457) of Franklin Blake's behavior under the influence of opium is part weird science and part dramatic performance—it is a stagey device that would never pass muster in a court of law, even though it persuades both the lawyer and the detective who witness it.[36] Franklin Blake, whose persistence and resourcefulness are crucial to solving the mystery, is a dilettante, as well as an experimental chemist, whose liberal continental education in the arts was triggered by his father's frustration with the corrupt side of English law. By contrast, the novel's chief antagonists are a crooked lawyer, Ablewhite, and an inept doctor, Mr. Candy, whose practical joke in giving Franklin Blake opium (in revenge for Blake's abuse of the medical profession) actually causes all the mischief.

To be sure, Collins's fringe characters, in their deciphering of the novels' mysteries, always model themselves extensively on professional methods. They emulate professionalism's standards of rationality, codes of self-regulation and disinterest, clinical familiarity

[36] See Welsh on this point, in *Strong Representations*, pp. 225–26. Taylor speculates on the relation of this device to mesmerism (*Secret Theatre of Home*, p. 187).

with criminal mentalities, and discretion in the management of intimate affairs.[37] They often use the medical, psychological, and legal ideas Collins feverishly gleaned from contemporary professional discussions.[38] They also imitate the exceptional moral transgressiveness of the novels' more canny professional figures. But Collins distinguishes his protagonists from professionals in several important respects, which locate their moral and psychological sophistication on nonprofessional social terrain and which suggest, finally, that these fringe intellectuals extend and surpass the various social, moral, and psychological powers of professionals.

Perhaps the most obvious of these differences has to do with receptivity to sensation. Godfrey Ablewhite may be joking when he claims that "Nervous Force" is something that "the law doesn't recognize as property" (227), but Collins's novels are full of lawyers who fail by miscalculating the power of love. Mr. Pedgift's lack of understanding of both Allan's and Bashwood's love for Lydia Gwilt, for example, contrasts strikingly with his comprehension of Lydia's mercenary character. More generally, Collins's protagonists always resist the authority of mere reason, especially when it is embodied in professional assumptions that they dispute. Gabriel Betteredge's one advantage over Sergeant Cuff, it turns out, is his skepticism about rationality: "It was downright frightful to hear him piling up proof after proof against Miss Rachel, and to know, while one was longing to defend her, that there was no disputing the truth of what he said. I am (thank God!) constitutionally superior to reason" (186). Similar sentiments move Franklin Blake to tell Mr. Bruff that he has "no more imagination than a cow" (466), and it is crucial to Blake's receptivity to Ezra Jennings than Blake acknowledges other "credible realities," being "an imaginative man" (43).

But their emotional resources, including their familiarity with sensation, are actually the least specific of the protagonists' nonprofessional skills. Collins also stresses the importance of their aesthetic

[37] Magali Sarfatti Larson stresses this last sphere of competence, in explaining how the professional was conceived as a kind of supersubject, in *The Rise of Professionalism: A Sociological Analysis* (Berkeley: University of California Press, 1977).
[38] Taylor documents how Collins borrowed the paradigms of mid-Victorian psychology (*Secret Theatre of Home*, pp. 27–70). Peters recounts his thirst for medical and legal knowledge (*King of Inventors*, esp. pp. 109–10, 267).

talents and methods—entirely disproving Cuff's contention that "the nature of a man's tastes is, most times, as opposite as possible to the nature of a man's business" (108). Though visual observation is crucial to Walter Hartright's quest and performative skills distinguish characters like Marian Halcombe and Magdalen Vanstone, the most important of these methods is the power of narrative itself. The narrative skills of both Walter and Marian prove indispensable in their piecing together of the conspiracy in *The Woman in White*. In *The Moonstone*, as I have noted, Ezra Jennings solves the novel's riddle by constructing a narrative out of what seemed to be the incoherent babbling of a delirious patient. Jennings is able to piece together verbal fragments, through the aid of both memory and imagination (the two indispensable creative powers behind narrative in Collins), to produce a unified narrative of Mr. Candy's actions. "Admiration of the ingenuity which had woven this smooth and finished texture out of the ravelled skein, was naturally the first impression that I felt" (430), says Franklin Blake. And in *Armadale*, it is the written narrative of Allan's dream—as well as the narrative of the original crime dictated by Midwinter's father—which guides Midwinter's rescue of his friend.

Rather than just validating the power of individual narrators, Collins's novels affirm the authority of a force often designated as "fatality"—a force that is invisible to professional investigation but is crucial to the progress of both Collins's protagonists and his readers. The novels' sensationalistic exploration of superstitions, dreams, and nervous forebodings are, at root, a preoccupation with the interconnections and the linear force of a kind of superrational narrative force mysteriously embodied in human events. The novels are preoccupied with "unreasonable" forebodings that are nevertheless fulfilled—the curse of the moonstone, the ambiguous prophecy of Allan Armadale's dream, Marian's dream about Walter in Central America, Walter's nervous premonitions about the woman in white. In all these cases, what Collins affirms is not superstition per se but the importance of his characters' *suspicion*—their liberation from morally indoctrinated credulity—when it comes to recognizing the unfolding story embedded in a particular sequence of events. The omnipresence of narrative "fatality" legitimates a hermeneutics of suspicion—or, as D. A. Miller puts it, linking suspicion with sensation itself, Collins "makes nervousness a metonymy for read-ing."[39] Collins is satirical about any mechanical reliance on supersti-tious texts—like Gabriel Betteredge's belief that the text of *Robinson Crusoe* can predict all future events. But what Collins takes much more seriously is the power of those who suspect that plots, both human and superhuman, are constantly unfolding beneath the surface of apparently disconnected events. In this sense, the power of his narrators rests not so much in paranoia (since suspicion in Collins is always well founded), as in the crucial ability to negotiate the transgressive space between a scrupulous, faithful, honest obser-vation of facts and unwarranted suspicion about how to link those facts together. One of the shared pet phrases of Collins's narrators is their invocation of a teleological "chain of events" (*Woman in White*, 112–13). The power of cultural intellectuals rests precisely on their talent for suspecting the secret narrative beneath isolated appearances, the narrative that might expose the significance of this chain. The form of many of Collins's novels—the presentation of fragmentary accounts and scattered pieces of textual evidence (let-ters, diaries, depositions) that the novel as a whole stitches to-gether—points toward Collins's conception of narrative as an instrument for deciphering random evidence and, ultimately, for producing truth out of it. This sense of narrative as decipherment, I am arguing, is a sign of moral as well as epistemological sophisti-cation.

Of course, professional competence is generally represented in Victorian culture as an ability to piece together a comprehensive understanding from fragmentary or circumstantial evidence—what Alexander Welsh would call "strong representations."[40] Praising Collins's work, a contemporary wrote that the "fascination" of his method lay in "the power of throwing down . . . a hundred incidents which appear to be perfectly unconnected, and gradually gathering them together to produce the circumstantial or cumulative evidence which removes a veil from a great mystery. . . . This is to possess the

---

[39] Miller, "*Cage aux folles*," p. 110. Miller's gendering of such nervousness as "female" is echoed by Taylor and a number of other critics, though I believe it is important to recognize how male cultural intellectuals appropriate the domain of sensation, especially in their narrative powers.

[40] See Welsh, *Strong Representations*, esp. p. x.

legal mind in one of its most remarkable qualities, which, after all, is essentially dependent upon the imaginative faculty, whether in a lawyer or a novelist."[41] One might just as easily link Collins's use of dreams and the unconscious—the devices of "sensation" which became the staples of the psychological thriller—to the pre-Freudian psychological theorists with whom Collins was familiar.[42] John Elliotson, William Carpenter, John Conolly, and other psychologists known to Collins drew on the associationist psychology pervasive in mid-century psychiatric circles and grounded their theories about mental processes on the interpretation of circumstantial and fragmentary evidence. Ezra Jennings himself announces that his interpretive methods are based in models of the unconscious developed by Carpenter and Elliotson. But Collins's representation of narrative as a superior "sensational" method, more synthetic than the rational methods of his novels' mainstream professionals, indicates his competitive desire to distinguish aesthetic practices—however disingenuously—from the professional models on which he has quite plainly modeled them.[43]

Narrative power, rooted in convictions about "fatality," is often presented polemically as the skillful suspicion that distinguishes the methods of the cultural intellectual from the methods of the professional sifter of evidence. This distorted, competitive distinction is dramatized explicitly in *Armadale*, when Midwinter and Dr. Hawbury match wits in the deciphering of Allan's dream. The "rational theory of dreams" (143) propounded by the doctor, which he represents as "the theory accepted by the great mass of my profession" (137), holds that dreams can be explained away by random events and associations of the previous day. This theory,

[41] Charles Knight, *Passages of a Working Life*, 3 vols. (London: Bradbury and Evans, 1865), 3:185–86.

[42] See Taylor, *Secret Theatre of Home*, esp. pp. 174–206.

[43] John Sutherland suggests that Victorian fascination with sensation fiction corresponded to a popular sense that new types of crime were resistant to traditional legal practices, requiring new methods of detection ("Wilkie Collins and the Origins of the Sensation Novel," *Dickens Studies Annual: Essays on Victorian Fiction* 20 [1991], 243–57). Christopher Kent has shown how Collins redefines rational standards of probability by crossing them with new ideas about subjective perception, change, and coincidence ("Probability, Realism and Sensation in the Novels of Wilkie Collins," *Dickens Studies Annual: Essays in Victorian Fiction* 20 [1991], 259–80).

which explodes the narrative continuity of the dream itself, turns out to be a poor method in comparison with the more prophetic approach of Midwinter, who sees the dream, mistrustfully, as a narrative of events to come—precisely what it proves to be. Midwinter himself scorns the doctor's approach to dreams as a symptom of professional fetishization of fact: "The view of a medical man, when he has a problem in humanity to solve, seldom ranges beyond the point of his dissecting-knife" (136). However, Collins appropriated Midwinter's ideas about the prophetic potential of dreams from John Addington Symonds's *Sleep and Dreams* and uses a bohemian protagonist to disguise the fact that he is actually playing one perfectly respectable medical faction off against another by choosing sides in the contemporary debate about the significance of dreams— the obtuseness of "the great mass" of the medical profession is actually Collins's willful misrepresentation.[44] Conflicts like this demonstrate Collins's jealous desire to disavow his debts to newly emergent professional discourses and to define the synthesis of circumstantial evidence as the exclusive province of the aesthetic.[45] His own novels, in other words, manage to "lie" about their relationship to professionalism.

Collins's apprehensions about defending his fringe of cultural intellectuals, and their tenuous cultural authority as good narrators, is reflected in his striking preoccupation with quacks. The novels obsessively expose and ridicule imitation professionals who pervert legitimate branches of professional knowledge—Captain Wragge in *No Name*, who bewitches Mrs. Lecount with bogus talk of science; Doctor Downward, in *Armadale*, whose facile knowledge of chemistry and psychology leads to the farcical schemes of his asylum; and even Count Fosco, who, as an amateur medical practitioner, exploits his knowledge of chemistry for sinister purposes. These figures, by scapegoating the quack, carry off some of the risk of Collins's

[44] John Addington Symonds, *Sleep and Dreams* (London: J. Murray, 1851). Taylor discusses Symonds's theory that dreams could predispose individuals to imitate them in waking life, and thus to make them "come true" (*Secret Theatre of Home*, pp. 157–62).

[45] Lawrence Rothfield has shown how medical discourses supplied British novelists with paradigms of realism and models of professionalism which played to the advantage of naturalistic writing, especially detective fiction (*Vital Signs: Medical Realism in Nineteenth-Century Fiction* [Princeton: Princeton University Press, 1992]).

affirmation of a counterprofessional realm affiliated with aesthetic practices. It is crucial that Collins's protagonists be suspected and then exonerated of quackery—as when Mr. Bruff underestimates the legitimacy of Jennings's methods: "it looked like a piece of trickery, akin to the trickery of mesmerism, clairvoyance, and the like" (445). This scapegoating of quackery deflects, to some extent, the problem of the protagonists' unusual methods, since one consistent tendency that distinguishes Collins's nonprofessionals from their professional kin—however inaccurately, from a historical viewpoint—is their reliance on experimental methods. It also deflects the dangerous resemblance between the rising social aspirations of cultural intellectuals and those of quacks. Furthermore, when Collins pathologizes the dangers of law and medicine as institutions, he usually attributes those dangers to the perversion of medical methods by quacks—as in his description of Dr. Downward's mental asylum, an institution that practices absurd mechanisms of surveillance and control. Downward's asylum is a transparent parody of systems of "moral management" advocated by John Conolly (a figure ridiculed by Charles Reade as a quack in his 1863 *Hard Cash*) in the mid-century debate about treatment of the insane.[46] While the specter of professional knowledge as a vehicle of social control is constantly raised in Collins's work, it is rarely associated with figures of legitimate medical and legal authority. The paranoia about surveillance in *The Woman in White*, for instance, comes not from apprehensions about legal institutions, but from the protagonists' fear of imposters. The quack thus absorbs some of Collins's apprehensions about both insiders and outsiders.

The complex social tensions set up in Collins's novels by the opposition of professionals to cultural intellectuals is finally a highly distorted quarrel. It amounts to a dispute between two competitive but equally elevated middle-class elites—roughly, between the "scientific" and "humanistic" branches of what has come to be called the "New Class."[47] In his own life, Collins was reverential toward

[46] On Conolly and quackery, see Taylor, *Secret Theatre of Home*, p. 41.

[47] The founding sociological study of these two competing elites is Alvin W. Gouldner, *The Future of Intellectuals and the Rise of the New Class* (New York: Seabury Press, 1979). Frank Heuberger provides an excellent overview of theories of the "New Class," in "The New Class: On the Theory of a No Longer Entirely New Phenomenon," in *Hidden Technocrats: The New Class and New Capitalism*, ed.

his professional friends, and he always advertised his consultations with legal and medical authority quite proudly, in the introductions to his novels, as proof of their technical accuracy. *No Name* is dedicated to Francis Beard, the surgeon who served as amanuensis during one of Collins's illnesses. More important, Collins was insistent in claiming professional respectability for his own craft. As early as *Basil*, he distinguished himself from "the mob of ladies and gentlemen who play at writing," by numbering himself among "those who follow Literature as a study and respect it as a science."[48] He was a founder-member of the Society of Authors in 1884, and he later served as its vice-president. Collins's competition with professionals for social authority thus has the character of a family dispute, in its ambivalent identifications and differentiations; it resembles the internal professional bickering that he loved to dramatize in the novels themselves—the showing up of Mr. Dawson by the young London surgeon, the jockeying of the Pedgifts with Mr. Darch, the humiliation of Superintendent Seegrave by Sergeant Cuff. The novels always end in a cooperation between professional figures and Collins's more marginal elite of cultural intellectuals. Ezra Jennings does not replace Cuff entirely, in the pursuit of the moonstone, but he does furnish Cuff with the information that allows him to finish the job. In *The Woman in White*, the relationship is reversed when the diligence of an overly scrupulous (and conveniently deceased) law clerk provides Walter with the legal information he needs to uncover Sir Percival's secret. The cultural intellectual always "proves" his case to lawyers and detectives, as Jennings does for both Cuff and Bruff, and as Walter does for Mr. Kyrle. But at the same time, the limitations of professionals, in the realms of secrecy, sensation, and the detection of crime, are constantly and jealously dramatized in Collins's novels, in order to claim the greater expertise of the cultural intellectual. The differences in methods of cultural intellectuals and professionals—particularly the

---

Hansfried Kellner and Frank W. Heuberger (New Brunswick, N.J.: Transaction Publishers, 1992), pp. 23–48.

[48] William Wilkie Collins, "Letter of Dedication," in *Basil: A Story of Modern Life* (London: Richard Bentley, 1852), pp. xv, xvii. These lines were cut in later editions.

greater skills of cultural intellectuals at negotiating the gap between honor and suspicion—are adamantly maintained.

It is a measure of the precariousness of the cultural intellectual class, a precariousness that seems both flaunted and resented by Collins's protagonists, that his cultural intellectuals cross the boundaries of social class quite freely. Walter Hartright, received at Limmeridge "on the footing of a gentleman" (11) and paid the honor of being challenged to a duel by Fosco, is by turns a failed denizen of Clement's Inn, an illustrator for cheap periodicals living in East London, and a foreign emissary for an illustrated newspaper. The liminality of his class position—echoed by the instability of Marian's and Laura's social identities—is repeated through Midwinter in *Armadale* and by the frequent cross-class-dressing of characters like Magdalen Vanstone and Lydia Gwilt. The social transcendence—or transgression—of such figures reinforces the moral sophistication of the outsider/insider by highlighting the cross-class appropriations of moral behavior these figures achieve. By exaggerating the ways in which cultural intellectuals vaporized the social boundaries of bourgeois culture, Collins sought to stress the transgressive moral and psychological potency of such figures, a symbolically generalized potency that rendered them superior to the "insider" professionals that—in fiction at least—they actually outperform.

The Woman in White is enormously allusive when it comes to the arts—the visual arts, in particular, but also music, architecture, drama, and, of course, narrative. Although Collins's novel is a far cry from the self-reflexive aesthetic projects of the modernists and is not as centrally concerned with the power of creative imagination as were earlier novels by Scott, Shelley, or Charlotte Brontë, *The Woman in White* is unprecedented in its use of the arts as reference points for class tensions of various kinds. It is also ground-breaking in its concern with the social authority of cultural intellectuals. Its eagerness to explore the class structures embedded in various aesthetic practices anticipates, albeit remotely, the demystified self-awareness of postmodernism, although the particular social drama Collins's novel foregrounds is decidedly Victorian. The defining episodes of this drama occur when both villains meet their downfall in scenes laden with cultural and aesthetic significance—Sir Percival in a conflagration of unrestored, ecclesiastical wood carvings and Count Fosco in a stagey recognition scene that transpires between the acts of *Lucrezia Borgia*. The novel's vengeance against aristocrats, figured in part through these aesthetically coded scenes of retribution, underscores the triumph of a culturally specific outsider class, a mobile segment of middle-class society which is fundamentally, if nebulously, allied with the arts. But the melodrama of the cultural intellectual is not just a crusade against aristocratic authority. The novel maps aesthetics onto social class by opposing cultural intellectuals to both the landed gentry and a professional class that turns out to be comparatively less skilled at solving the mysteries of the human heart, as well as the mysteries of social justice and moral principle.

In this last section, I explore the exceptional social space Collins defines in *The Woman in White* through various aesthetic practices, a liminal space that he reserves for those fully empowered by moral transgression. I mean to show both how Collins explicitly opposes aesthetic practices to professional ones and how these deprofessionalized practices are affiliated with morally transgressive agents, whose skill with a hermeneutics of suspicion places them ethically somewhere between honesty and dishonesty. This linkage of two different violations of insider/outsider symbolic boundaries, one cultural and the other ethical, is designed to shore up the transgressive sophistication of cultural intellectuals at the expense, primarily, of their professional kin.

In Collins's novel, art is marked by class as much as class is marked by art. For *The Woman in White* does not at all celebrate what it designates as high art. Through Frederick Fairlie, high art is elided with the selfishness, enervation, and exclusivity of the landed gentry—it is something to "possess" (33), whether as the art object that can be photographed and labeled or in the person of the drawing master himself.[49] Marian herself shares Collins's antipathy to artistic hierarchies. Refusing to tour the Elizabethan bedrooms and the Elizabethan wing at Blackwater, even though "the architecture of

[49] Collins spoofed the pretensions of the world of high art in "A Passage in the Life of Mr. Perugino Potts," an anonymous piece in *Bentley's Miscellany* 31 (1852), 153–64.

'the old wing,' both outside and inside, was considered remarkably fine by good judges" (182), Marian earns the housekeeper's "undisguised admiration of my extraordinary common sense." This common sense compels Marian to value the efficiency and comfort of "the bright modern way" (183) in the building's new wing over what she calls the "architectural jumble" of Blackwater and the "barbarous lumber" of its antique furnishings. Cavalierly aligning herself with the cultural perspectives of the housekeeper, Marian refuses to let any reverence for architectural significance tyrannize the needs of everyday life.

Collins is no philistine, however. In his indefatigable animation, Count Fosco displays another kind of cultural taste with which Collins has more sympathy—a cultural hybridity that ranges freely over the aesthetic languages of both social insiders and social outsiders. Despite his elevated taste in music, which allows Fosco to direct—with "critical supremacy" (530)—the audience response to Donizetti's opera from his own seat in the pit, Fosco's musical talents are extremely diffuse. He plays Italian "street-songs" (286) on the piano and Figaro's aria from *The Barber of Seville* on the concertina. Similarly inconsistent, his grandiose personal manner is compared to that of "a play-actor" (368) by Hester Pinhorn, and Fosco himself links his sense of humor to "the illustrious nation which invented the exhibition of Punch" (305). Fosco's literary range allows him to quote Sheridan and refer to Chatterton in his elaborate theory of masks, while he also boasts about having written "preposterous romances, on the French model, for a second-rate Italian newspaper" (232). He offers the story of his own crime to "the rising romance writers of England" (568) at the same time that he longs for a "modern Rembrandt" (565) to do pictorial justice to his conspiracy. Fosco's mixed allusions draw attention both to the popular status of Collins's novel and to its affinities with Fosco's cultural hybridity. In Victorian culture, of course, the appeal of sensation fiction rested largely on its transgressive situation between high and low culture.[50]

Walter's representative identity as cultural intellectual depends on his sharing in these mixed aesthetic registers. While Walter, as

[50] For a good discussion of the hybrid location of sensation fiction, see Cvetkovich, *Mixed Feelings*, pp. 15–16.

drawing master, is the envoy of high culture in genteel society, his talents also prepare him to serve more humbly as the draughtsman for an expedition to Central America and as an illustrator for cheap periodicals. Less a matter of taste than of necessity, Walter's movement between aesthetic privilege and hackwork nevertheless gives his talents an improvisatory potency, a relatively unbounded cultural power appropriate to the social insider/outsider. Walter reinforces the doubleness of his social position through bitter complaints about the undeserved exclusion of artists, which he tempers with the conviction that he is above concerns about status. "I am only a drawing master" (18), Walter tells Anne Catherick, "a little bitterly." But in his later achievement of manly resolution, he feels that "I had done with my poor man's touchy pride; I had done with all my little artist vanities" (96). His ambiguous reward is Gilmore's praise for his being "gentlemanlike" (113). The social homelessness of cultural intellectuals, as represented in this novel through Walter's location between high and low culture, as well as between high and low society, is precisely the condition of both marginality and sophistication.

The protagonists' mixture of refined taste and aesthetic pragmatism is not figured solely through Walter's employment, however. All three protagonists consistently bring visual skills to bear on the realm of the everyday, both as an aid to their detective project and as a crucial component of their psychological depth. In this way, the novel makes aesthetic aptitude more a matter of practices than of products. Aesthetic talents become deprofessionalized, in other words, as they are appropriated for more private, more interpersonal uses. Laura's treasured book of sketches, a token of Walter's presence, and her performances of Mozart for him at the piano have a value quite apart from their purely aesthetic merits, and this transformation of aesthetic products into personal terms demonstrates a hybridizing of the aesthetic with the everyday, the culturally elevated with the culturally insignificant, which the novel associates with the heightened sensitivity of cultural intellectuals. Such hybridity becomes a sign of the cultural intellectual's undervalued but very real intellectual potency. Domesticating high culture in the realm of the everyday empties the aesthetic of its professional identity and divorces it from particular crafts and objects "possessed" by the wealthy. It signals an escape from the sterile world of Mr. Fairlie's "art-treasures" (310) and an entrance into the "minutely observant" (103) world of declassed sensitives.

The most important aspect of this transposition of aesthetic abilities into everyday life is that, in *The Woman in White*, sight itself (rather than "aesthetic" sight as conventionally or professionally understood) is rarefied as the opposite of thought. The cultural intellectual's acute sight is thus allied with a receptivity to sensation as an alternative to the rationality that so constrains the novel's legal minds. Just before Walter meets Anne Catherick, in the novel's Ur-sensation scene, he empties his mind of thought by filling it with visual matter, either real or imaginary: "my mind remained passively open to the impressions produced by the view; and I thought but little on any subject—indeed, so far as my own sensations were concerned, I can hardly say that I thought at all" (14). Abandoning the Heath, Walter surrenders his attention to "fanciful visions of Limmeridge House" and musings about "what the Cumberland young ladies would look like" (15). It is in this state of visual preoccupation that he is arrested by the reason-numbing sight of the woman in white. The image of this "extraordinary apparition" (15) returns to Walter in "a sensation, for which I can find no name" (50), when he sees the "living image" (51) of Anne in Laura as he watches her walk back and forth on the terrace at Limmeridge. Throughout the novel, sight is constantly allied with sensation and functions as a nonrational form of intelligence. The novel is full of memorable scenes of spectatorship that abrogate rational understanding by appealing instead to sensation—Walter's first view of Marian (which inspires "a sensation oddly akin to the helpless discomfort familiar to us all in sleep, when we recognize yet cannot reconcile the anomalies and contradictions of a dream" [25]); Marian's dream vision (later fulfilled) of Laura rising out of a grave to meet Walter; and Walter's first glimpse of Laura. In this last visual encounter, Walter explicitly equates the sensation of love with sight of the beloved, and he appeals to universal (male) experience by locating the "mysteries" (42) of the human heart in the realm of the visual. Speaking with an air of profundity about "the sensations that crowded on me, when my eyes first looked at her," he asks the reader to remember that same "matchless look" from his own experience.

"Look" (270), Anne Catherick writes in the sand, marking the placement of a written message that fails to convey rational understanding. *The Woman in White* is insistent throughout about the power of the visual to transcend rational inquiry and explanation. "I trust nothing, Laura, but my own observation of your husband's conduct" (257), says Marian, once she has become educated in distrust. "Where are your eyes?" (296), says Count Fosco to Sir Percival, impatient with the latter's lack of imagination. The law, in particular, is constantly given eyes that do not see: the Inquest into Sir Percival's death finds nothing, "no explanation that the eye of the law could recognize having been discovered" (485). "In the eyes of law and reason" (124), as Mr. Gilmore tells Walter, Laura has no cause for refusing Sir Percival's offer of marriage. And again, "in the eye of reason and of law" (380), Laura lies buried in the churchyard. Differences in visual acuity among the main characters are constantly measured, from Mr. Fairlie's habitual closing of his eyes and his appeal to Walter to look out the shuttered window for him, to the "sharp eyes" (130) of Marian. For it is not as if appearances never deceive. As the "living image" of Anne, Laura foregrounds the problem of deceptive appearances and serves as embodied proof that other characters do not look as observantly as the protagonists. Laura's uncle and her servants may not know her, but when Marian comes upon Laura in the asylum, Laura "looked eagerly" at her, and "in that moment Miss Halcombe recognized her sister" (387).

In his first visual encounter with Laura, Walter is careful to distinguish an active and personal orientation to the visual from the colder, more professional cultivation of the visual arts themselves, even though the two are related. When he looks at his first sketch of her, he is appalled at how few of his sensations "are in the dim mechanical drawing, and how many in the mind with which I regard it" (41). Walter goes on to apply his personal experience in love to the general difference between cultivated aesthetic sight and everyday observation, explicitly rejecting the clichés of romantic naturalism. Valuing the link between vision and emotional immediacy, to the detriment of artistic conventions, Walter treasures his viewing of Laura herself more than he does the orthodox subjects that he must teach her to paint: "the slightest alterations of expression in the lovely eyes that looked into mine, with such an earnest desire to learn all that I could teach and to discover all that I could show, attracted more of my attention than the finest view we passed through, or the grandest changes of light and shade, as they flowed into each other over the waving moorland and the level beach" (44). Celebrated as more authentic than aesthetic sight, the personal power of everyday observation becomes, in some larger sense, the very definition of sanity in the novel. Laura is restored to her right mind by the therapy of sketching, not because of the healing power of art itself, but because in exercising her vision in the present she recovers her memory of past sights—"we helped her mind slowly by this simple means" (400). Earlier, the healthy views of Limmeridge—"I seemed to burst into a new life and a new set of thoughts the moment I looked at it" (24), says Walter—are contrasted to the debilitating enclosure of Blackwater Park, with its "trees that shut out the view on all sides" (181).

As is the case with narrative assemblage, Collins celebrates the visual acuity of the cultural intellectual by erasing the real historical connections between visual skill and Victorian professionalism. Particularly in the case of medicine, technologies such as photography and the speculum (and, later, the x-ray) were coming to define medical positivism in largely visual terms. Collins would have been familiar with a popular illustrated book called *The Mind Unveiled*, which depicted mentally retarded children, and in *Armadale*, Dr. Downward invokes the methods of John Conolly, who, along with Hugh Diamond, pioneered psychiatric photography in the 1850s.[51] Michel Foucault has explicitly connected the rise of visual technologies in nineteenth-century medicine to the emphasis on everyday sight that Collins has tried to deprofessionalize: "That which is not on the scale of the gaze falls outside the domain of possible knowledge. Hence the rejection of a number of scientific techniques that were nonetheless used by doctors in earlier years. . . . The only type of visibility recognized by pathological anatomy is that defined by

[51] Isaac Newton Kerlin, *The Mind Unveiled* (Philadelphia: U. Hunt, 1858). On the rise of visual technology in the nineteenth century, see Stanley Joel Reiser, *Medicine and the Reign of Technology* (Cambridge: Cambridge University Press, 1978), pp. 45–68. On nineteenth-century medical photography, see Sander L. Gilman, *The Face of Madness: Hugh W. Diamond and the Origin of Psychiatric Photography* (New York: Brunner/Mazel, 1976).

everyday vision."[52] Visual technologies aside, notions of physiognomy as a reliable index of moral and psychological traits were well established early in the nineteenth century, having been systematized late in the eighteenth century by the work of Caspar Lavater. Victorian interest in criminal physiognomy was widespread—studies of the physiognomies of prostitutes and criminals were popularly available as early as the 1830s—and Collins's physical descriptions of incorrigible villains owe something to commonplace Victorian convictions about the visual appearance of criminal types.[53]

While Collins obscures these developments by systematically blinding his professionals, he was willing to preserve the link between acute sight and professional skill when it served his own interests. That is to say, in simple vocational terms, Collins marks the faculty of sight as the purely masculine preserve of the cultural intellectual. There is no mistaking the connection, for men at least, between visual sensitivity and social opportunity. Women are not so privileged—Marian confesses that "women can't draw" (28), and Laura is allowed only the delusion of competing professionally with Walter. Collins's masculinizing of his own cultural microelite is in some ways more pronounced than Trollope's, since Collins struggled harder to define the cultural intellectual against a uniformly masculine professional class. His deliberate exclusion of women from the public roles facilitated by aesthetic skills—drawing master, draughtsman, illustrator—is in no way exonerated by the "sympathy" he is alleged to have shown toward both "strong" and victimized female characters. Nevertheless, it is important to note that Collins tries to efface the sexual coding of the cultural intellectual to the degree that he generalizes visual skill, locating it partly in the everyday, rather than exclusively in the public profession of art. Walter's professional identity remains a transient one, defined throughout by the odd indifference that underlies his initial mismanagement of "professional resources" (2) and lack of enthusiasm about his job prospects at Limmeridge. His liminal status at the end of the novel, as the father of the heir of Limmeridge House, suspends his professional identity in oddly appropriate ways. Collins's male

[52] Michel Foucault, *The Birth of the Clinic: An Archaeology of Medical Perception*, trans. A. M. Sheridan Smith (New York: Vintage, 1973), p. 166.
[53] See Taylor, *Secret Theatre of Home*, p. 50.

protagonists always tend to be dilettantes, amateurs, or, like Walter, only marginally successful artists. Their paraprofessional status is what allows them to blend the male world of artistic endeavor with the feminized world of "minutely observant" interests.

Collins never plays the status of narrative off against the visual. Rather, he tends to link visual skill and narrative skill in their common ability to supersede rationality's dependence on factual evidence, and in their affinity with suspicion, which makes them both superior modes for understanding human experience.[54] When Marian gives Walter a verbal "sketch" of Mrs. Vesey's character, Walter is impressed with its "truthfulness" (38). In this novel, the superrational "fatality" (416) that drives so many of Collins's plots is also referred to repeatedly as a "Design" (248)—a design that is usually "yet unseen." Narration and vision (or the visionary) are complementary skills, both allied in their ability to penetrate the deceptions that rationality cannot, both able to piece together the fragmented elements of the novel's fatal design. Visual and narrative skills are made to depend equally on distrust and on the willingness of characters to penetrate appearances that such distrust inspires. Both these skills allow Walter to suspend "the ordinary rules of evidence" (65) in order to exercise his suspicions, an achievement not matched by the many failed narrators of the novel. Walter repeatedly resorts to visual metaphors for his skillful suspicion: refusing to accept "the guilty appearances described to me, as unreservedly as others had accepted them" (435), he is able to see "something hidden beneath the surface" (434). We have noted earlier how narrative in Collins incorporates suspicion as the link to the power of moral transgression. But in *The Woman in White*, suspicion is made more broadly the condition of all aesthetic intellection. It is suspicion—the mainspring of "the sensational"—that comes to stand in for more conventional theories of aesthetics which are less troubled by their affinity to professional methods of investigation.

Ultimately, both vision and narration, as vehicles of sensational suspicion, allow Collins's protagonists to outdistance the novel's

---

[54] Collins was himself an accomplished amateur painter, having had a picture accepted for the Royal Academy exhibition of 1849. In the preface to *Antonina*, he uses painterly terminology to describe narrative effects.

lawyers in pursuit of truth, and it is in relation to the failures of the legal profession that aesthetic skills are most clearly celebrated. The mystery that legal "machinery" (1) in this novel does not even go so far as to suspect must finally be solved through a series of narratives based on eyewitness accounts. Given the blindness of legal justice, Walter is fully warranted in taking on the task of administering justice, both in tracking down and "sighting" two men he had never previously seen (and whom he finally sees as corpses—in Sir Percival's case, for the very first time) and in forcing the law to hear and confirm his own narrative. His assumption of this authority is a specific challenge to the social authority, not to mention the competence, of all those who represent the legal profession: "Those two men shall answer for their crime to ME, though the justice that sits in tribunals is powerless to pursue them" (410). For Collins, the authority of the cultural intellectual is based on a linkage between certain aesthetic skills—vision, narration—and the morally transgressive conduct those skills enable. As Walter tells us, "The Law would never have obtained me my interview with Mrs. Catherick. The Law would never have made Pesca the means of forcing a confession from the Count" (578). The law could never do these things because the law is bound both to rigid codes of conduct—unless it is completely perverted by criminals and quacks—and to rational methods that are shown to be inadequate to synthesize human experience in a number of domains generally linked by the intersection of truth-telling and deceit.

The Woman in White links aesthetic sophistication and moral sophistication in competitive opposition to the cultural and moral impoverishment of the "insider" professional class, but only through the transgression of various boundaries that segregate the inside of Victorian culture from the outside. Collins's novel is not rooted in some absolute socio-symbolic terrain, either within or without mainstream Victorian culture. It is, instead, an argument for the social authority of a specific subclass—very different from Trollope's—located in a particular social and cultural limbo. It attempts to produce the sophistication of cultural intellectuals primarily through a tenuous antiprofessionalism—a strategy as new for the aesthetic fringe as was the rising authority of professionals themselves in mid-Victorian England. This ambiguous antiprofessionalism ulti-

mately laid a new foundation for middle-class aesthetic sophistication that would later support modernism's delicate appropriations of
scientific and technical authority. In the symbolic terms of Victorian
culture, however, it is not simply the cultural intellectual's scientific
knowledge or methods, but his affinities with transgressive moral
sophistication—underlying his skillful suspicion—which endowed
him with the power of "outsiders" to see and to tell what professional
"insiders" most want to know, and to act in ways that insiders—
many of whom constituted the novel's audience—could barely scru-
ple to imitate.

PART II

SEXUAL INVERSION

CHAPTER THREE

Lying and Impulsiveness
in Elizabeth Gaskell

Though I did not explore gender issues in Trollope and Collins to any great extent, it has been evident, I hope, that they are inseparable from the symbolic logic of transgression. In this second group of chapters, I move gender issues more to the foreground, to demonstrate how Victorian sexual boundaries are grounded in conventional ethical distinctions mapped through truth-telling. In the novels of both Elizabeth Gaskell and Ellen Wood, sexual identity is rigorously defined in relation to an axis of honesty and dishonesty. In both these writers, to transgress against norms of truth-telling is always to transgress against gender norms as well. As a result, both writers explore the possibilities of sexual inversion—and the transgressive vitality such inversion can signify—precisely through violations of the truth-telling norms associated with either sex. Such violations are a central concern of their fiction, for Gaskell and Wood were preoccupied with very different sites of social instability and social power than were Trollope and Collins. As we will see, however, the dynamics of sexual inversion—present in varying degrees throughout Victorian fiction—remain implicated in some of the same conflicts over middle-class boundaries that my first two chapters have outlined.

The uses of sexual inversion itself varied enormously among

Victorian writers. Without trying to reduce the differences between Gaskell and Wood to a debate about which one of them was more "feminist," I want to explore the different conceptions of female identity each writer generated out of the discourse of sexual inversion. Further, I want to expose their different attitudes toward the symbolic logic of transgression itself, as a tool for thinking about the relationships among gender, class, and power. After all, dominant middle-class notions about the expression of sociosexual power were not accepted universally, or without qualification. While Gaskell found ways to exploit the power and the implicit sophistication of what I have been calling "antibourgeois" transgression, Wood was more inclined to distance the terms of this symbolic dynamic altogether. In particular, Gaskell was able to adapt middle-class concepts of transgression for purposes of sexual reform, while Wood tended to protest—without supplying an alternative—against the class-bound options such transgression seemed to leave for women. These two writers thus define extreme positions on the question of how "exceptional" middle-class transgression might have been useful for Victorian women. Taken together, they can help mark out the different kinds of possibilities—or the lack of them—that women saw for themselves within this fundamental symbolic logic of middle-class culture.

For Gaskell, these possibilities included aggressive, class-coded claims to social authority, like those we have seen in Trollope and Collins, but they also included a feminine moral and psychological creativity identified with deceit, but sanctioned, in turn, by such authority. Ironically, both potentials depend on Gaskell's having defined transgression in relation to surprisingly dogmatic norms of sexual difference. However Gaskell settled particular questions about the advancement of women, her system of sexual difference established a strictly gendered division of moral conduct, particularly in the realm of truth-telling. This ideological division of labor stays entirely within the bounds of middle-class ideology and the opportunities for expressing desire which its symbolic logic of transgression made possible. As a result, sexual difference in Gaskell's novels is as much a site of ideological cooperation as it is a site of conflict between men and women. Without forgetting that gendered symbolic oppositions are never symmetrical, that they always lend themselves to hierarchies of domination, we must also remember that gender roles can complement each other within particular ideological formations. The point is all the more important in Gaskell's case, since her polarization of sexual identity limits the terms in which she can imagine challenges to middle-class ideology.

Norms of sexual difference in Gaskell's novels also create a set of productive tensions, however, between the laws of sexual identity and the significance attached to violating them—tensions that Gaskell exploits for a number of different purposes. Many readers have linked Gaskell's apparently ambivalent treatment of sexual conflict (was she a protofeminist or a sexual collaborator?) to her supposed ambivalence about social change, in an increasingly standard view of her as a self-conflicted social analyst.[1] But the focus of gender-oriented criticism on questions of straightforward sexual conflict—on Gaskell's attitude toward female independence and confining female roles dictated by patriarchal norms—has deflected attention from her fundamental and remarkably rigid conception of sexual difference, and what its reversals indicate about her ideological intentions. Gaskell's apparent ambivalence about social and sexual change needs to be reunderstood as an ideological dynamic driven, in part, by the productive tensions she found within fixed categories of sexual difference, particularly ethical ones, and the symbolic significance she found in violating or inverting them. If her

---

[1] Among feminists, there is a long history of arguments on either side. Both Aina Rubenius and Coral Lansbury cite Gaskell's empathy for working-class women and her respect for new female vocations such as nursing and teaching, along with her critiques of the sexual double standard, of patriarchal tyranny in the family, and of confining female stereotypes, as proof of her feminist views. See Rubenius, *The Woman Question in Mrs. Gaskell's Life and Works* (Cambridge: Harvard University Press, 1950); and Lansbury, *Elizabeth Gaskell: The Novel of Social Crisis* (New York: Barnes and Noble, 1975). But Françoise Basch sees the novels flatly as "based on a conventional notion of the woman's realm" (*Relative Creatures: Victorian Women in Society and the Novel*, trans. Anthony Rudolf [New York: Schocken Books, 1974], p. 185). Judith Lowder Newton also dismisses Gaskell as a proponent of "woman's sphere" (*Women, Power and Subversion: Social Strategies in British Fiction, 1778–1860* [Athens: University of Georgia Press, 1981], p. 164). Arguments about Gaskell's social and sexual self-contradictions include Margaret Ganz, *Elizabeth Gaskell: The Artist in Conflict* (New York: Twayne, 1969); and Shirley Foster, *Victorian Women's Fiction: Marriage, Freedom, and the Individual* (London: Croom Helm, 1985). Foster finds that "even while upholding intrinsically orthodox romantic attitudes [Gaskell] voices her own dissent from contemporary mores" (p. 137).

thinking about sexual difference seems confused, the confusion is not hers alone—it is embedded in the heterogeneous dynamism of bourgeois culture itself.

We can begin to recover the ideological uses served by Gaskell's system of sexual difference by looking at instances of sexual disorder in her work. Often, a writer's norms for sexual identity are revealed by his or her diagnosis of sexual pathology. And as it turns out, one of the more curious patterns in Gaskell's work is the frequent inversion of her protagonists' sexual identity. In many of her characters, gender traits are not qualified or revised; they are flatly reversed. Women are rigidly masculinized, and men rigidly feminized, in static and stereotypical ways. Faith Benson in *Ruth* has "a more masculine character than her brother," because she tends toward "quick, resolute action," while he often "deliberated and trembled."[2] Osborne Hamley in *Wives and Daughters* is "almost as demonstrative as a girl" and "almost effeminate in movement."[3] Mr. Hale in *North and South* has eyes that have "a peculiar languid beauty which was almost feminine" (10.121), and his cowardice and secrecy mark him as unmanly. Inversions of sexual identity in these characters are often reinforced by unusual cross-sexual affinities between fathers and daughters or mothers and sons. Miss Deborah Jenkyns, Sylvia Robson, Phillis Holman, and Margaret Hale are all said to resemble their fathers physically and to have pride of place in their affections; Peter Jenkyns, Philip Hepburn, and Osborne Hamley are as pointedly identified with their mothers, or with mother-figures. The strict polarity of these inversions is further reinforced by striking contrasts between paired siblings—stalwart Roger and effeminate Osborne Hamley, dictatorial Miss Jenkyns and timid Miss Matty, headstrong Faith and vacillating Thurstan Benson, rugged Molly Gibson and precious Cynthia Kirkpatrick.

Sexual inversion is a regular feature of Gaskell's novels, playing a

[2] Elizabeth Gaskell, *Ruth*, World's Classics (Oxford: Oxford University Press, 1985), 19.205.

[3] Elizabeth Gaskell, *Wives and Daughters* (Harmondsworth: Penguin, 1969), 4.75; 14.203. References to the novels are to chapter and page numbers in the Penguin edition, unless otherwise noted.

crucial role in virtually every plot. Its frequency suggests a preoccupation with sexual disorder which has very large dimensions. Not all
of these dimensions are encompassed by viewing such inversions as
a challenge to patriarchal norms of sexual difference, which is
the usual way in which Gaskell's various manipulations of gender
difference have been understood.[4] Readers who adopt this sympathetic view do not, of course, isolate instances of sexual disorder, as
I have termed them, in Gaskell's work. Rather, they call attention
to what appear to be instances of sexual liberalization. Gaskell
certainly does affirm women in assertive interpersonal roles, while
encouraging men to become more compassionate or nurturing. The
novels tend to celebrate the kind of transformation heralded by
active heroines like Mary Barton and Margaret Hale, and by the
conversion of men like Mr. Thornton to a heightened capacity for
sympathy. There is no denying that Gaskell wanted to "strengthen"
women and "soften" men. But this pattern in her work verges very
closely on repressive Victorian myths about sexual identity. Gaskell's
thematics of sexual liberalization can be seen—and often is seen—to
reinstate the Victorian cult of domesticity, in which feminine
compassion is affirmed as a principle of social redemption and as an
improving influence on overly aggressive men.[5] Such a program of
amelioration fits quite comfortably with traditional notions about

[4] Rubenius sees Gaskell's "strong" women and "weak" men as a valorization of
women's abilities (*Woman Question*, pp. 14–15). In Lansbury's optimistic view,
Gaskell had an awareness of "psychological complexity" that "inclined her to an
androgynous view of human nature" (*Elizabeth Gaskell*, p. 211). Patsy Stoneman
makes the most thorough case for this affirmation of sexual synthesis (*Elizabeth
Gaskell* [Sussex: Harvester Press, 1987]).

[5] This is a recurrent problem for a tradition of Anglo-American feminist readings
of Gaskell. Patricia A. Wolfe sees Miss Matty's "genuine femininity" (which she
equates with tenderness and understanding) as a corrective to the misguided,
militant feminism of Miss Jenkyns ("Structure and Movement in *Cranford*," *Nineteenth-Century Fiction* 23 [1968], 161–76). Barbara Weiss argues that Gaskell's
feminine stereotypes did, in fact, help modify patriarchal culture ("Elizabeth
Gaskell: The Telling of Feminine Tales," *Studies in the Novel* 16 [1984], 274–87).
Stoneman argues, in *Elizabeth Gaskell*, that Gaskell's novels seek to revise sexual
ideology by insinuating "feminine" psychological capacities—by which she means
capacities for nurturing or "caring"—into male characters. In Stoneman's sexual
psychology, "caring is the authentic voice of woman" (p. 205). She argues that, as
"the progressive force of change" (p. 14), women induce men to be better nurturers.
Margaret Homans tries to recast Gaskell's idealization of the attributes of the
mother in symbolic terms (*Bearing the Word: Language and Female Experience in*

the separation of spheres, a separation that Gaskell herself seems to support in her general convictions about women's duties in the home.[6] Dickens, Trollope, Thackeray, and other nineteenth-century novelists all took similar, nonthreatening stands, urging women to be strong in their compassion and men to be compassionate in their power. Criticism of Gaskell's ambivalence about sexual change is often attuned closely to the limitations of this particular reformist strategy.

But Gaskell manages to transform her sexual liberalism by splicing it with the cultural power available through the symbolic logic of transgression. Her particular version of sexual liberalism cannot be fully understood without attending to the volatile symbolic possibilities she creates by linking ideals of strengthening/softening to the transgressive energies she found in the symbolic lexicon of elite middle-class culture. That is to say, Gaskell's liberal, ameliorative ideas about sexual difference incorporate the simultaneous reverence for middle-class moral norms and transgression of those same norms that characterize what I have been calling exceptional middle-class elites, with their special claims for authority over middle-class culture and their privileged moral, social, and psychological flexibility.

The dynamism underlying Gaskell's liberal attitudes depends on her keeping the strengthening/softening of her protagonists quite distinct from patterns of pathological sexual inversion. The stark, polarized reversals of sexual identity in Miss Jenkyns, Osborne Hamley, Philip Hepburn, Sylvia Robson, and other characters violate basic Gaskellian conceptions of sexual difference in ways that the softening of Mr. Thornton or the strengthening of Mary Barton do not. Partly as a phobic limit set upon her modest tamperings with sexual identity and partly as an establishment of the boundaries

---

Nineteenth-Century Women's Writing [Chicago: University of Chicago Press, 1986]). A balanced account of the implications for feminism of Gaskell's exploration of motherhood and the values traditionally associated with it is Deanna L. Davis, "Feminist Critics and Literary Mothers: Daughters Reading Elizabeth Gaskell," *Signs* 17 (1992), 507–32.

[6] On this Gaskellian orthodoxy, see Rubenius, *Woman Question*, pp. 58–60; Basch, *Relative Creatures*, pp. 88, 185, 191, 270; Foster, *Victorian Women's Fiction*, p. 139; and Winifred Gérin, *Elizabeth Gaskell* (Oxford: Oxford University Press, 1980), pp. 54, 262.

that might define more dramatic transgressions, such inversions are presented in Gaskell's novels as signs of abnormality. They are rarely seen as constructive. The fruits of sexual inversion are not self-confident women and sensitive men, but tyrannical, headstrong, indiscreet women and weak, indecisive, cowardly men. The novels' plots underscore the abnormality of sexual inversions by occasionally using them to prevent satisfactory romantic resolutions—which are so important to Gaskell's novelistic imagination. In *Sylvia's Lovers*, Sylvia Robson—perhaps the most tomboyish of Gaskell's heroines—prefers the manly but shallow Charlie Kinraid to the more faithful but effeminate Philip Hepburn, who is "as shy . . . as a girl" and who cherishes the approach of New Year's Parties "as much as any young girl."[7] Hepburn, in many ways the superior lover, disgusts Sylvia by being fastidious about clothing and disappoints her by being shyly reserved: "he could not be merry and light-hearted like other young men" (13.160). Similar sexual inversions divide Jemima Bradshaw from Mr. Farquhar in *Ruth*, and Phillis Holman from Paul Manning in "Cousin Phillis." Gaskell's plots always pressure us into seeing these divisions as unnatural, and often as regrettable.

To discover what is endangered by sexual inversions, how they are different from Gaskell's more moderate sexual liberalizations, and how sexual inversion plays on the ideological necessity of "normal" sexual difference, we must look at large-scale patterns of truth-telling in Gaskell's oeuvre. The pathology of sexual inversion in her work is most visible on the level of general narrative polarizations of honesty and dishonesty, which coalesce only from a relatively distant critical viewpoint. I will qualify these generalizations later, through a close reading of Gaskell's transgression of these very same polarizations in *Cranford*. Rather than confining Gaskell to conventional Victorian notions of sexual improvement—to the ideology of strengthening/softening—or to simple ambivalence about questions of sexuality, I look at the underpinnings of sexual difference which she dynamically disorders through sexual inversion. These disorderings, structured in relation to gendered notions about truth-telling, allow her to express social and sexual desires that normative gender

[7] Elizabeth Gaskell, *Sylvia's Lovers*, World's Classics (Oxford: Oxford University Press, 1982), 14.167; 12.133.

difference, even when liberalized, seems to exclude. What is ultimately at stake is Gaskell's ability to link liberal feminist thinking
to the kinds of transgressive energies claimed by elite, empowered,
and morally creative segments of Victorian middle-class culture. For
her much-debated challenges to conventions of sexual difference
must be understood as attempts to activate transgressive energies
shaped by their specific class location within the logic of middle-
class power.

One of the underpinnings of sexual difference in Gaskell's work is
her tendency to locate symbolically opposed vices within the normal
range of behavior of each sex. These vices are then displaced across
gender and made to appear as the primary personality flaws of
sexually inverted characters. Throughout the novels, for example,
lying is defined as a characteristically female transgression. This
premise obviously echoes a misogynist tradition that predates the
nineteenth century, but the traditional stereotype was a powerful
one in Victorian culture. Victorian fiction thrives on the figure of
the woman as deceiver, giving it such monstrous forms as Thackeray's
Becky Sharpe, Trollope's Lizzie Eustace, Collins's Lydia Gwilt,
Braddon's Lady Audley, and Eliot's Rosamond Vincy. In Gaskell's
novels, too, lying—an obsessional subject in her work—is always
viewed as a feminine defect.[8] Both Mary Barton and Margaret Hale,
for instance, suffer pivotal crises of conscience over lies that they
tell, lies that break their unconventional, unmaidenly confidence in
themselves and that ultimately weaken or feminize them. Margaret
Hale's debilitating guilt over a lie told to save her brother's life—a
guilt that restores Mr. Thornton's manly power over her, when he
discovers the lie—has seemed so excessive, given the circumstances,

---

[8] The prominence of lying as a theme is occasionally noted in passing by Gaskell
critics, but almost never in the context of sexual difference. An exception is Nina
Auerbach, who briefly comments on the connection in "Elizabeth Gaskell's 'Sly
Javelins': Governing Women in Cranford and Haworth," *Modern Language Quarterly*
38 (1977), 284–85. But Auerbach sees lying only as an approved weapon in
Gaskell's feminist arsenal. Stoneman claims, somewhat extravagantly, that lying
always results from a denial of female sexuality (*Elizabeth Gaskell*, p. 149). P. N.
Furbank comments on the ways in which deceitfulness infects Gaskell's narrative
voice ("Mendacity in Mrs. Gaskell," *Encounter* 40, no. 6 [June 1973], 51–55).

that many readers have tried to explain it away as a flaw of plot construction.[9] Mary Barton's withholding of evidence that would incriminate her father, during the trial of Jem Wilson, is a lie of omission which leads directly to the feminine delirium that marginalizes her in the novel's climactic events and makes her dependent, during her recovery, on Jem's care. Mary's mental crisis and delirium are caused by her inability to adopt Jem's manly admonition to his mother that she "tell the truth" (32.386) on the witness stand, even if it happens to incriminate him, or Will Wilson's declaration before the court that he "would scorn to tell a lie" (32.397). "I must not go mad. I must not, indeed," Mary mutters to herself bitterly after her own testimony. "They say people tell the truth when they're mad; but I don't. I was always a liar" (32.394). In both cases, lying emerges as the conventional, almost therapeutic sign of the heroines' essential femininity and their need for male guidance and support.

Throughout Gaskell's novels, lying defines "normal" female depravity. In *Cranford*, the pretences and the genteel lies (not to mention the sexual repression) of the Cranford ladies have a legendary charm; nevertheless, they are sometimes in sharp contrast to the unaffected masculine honesty of men like Captain Brown and Mr. Holbrook. Gaskell considered it a wonderful joke to have her Cranford ladies profess themselves "superior to men . . . in the article of candour" (10.147) at a moment when they are terrifying each other with stories of imaginary robbers, hopelessly mangling the facts. Clare Gibson and her daughter Cynthia, in *Wives and Daughters*, are perhaps the most extreme examples of the duplicity Gaskell identified with women, especially since these two characters have an enormously disruptive impact on the unambiguously masculine Dr. Gibson, who is sternly dedicated to personal and professional honesty. Cynthia's "exaggerated desire for . . . secrecy" (35.434)—an authorial euphemism for her love of maneuvering room—puts her in open conflict with Dr. Gibson, whose promise to tell Squire Hamley if his son and Cynthia become engaged is the very fact that she wishes to keep secret. Often, these gendered ethical tendencies define the basic terms of sexual conflict. "A man's

---

[9] Ganz ascribes Margaret's guilt to sensationalistic and evasive melodrama (*Elizabeth Gaskell*, p. 102); and Edgar Wright to "pure plot-spinning" (*Mrs. Gaskell: The Basis for Reassessment* [London: Oxford University Press, 1965], p. 144).

promise is to override a woman's wish, then, is it?" Cynthia asks Dr. Gibson defiantly. Phrased in slightly different terms, this general opposition between masculine forthrightness and feminine concealment or deceit might define the battle lines between adversaries like Captain Brown and Miss Jenkyns (who differ on whether to be honest about one's poverty) in *Cranford*, or Mr. Bradshaw and Ruth Hilton (who part stormily over her "hypocritical" [26.337] concealment of her son's illegitimacy) in *Ruth*.

That lying is female and honesty male is only underlined, then, by Gaskell's displacement across gender of these ethical tendencies in characters who are explicit instances of sexual inversion. It is the feminized Osborne Hamley who wreaks havoc in *Wives and Daughters* by concealing his marriage from his father, and by obliging others to help him live this lie. Conversely, Molly Gibson, with her "tom-boy ways" (21.276), is distinguished for her honesty: "why, the child is truth itself," says Lady Harriet (49.578). In *Sylvia's Lovers*, effeminate Philip Hepburn tells the dramatic lie on which the plot of the entire novel turns, when he conceals Kinraid's impressment and his promise to return to Sylvia (which, being manly, Kinraid keeps). Masculinized Sylvia, in contrast, claims to "allays keep to [her] word" (12.150). In "Cousin Phillis," the pivotal deception is manufactured by the partially feminized Holdsworth ("almost like a girl" [2.256] in his illness and characterized by habitual facetiousness) and the unmanly narrator, ironically named Manning, who dreams, in a classic case of wish fulfillment, "that I was as tall as cousin Phillis, and had a sudden and miraculous growth of whisker, and a still more miraculous acquaintance with Latin and Greek" (1.240). These two problematically gendered men blunder into a romantic deception that breaks the heart of the straightforward, masculinized Phillis. "She's more like a man than a woman" (2.252), Manning tells his father frantically, when the latter suggests that they marry, and one consequence of this manliness is that Phillis is unable to understand or to ward off the fascinating "badinage" (3.270) and the "beguiling" (4.299) ways of Holdsworth.

If lying—along with conceptual relatives like concealment, deception, secrecy, and, ultimately, simple reserve—is the normal province of feminine vice and a sign of abnormality in men, Gaskell defines masculine vice, by contrast, in terms of excessive impulsiveness. Sometimes this impulsiveness takes the form of violence, but sometimes it takes the subtler form of an uncompromising honesty or expressiveness so extreme that it can lead to indiscretion, cruelty, or even self-destruction. To conceive the opposition in this way, using a nonethical term like "impulsiveness," is to show how larger psychological categories than "lying" and "honesty" are implicated in Gaskell's system of sexual difference. It is also, of course, to show the sexual hierarchy embedded in this opposition, since lying is at once a more trivializing and a more insidious characterological flaw. Myths of impulsive male honesty also help justify male authority in the realm of speech, supporting the systematic male usurpation of linguistic authority which contemporary feminism has exposed in nineteenth-century texts. But the lopsidedness of the opposition can suggest as well an important interlocking of the psychological and the ethical. For the ethical axis in Gaskell's novels is tied to opposed psychological potentials, which I term "calculation" and "anticalculation"—that is, psychological dispositions toward either craft or impulsiveness. This broadened opposition between "calculating" feminine deceit and impulsive or "uncalculating" masculine honesty generates a number of ideological premises in the novels which help support such a connection between ethical tendencies and psychological ones.

One of the cultural clichés invoked repeatedly by Gaskell's narrators, for example, is that women's concealed, secret, and sometimes deceptive feelings necessarily run much deeper and are thus less changeable than those of men. "Feyther's liker me, and we talk a deal o' rubble," says tomboyish Sylvia; "but mother's words are liker to hewn stone. She puts a deal o' meaning in 'em" (2.12). According to this logic, if women lie in a "deep" spirit of calculation, they also calculate long-term commitments; while men—being more impulsive, and less governed by foresight—are inconstant. This notion is borne out in *Sylvia's Lovers* by an odd complication of sexual difference: the effeminate liar Philip turns out to be more faithful than the manly, truthful Kinraid. In *Wives and Daughters*, Osborne is a liar but faithful; Roger's manhood, on the other hand, is only reinforced when he is found to be "not a model of constancy" (60.699), for his inconstancy—about which he is perfectly honest, confessing it freely—links him to several other virile suitors in the novel (Mr. Preston, Edward Coxe). Honesty, in other words, is not at all compatible, in terms of Gaskellian sexual psychology, with fidelity. Honesty is a male virtue because it is opposed to calculation, but fidelity is a female virtue because it is opposed to acting on immediate impulse. This explains how the association of lying with the feminine is compatible with Gaskell's convictions about other kinds of feminine moral integrity. Whatever her affiliation of women with lying, Gaskell also participated in the Victorian revision of traditional stereotypes about women's fickleness. This revision produced the reverse Victorian stereotype of sublime feminine constancy, found in Dickens's Agnes Wickfield, mocked in Trollope's Lily Dale (though his readers missed the irony, to his dismay) and daringly broken by Charlotte Brontë (to howls of protest) in *Villette*. Ruskin, in his veritable dictionary of sexual stereotypes, "Of Queens' Gardens," epitomizes this revision when he defines "the true changefulness of woman" as "an infinitely variable, because infinitely applicable, modesty of service" to her husband.[10] Having taken considerable criticism from reviewers because of Mary Barton's inconstancy, Gaskell herself was careful never again to let her heroines love twice.[11] In general, the polarized distribution of moral strengths which a novelist like Gaskell employs should make us wary of arguments that Victorian culture identified moral authority monolithically with the feminine.

A correlative of this distribution of constancy/inconstancy is that, because of their greater ability to calculate consequences, women are much more likely to feel compassion than men. Calculation, in other words, is not always selfish, any more than impulsiveness is necessarily disinterested. Male emotion in Gaskell's novels tends generally to be more superficial, more reflexive, more violent—and more often, therefore, insensitive or destructive to others. In *Cranford*, the impulsive violence of Mr. Jenkyns, who publicly beats his son Peter, is what drives Peter out of the family and, indeed, out of England, hastening Mrs. Jenkyns's death. In *Mary Barton*, the violent moods of John Barton—sometimes impulsively and unreasonably vented against Mary herself—lead him into a hasty conspiracy

[10] John Ruskin, *The Works of John Ruskin*, 12 vols. (New York: John Wiley and Sons, 1885), 11:101.

[11] See Rubenius on this issue (*Woman Question*, p. 78).

formed in the heat of anger, and then to murder. In *Sylvia's Lovers*, Sylvia's father acts on impulse when he leads the attack on the press-gang's headquarters—the affair is only "an adventure . . . a rough frolic" (23.258). As for the tomboyish Sylvia herself, "All Sylvia's persistent or enduring qualities were derived from her mother, her impulses from her father" (29.334).

Gaskell does not simplistically oppose the aggression of men to the compassion of women, as critics of her "cult of domesticity" often maintain. She identifies violence with an impulsive spontaneity—an uncalculating openness of expression—that she sees as quintessentially male and that can lead as easily toward honesty as toward violence. Even male compassion, when it is finally achieved in Gaskell's novels, must be expressed impulsively, decisively, publicly. And only through emotional impulsiveness can Gaskell's more active, independent women be linked to masculine forms of power. Her inverted heroines experience psychological power (though not, of course, political or economic power) through their spontaneous, candid, sometimes violent outbursts of emotion. Aroused by the passions of the male mob at Thornton's house, Margaret Hale acts out those passions heroically—as many readers have noticed—when she throws her body between the mob and Mr. Thornton. What she does not foresee—and this lack of foresight will later chasten her from such impulsiveness—is the sexual interpretation that will be attached to her action. Mary Barton publicly confesses her love for Jem Wilson in an unmaidenly courtroom outburst that resembles Margaret's lack of premeditation, her spontaneous expressiveness: "Suddenly her resolution was taken. The present was everything; the future, that vast shroud, it was maddening to think upon; but *now* she might own her fault, but *now* she might even own her love" (32.390). Both these women are remarkable, too, for their inability to ascertain the state of their own romantic inclinations—readers know which men these women really love before they know themselves. Both have a life of feeling which is beyond their own control. Similarly, when Sylvia declares to Philip Hepburn that she can never live with him, after discovering his deception about Kinraid, it is with an impulsive vehemence that she later comes to regret. Sylvia is a creature "governed by impulse," according to one critic, and her unmitigated hatred for Philip shocks her friend Jeremiah

Foster, who "had never met with any one so frank and undisguised in expressions of wrong feeling" (36.412).[12] Her verbal assault on Philip is the nearest thing to female violence in the novels.

In all these cases, the openly labeled, extreme inversion of sexual identity in Gaskell's protagonists is accompanied by gender-specific vices that are also inverted—that is, in men who lie and in women who act out violent, passionate, "honest" impulses. These inversions, and the ethical defects that accompany them, cannot be understood solely in relation to sexual conflict. They must be explained in relation to political ideology as well. Gaskell's notion of the "normal" vices to be found in male and female behavior supports a sexual division of labor in the realm of one of the most fundamental contradictions of bourgeois consciousness. Middle-class Victorian culture was preoccupied with resolving incompatible, opposed psychological strengths as the twin signs of its moral authority: in very general psychological terms, it needed to see itself as supremely "calculating" and supremely "uncalculating" at the same time. This prominent ideological doubleness is not surprising in a class that sought to supplant a social hierarchy of birth with its own double, and potentially contradictory, hierarchy of merit and morality and in a class that sought to distinguish itself, alternately, against both the calculating selfishness and the uncalculating profligacy it claimed to see in other social classes. Nevertheless, the culture that made a bible of Samuel Smiles's *Self-Help*, with its rationalization of greed, but that sentimentalized diatribes against self-interest such as Dickens's *A Christmas Carol*—both with equal fervor—remained troubled in various ways with its ideology of contradictory psychological strengths.

These particular terms—calculation and anticalculation—describe quite plainly, for example, the dominant philosophical dualism employed by a number of writers who crusaded to improve the philistine, commercial classes. Carlyle, Arnold, Mill, Ruskin, and others all struggled to incorporate Bentham's utilitarian emphasis on the rational calculation of pleasure and pain within a more balanced psychological model, reconciling calculation (or "analysis" or "the mechanical") with opposed psychological ideals like Mill's "cultiva-

[12] Ganz, *Elizabeth Gaskell*, p. 246.

tion of the feelings" and Carlyle's "anti-self-consciousness" or "dynamic science."[13] In middle-class fiction, the appropriate terms for this opposition might more properly be "reason" and "feeling." If Victorian novelists stressed one-sidedly an Eliotic enlargement of sympathy, along with an ethos of self-sacrifice born of compassion, it is only because they sought to balance what they saw as a dominant social emphasis on rational self-interest. Retaining the more abstract terms, "calculation" and "anticalculation," however, can help us perceive this conflict about psychological ideals as a general ideological one, absolutely central to middle-class culture, but with various specific manifestations. Harold Perkin has shown, for example, how middle-class economics were sublimated into both an entrepreneurial ideal, based on competition, and a professional ideal, based on disinterest, which were allied against aristocratic concepts of patronage but in constant tension with each other.[14] More crudely, standard histories of Victorian cultural values resort to similar dichotomies, which they also attribute to ideological tensions, whenever they claim that middle-class Victorians confusedly (or hypocritically) prized both competition and compassion, worldly prudence and spiritual self-sacrifice, the hard head and the soft heart.[15]

The broad psychological opposition of calculation and anticalculation, as an axis of cultural idealism, could be separately distributed to men and women, however, as one way of resolving potential contradictions. Such a distribution avoids the need to represent middle-class psychological and ethical strengths exclusively in terms of either one principle or the other, or as a muddled ideal that tries to synthesize the two. As Nancy Armstrong has demonstrated, one

[13] See John Stuart Mill, *Autobiography*, in *Collected Works of John Stuart Mill*, ed. John M. Robson, 33 vols. (London: Routledge and Kegan Paul; Toronto: University of Toronto Press, 1963–91), esp. 1:145–49; and Thomas Carlyle, "Characteristics," in *The Collected Works of Thomas Carlyle*, 16 vols. (London: Chapman and Hall, 1858), 3:1–33.

[14] Harold Perkin, *Origins of Modern English Society* (London: Routledge and Kegan Paul, 1969), pp. 218–70.

[15] For example, see Walter E. Houghton, *The Victorian Frame of Mind, 1830–1870* (New Haven: Yale University Press, 1957). Houghton claims that "the revival of Evangelical Christianity existing side by side in the middle classes with the new commercial spirit and a political economy of self-interest and unlimited competition" (p. 405) was responsible for much of what we now diagnose as middle-class hypocrisy.

of the functions of sexual difference is precisely to resolve this kind of ideological self-contradiction. Gender is constructed differently in middle-class culture, Armstrong argues, in order to embody seemingly incompatible cultural ideals, to effect a proper "division and balance of authority."[16] So abstract an opposition as that between calculation and anticalculation was by no means distributed neatly along sexual lines. In most social or public behavior, for example, Victorian men could be represented as calculatedly commonsensical, practical, and prudent; Victorian women as sympathetic, generous, self-sacrificing. But in terms of private emotional expression, especially involving sexual desire, the opposition of calculation/anticalculation could be reversed: men were conventionally seen as extravagant and uncontrolled; women as reserved and cautious. The sexual distribution of contradictory behaviors and symmetrically opposed psychologies follows complicated paths that are well beyond the scope of this study. What is more important to our present purposes is that, in the realm of morals alone, vices that indicate an unbalanced exercise of opposed psychological tendencies—lying as calculation taken to extremes and impulsiveness as anticalculation taken to extremes—could be represented as the kind of ideological disorder that occurs when one sex begins to act like the other. In the work of a novelist such as Gaskell, the inherent contradictions of bourgeois consciousness are controlled in this particular way by sexual difference, and disorderings of sexual norms for moral behavior signal the explosive potential of ideological principles that need to be kept carefully separate.

Largely for this reason, and not because of her supposed concessions to patriarchal conventions, sexual disorder is understood as pathological by Gaskell, rather than as a liberation. The movement of the novels' plots is always to heal these disorders. However much Gaskell wanted to soften men and strengthen women, a more fundamental project of her novels is to clarify middle-class consciousness by correctly dividing moral misconduct along sexual lines—that is, by banishing deceit from masculinity and by purging the feminine

---

[16] Nancy Armstrong, *Desire and Domestic Fiction: A Political History of the Novel* (Oxford: Oxford University Press, 1987), p. 42. My emphasis on the distribution of particular sexual characteristics may differ from Armstrong's, but I am very much indebted to her theoretical paradigm.

of impulsiveness, Gaskell's middle-class women must eventually become reserved rather than impulsive. Margaret Hale not only becomes a liar; she is also so humbled out of impulsiveness that she expresses her love for Mr. Thornton, at the end of *North and South*, in the muted, indirect form of a proposal to form a business partnership—a striking contrast to her earlier display of sexual emotion before the mob. A similar transition produces the eventual reserve of Mary Barton (who, as many have noticed, is closer to Gaskell's middle-class readers in speech and awareness than the other characters of *Mary Barton*).[17] When she awakens from her delirium (and in her subsequent behavior as well), Mary is consumed by a proper maidenly shame about her courtroom declaration: "Her white face flushed the brightest rosy red, and with feeble motion she tried to hide her head in the pillow" (34.416). Jemima Bradshaw, too, is initially "more headstrong and passionate by nature" (28.365) than even the sinning Ruth Hilton, and Mr. Farquhar fears to marry such an "impetuous" girl, who is "only guided by impulse" (20.215). But Jemima eventually finds herself "attaining to that just self-control which can distinguish between mere wishes and true reasons" (29.382). She goes through a gradual development, adopting at first only a "sullen reserve" (20.224) that resembles the "deceit" (19.211) of her mother's pretended submission, before she achieves a more genuine reserve. All three of these heroines pass through an initial period of masculine impulsiveness, then through an initiation into undesirable feminine deceit (Margaret's lie, Mary's omission of testimony, Jemima's "deceitful" reserve), before arriving safely in feminine humility.

Middle-class men, on the other hand, leave the realm of the lie—which is, for them, the territory of indirection and weakness—and acquire instead the proper amount of impulsiveness necessary to decisive action. Philip in *Sylvia's Lovers* does not just assume the uniform of honest masculinity when he enlists in the army, he also rejoins the ranks of the spontaneous. He saves Kinraid's life in the heat of battle; then, in a melodramatic overcompensation for his prior unmanliness, he wanders throughout England without plan,

---

[17] See Gillian Beer, "Carlyle and *Mary Barton*: Problems of Utterance," in *1848: The Sociology of Literature*, ed. Francis Barker et al. (Essex: University of Essex Press, 1978), p. 251.

merely following his impulses. Philip's heroic action during the siege of Acre is in dramatic contrast to his paralysis during the scene of Kinraid's impressment, in which the difference between the two men is starkly drawn in terms of manly "quickness" and unmanly "indecision":

> Philip was coming towards them slowly, not from want of activity, but because he was undecided what he should be called upon to do or to say by the man whom he hated and dreaded, yet whom just now he could not help admiring.
>
> Kinraid groaned with impatience at seeing one, free to move with quick decision, so slow and dilatory.
>
> "Come on then," cried the sailors, "or we'll take you too on board, and run you up and down the main-mast a few times. Nothing like life aboard ship for quickening a land-lubber."
>
> "Yo'd better take him and leave me," said Kinraid, grimly. "I've been taught my lesson; and seemingly he has his yet to learn." (18.218–19)

Philip's admiration for the more spontaneous, manly Kinraid guides his later development and shows him how to heal the disorder of his effeminate cautiousness. That Philip does "learn his lesson" in the army is quite clear in his rescuing of Kinraid: "One man left his fellows, and came running forwards . . . he seemed to understand without a word; he lifted him up, carrying him like a child; and with the vehement energy that is more from the force of will than the strength of body, he bore him back to within the shelter of the ravelin" (38.431). With a somewhat better sense of moderation, Thurstan Benson also becomes suddenly decisive by repudiating deceit in the final chapters of *Ruth*. After going along—falteringly— with the lie about Ruth's illegitimate child which grows out of his sister's feminine "talent for fiction" (14.150), Benson sheds his indecisiveness in dramatic fashion when the lie is finally exposed and renounced. He brainstorms the saving of Richard Bradshaw; he banishes Bellingham with uncharacteristic severity; he opens the doors of his church and the subjects of his sermons to the poor, without regard for consequences.

Working-class characters, we should note, are often exempted from these kinds of reordering and are even treated with authorial affection for sexual reversals that go unhealed. Martha in *Cranford* is viewed fondly for lacking "maidenly reserve" (6.95), for being "blunt and plain-spoken to a fault" (3.67), and for having "such quick ways with her" (14.188) that she dominates, comically, the more indecisive Jem Hearn. Job Legh, who literally mothers his infant granddaughter in a long comic passage in *Mary Barton*, accuses himself of being "an arrant liar" (30.373) when he misleads Mrs. Wilson for her own good. But this tolerance for inversion is often of a patronizing kind and defines working-class supporting roles for middle-class power—through images of female servants, such as Martha, who mannishly protect middle-class women or through feminized working-class men, like Job, whose patience and compassion (and antiunion sentiments) make them less of a threat to middle-class authority.[18]

The return to sexual order in Gaskell's novels also requires that lying and impulsiveness, as signs of femininity and masculinity, be properly domesticated. Obviously, vices of any kind must be tempered in emotionally well-developed Victorian protagonists. Excessive feminine lying or male impulsiveness, though sexually "normal," remain, in themselves, forms of psychological imbalance or disorder. Therefore, the specific potentials for vice associated with either sex must be moderated and channeled into more appropriate versions of these psychological dispositions. Female lying is reduced to reserve; male impulsiveness is reduced to candor and decisiveness. At the end of *Wives and Daughters*, the lies of Clare Gibson and Cynthia give way, in the novel's plot, to the acceptably feminine reserve of Molly Gibson. Similarly, the pretensions of Deborah Jenkyns in *Cranford* give way to the "quiet dignity" (8.116) of the conventionally feminine Miss Matty, who is deeply skilled in repression. More directly, the increased reserve of characters like Margaret Hale and Mary Barton redeems these women from their previous initiation

---

[18] Stoneman's *Elizabeth Gaskell* was the first thorough reading of the relation between class and gender in Gaskell's works. Unfortunately, in her impatience to lionize Gaskell as a radical feminist and to forgive her anything that resembles conventional thinking, Stoneman identifies Gaskell's workers with a "female ethic" that she claims is a challenge to patriarchy. Armstrong is much more convincing about the powerlessness of the feminized worker (*Desire and Domestic Fiction*, p. 20). Hilary Schor approaches class and gender problems in terms of Gaskell's status as a professional woman writer (*Scheherezade in the Marketplace: Elizabeth Gaskell and the Victorian Novel* [New York: Oxford University Press, 1992]).

into lying. Male impulsiveness, on the other hand, is often channeled into spontaneous forgiveness and affection—for example, in
the impulsive sympathy for workingmen expressed by Mr. Thornton's
and Mr. Carson's sudden, surprising acts of compassion. Often, it is
corrected by being channeled into acceptably decisive behavior.
Early in *Cranford*, for example, Peter Jenkyns impersonates women
twice, is the "darling of his mother" (6.93), and lacks masculine
earnestness and purpose, in a general feminization reflected by his
unmanly desire to play tricks on his father and sister. These tricks of
Peter's, however, oddly combine signs of femininity (cross-dressing,
deception) with a more mannish impulsiveness that is out of control:
"he could never resist a joke" (5.92) and "was not always so guarded
as he should have been" (6.94). At the end of the novel, however,
Peter impulsively sells off his land in India with "the odd vehemence
which characterized him in age as it had done in youth" (15.209).
Drawing on the more manly side of his personality, he returns—
impulsively ("I have been too sudden for you, Matty" [15.207], he
says repeatedly when his surprise return shocks his sister into a
faint), but with a purpose this time: he assumes the position of
patriarch in Cranford society. Peter protectively restores his sister to
gentility, and his ad hoc strategies for making peace between Mrs.
Jamieson and Lady Glenmire accomplish what months of female
deliberation had failed to achieve.

These reorderings of sexual behavior are accomplished, admit-
tedly, with very broad narrative strokes, and they are accompanied
by persistent ripples of inverted behavior: Peter Jenkyns's improvised
reconciliations, for example, are accomplished partly through the
tall tales with which he beguiles the Cranford ladies—in other
words, by his continued capacity for lying. The reordering of sexually
distributed ethical behavior—as we will see in greater detail in the
next section—is never absolute or mechanical. Nevertheless, the
movement of the novels in their broadest outlines is to correct sexual
disorder by correcting the behavioral excesses identified with it.
Sexual disorder in the realm of basic behavioral strategies occupies a
negative place in Gaskell's imagination, and it is not to be confused
with whatever needs she felt to expand the range of female action or
to moderate the business practices of men.

As we have seen, one of the reasons that sexual disorder is

conceived so negatively is that social order depends on a division of ideological labor between the sexes. In addition to controlling potential contradictions in bourgeois consciousness, however, sexual order also controls basic attitudes toward class boundaries themselves. Most readers would agree that whatever her desire for social change, Gaskell endorsed only unrevolutionary and nontraumatic change.[19] "No one can feel more deeply than I," she wrote, apropos of *Mary Barton*, "how *wicked* it is to do anything to excite class against class."[20] And in the novel, Job Legh claims that John Barton was not such a "fool" (37.455) as to be an Owenite, because he realizes that inequalities of station are inevitable. Like many Victorian writers, Gaskell's desire to ameliorate class tensions is inseparable from her desire to preserve existing social boundaries. Social reconciliation in her novels, to a great extent, means that, as John Lucas puts it, "all must be resigned to their places."[21] The novels harbor great underlying fears about the threat to the social fabric posed by social ambition, by political agitation, or by failure to respect and to uphold the duties of rank. Much more shocking

[19] Marxist critics have been severe with Gaskell on this point. See John Lucas, "Mrs. Gaskell and the Nature of Social Change," *Literature and History* 1 (1975), 3–27. Lucas attributes to her an "ahistorical view of change as able to accommodate and reconcile conflicting interests and energies" (p. 3). In "Mrs. Gaskell and Brotherhood," in *Tradition and Tolerance in Nineteenth-Century Fiction: Critical Essays on Some English and American Novels*, ed. David Howard et al. (New York: Barnes and Noble, 1967), pp. 141–205, Lucas argues that Gaskell's promotion of a "unity of interests" includes a guilty recognition that her beliefs are to the advantage of her own class. See Raymond Williams's comments, in *Culture and Society, 1780–1950* (1958; New York: Columbia University Press, 1983), pp. 89–90, about the limits of Gaskell's sympathy with the working class; and Arnold Kettle, "The Early Victorian Social-Problem Novel," in *From Dickens to Hardy*, ed. Boris Ford (Harmondsworth: Penguin, 1958), pp. 169–87.

[20] Elizabeth Gaskell, *The Letters of Elizabeth Gaskell*, ed. J. A. V. Chapple and Arthur Pollard (Manchester: University of Manchester Press, 1966), no. 36, late 1848, p. 67.

[21] Lucas, "Mrs. Gaskell and the Nature of Social Change," p. 10. Rosemarie Bodenheimer's contention, in "*North and South*: A Permanent State of Change," *Nineteenth-Century Fiction* 34 (1979), 281–301, that Gaskell endorses the value of conflict is faithful to some of the platitudes of Gaskell's characters, but not to the novels' evident concessions to liberal orthodoxy, as chronicled by Lucas, Williams, and others. If nothing else, the middle-class characters of *North and South* all agree that workers need authoritative guidance, as noted by Ganz (*Elizabeth Gaskell*, p. 93).

than their counseling of social resignation are reactionary authorial pronouncements like the narrator's remarks on the hanging of Daniel Robson: "So the authorities were quite justified in the decided steps they had taken, both in their own estimation then, and now, in ours, looking back on the affair in cold blood" (25.283).[22] This kind of coldhearted authoritarianism, which jars against Robson's generous, heroic actions during the riot against the press-gang, underscores the great fear underlying Gaskell's moral platitudes and confirms her consistent support for legal authority.[23]

One result of this political cautiousness is that the disordering of sexual identity, and behavioral excesses like lying and impulsiveness which such disorder unleashes, are firmly tied to threats against social class. Readers have often noticed how Gaskell's plots emphasize the restoration of familial relationships as a model for social stability. In Gaskell's novels, the family centralizes power, establishes subordinate ranks, and even incorporates a loyal servant class.[24] But coherent sexual difference is a metonymy for social stability as well. Lying men and impulsive women are consistently motivated in Gaskell's novels by desires that threaten the stability of class boundaries. The same is true of women whose lies have not been domesticated properly as reserve, and men whose impulsiveness is violent and aggressive rather than forgiving or purposeful. In general, lying and impulsiveness—the ethical and psychological signs of sexual disorder—are always also the signs of a threatened disruption of class boundaries.

In some cases, the connection is made directly. Clare Gibson and Cynthia are compulsive liars because they are constantly plotting their social rise. The effeminate, indecisive Mr. Hale willingly suffers a social fall. The most prominent male liars of the novels—Osborne

[22] This passage is singled out both by Terry Eagleton, "*Sylvia's Lovers* and Legality," *Essays in Criticism* 26 (1976), 26; and by Lucas, "Mrs. Gaskell and the Nature of Social Change," p. 19.

[23] See the comments of Wright, *Mrs. Gaskell*, p. 27; and Deirdre David, *Fictions of Resolution in Three Victorian Novels: "North and South," "Our Mutual Friend," and "Daniel Deronda"* (New York: Columbia University Press, 1981), p. 15.

[24] See Wright, *Mrs. Gaskell*, p. 63. A related argument is Catherine Gallagher's contention that Gaskell attempts to found social order on a metonymic conception of family order ("*Hard Times* and *North and South*: The Family and Society in Two Industrial Novels," *Arizona Quarterly* 36 [1980], 70–96).

Hamley and Philip Hepburn—are both alienated from their own class and attempting to marry women who are beneath them in rank, either by birth or inclination. In other cases, the connection is more figural. When men usurp the power of lying, for instance, an epidemic and amorphous destabilization of social order often follows. In *Cranford*, Signor Brunoni's conjuror tricks inspire a panic among the Cranford ladies over an imaginary threat from foreigners and robbers—in particular, from a woman who is "masculine-looking—a perfect virago; most probably a man dressed in woman's clothes" (10.145). In *Sylvia's Lovers*, the press-gang's fraudulent ringing of the church bell to assemble the men of Monkshaven leads directly to an outbreak of mob violence. "That comes o' ringin' t' fire-bell," says Daniel Robson, "It were shame for it to be tellin' a lie, poor oud story-teller" (23.264). Both incidents dramatize fears about working-class retaliation against middle-class privilege and authority by making masculine deceit the flash point for social disorder. Impulsive action—and, of course, violence—is even more obviously tied to disruptive social desires. This is most clear in the male violence of *Mary Barton* and *North and South*, where class conflict results in spontaneous physical assault, and in such scenes of frustrated ambition as the beating of Peter Jenkyns by his father in *Cranford*. But impulsiveness is associated with transgressions against class in Gaskell's women as well. Mary Barton, who is initially a "faulty, impulsive, lovable creature" (23.318), is infatuated with Harry Carson because she is blinded by the same dreams of wealth and gentility which have ruined her aunt Esther. The realignment of her attitudes toward class corresponds to her recognition that feminine constancy in love (she has known her working-class lover since childhood) is more to be trusted than sudden, errant impulses.

The rectification of social desire in Gaskell's novels—the banishment of calculating ambition or uncalculating irresponsibility—is thus consistently related to the discovery of proper sexual identification and behavior. In this sense, calculation and anticalculation—or lying and candor—as opposed middle-class psychological ideals, are presented as potential threats to social order when either one of them escapes symbolic control. The gendering of vice is one of the primary ways that Gaskell upholds the stability of middle-class cultural values. It is also her means of defining the explosive social implications of any permissible disruption of gender-coded moral norms.

The most interesting parts of Gaskell's novels are the areas in which her large patterns of social and sexual regulation, however persistent they may seem from the vantage of a synthesizing critical distance, are disrupted. For, like most middle-class writers, Gaskell is fascinated by the very same transgressive behavior that she stigmatizes. The kind of behavior that she expels as socially disordering is behavior that she fears, most of all, because of its promise of various kinds of power. That is to say, sexual inversion, lying, and impulsiveness—because of their intimate connection to symmetrically opposed middle-class ideals—are not at all alien to middle-class consciousness. Rather, they are the very springs of its desire, always threatening to break out of their tenuous ideological harmony. Gaskell demonstrates that lying has so strong a hold on the middle-class Victorian imagination because it expresses "calculation" as the force of a desire, rather than simply as a virtue. Lying transforms middle-class discipline, secrecy, and strategy into the stuff of romance. If impulsiveness has a similar hold, it is because impulsiveness likewise expresses "anticalculation" as a desire, rather than simply as a virtue. More important, both lying and impulsiveness, insofar as they are signs for socially disruptive desire, embody a dreaded, half-recognized connection between middle-class ambitions and social disorder itself. Both reveal the social aggression that underlies the cultural ideals of certain segments of the middle class. Both demonstrate the dangerous ambitions, the competitive individualism, and the anarchic social or sexual energies that lie just beneath the surface of middle-class cultural values, especially those appropriated by its vanguard elements.

The redemptive qualities of Gaskell's protagonists, both male and female, are always carefully but obsessively defined in terms of transgressive behavior, in order to emphasize the vitality, social power, and psychological strength generated by middle-class cultural ideals. Favored protagonists are always distinguished by some degree of sexual inversion. More important, they are distinguished by excesses of both impulsiveness and lying. If Gaskell's novels thus present to the modern reader a considerable degree of moral and sexual ambivalence, this confusion is endemic to bourgeois consciousness, which is hardly as static and ordered as it is usually made out to be, or as it makes itself out to be. The transgressive energies that Gaskell has expelled—capacities for lying and impulsiveness, and the sexual disorder or inversion they sometimes imply—are precisely the condoned libidinal, psychological, and social strengths with which she revitalizes her transformed yet recognizably middle-class sexual roles. Their transgressive potentials must be brought in secretly, carefully, in measured amounts, but they are an important part of Gaskell's cultural idealism. The result is a remarkably powerful and self-reinforcing symbolic logic. The logic of sublimated transgression makes bourgeois self-consciousness wonderfully immune to perceiving itself as repressive, while that logic carefully upholds bourgeois standards of social order. At the same time, it opens up possibilities for the progressive revision of conventional gender roles which writers like Gaskell were able to exploit by making new areas of transgressive experience available to either sex. Such revisions, in Gaskell's case, take place only in the context of the discriminating sophistication she securely identifies with middle-class elites. But this confinement does not condemn her revisions to insignificance, particularly in the social and psychological possibilities they opened up for women. We can see how these revisions work, and the uses they make of transgression against sexual norms, by looking closely at *Cranford*—a novel that is pivotal in Gaskell's gradual displacement, over the course of her career, of social conflict into problems of sexual disorder.

Cranford society is not "in possession of the Amazons" (1.39) simply because the nineteenth-century shift from a rural to an urban economy has marginalized it.[25] Gaskell emphasizes the sexual inversion of power in Cranford partly to diagnose a world that is ideologically disordered from within. The inversion of sexual power signals the presence of disruptive social desires within Cranford—and

[25] Critics commonly judge Cranford in realist terms, as the representation of conflicts specific to a provincial backwater. Even a Marxist like Lucas dismisses *Cranford* as a rural "idyll," in "Mrs. Gaskell and the Nature of Social Change," p. 14.

not merely outside of it—which threaten the stability of the community. The linkage between Cranford gentility and socially destructive desire is made clear by the parallels between Miss Jenkyns, the leader of Cranford's "strict code of gentility" (7.109), and her overly ambitious father. But to understand Cranford's internal corruption, we must recognize the way in which lying and impulsiveness distinguish sexually complementary disorders. An attention to the binary distribution of disruptive social desire can, if nothing else, help us avoid silly quarrels about whether the militant snobbery of Cranford is finally either a feminist or a patriarchal aberration.[26]

Mr. Jenkyns and his daughter, for example, enact dangerous social ambitions that are symmetrically gendered. On the one hand, Mr. Jenkyns's love of power is revealed by his masculine failure to control his impulses, by a potential for violent expression that will lead, ultimately, to the beating of his son Peter. Even in Mr. Jenkyns's love letters, in which the narrator finds, to her surprise, "the honest warmth of a manly heart" (5.86), social ambition is linked to male sexuality as an inability to control and conceal desire. Mary Smith tells us, for instance, that "he could hardly write a letter to his wife without cropping out into Latin" (5.88). This "cropping out," she then tells us, "was nothing to a fit of writing classical poetry, which soon seized him." These upscale moments of literary inspiration, however they are satirized, take the same psychological form as the "eager, passionate ardour" (5.86) of the love letters: Jenkyns's bride-to-be is said to be annoyed at his repeated "demands upon her for expressions of love." Publication of Mr. Jenkyns's sermon, then, is "the event of his life" (5.87) precisely because excessive needs for self-display constitute his social and sexual identity equally. Deborah's social ambitions, on the other hand, follow a female course: dedicated to the restriction of impulse, Deborah dictates the social "rules and regulations" (1.49) that identify refinement with pre-

---

[26] Martin Dodsworth began this debate by arguing that Cranford disharmony results from the repression of sexual needs for feminist purposes ("Women without Men at Cranford," *Essays in Criticism* 13 [1963], 132–45). Auerbach, among others, countered by attributing Miss Jenkyns's tyranny to "her father's patriarchal code" ("Elizabeth Gaskell's 'Sly Javelins,'" p. 280) and by claiming Miss Matty as a virulently feminist heroine. Margaret Tarratt traces all social ills to Mr. Jenkyns's "repressive sense of propriety" ("*Cranford* and 'The Strict Code of Gentility,'" *Essays in Criticism* 18 [1968], p. 158).

tence—that is, with deceit. Her letters, written in an "admirably calculated" (5.90) hand, contrast her phony stateliness to her father's impulsive ardor. Her excessive feminine dedication to pretence and repressed desire takes an unnatural sexual turn in her vow to refuse "a hundred offers" (6.102) for her father's sake—a vow that is itself deceitful, since, as Miss Matty puts it, "It was not very likely she would have so many—I don't know that she had one; but it was not less to her credit to say so."

Excesses of both male impulsiveness and female deceit together reflect an excess of ambition for genteel status that threatens social order. Peter, who is "ungenteel, and not careful enough about improving his mind" (6.95), is driven off, in effect, by both kinds of ambition. The crueler manifestation of Mr. Jenkyns's and his daughter's ambitions, though, is their combined intervention, in the name of class standing, against Matty's marriage to Mr. Holbrook: father and daughter ally themselves against two characters expressly singled out for their lack of social guile. The telling irony is that the Holbrook and Jenkyns families are much closer in the social hierarchy than Mr. Jenkyns and his daughter would like to pretend. Both belong to classes that are collectively struggling to improve their social status early in the nineteenth century and to climb above the middle ranks—the one by riding the crest of nineteenth-century professionalism, the other through the increased economic efficiency brought by the agricultural revolution. The difference between the two families has much more to do with their attitudes toward these similar collective struggles than with official rank. While Mr. Jenkyns cherishes the sign of his professional expertise—his published sermon—and even poses for his portrait with his hand on a copy of it, Mr. Holbrook refuses the title "Squire" that other yeomen are claiming. The interference of Mr. Jenkyns and Deborah, then, is the sign of an aggressive ambition, both individual and collective, and not of desires simply to preserve rank—desires that Gaskell would presumably have found much more forgivable.

The genteel lies of Cranford society are merely the female expression of these dangerous drives toward social elevation. The collective lies the ladies tell, whether direct (saying that they *prefer* walking to sedan chairs) or indirect (acting "as if we all believed that our hostess had a regular servants' hall" [1.41]), are comic because of their relative impotence. But they are nevertheless signs of excessive ambition which are firmly linked to the catastrophes precipitated by Mr. Jenkyns and his daughter. Readers sometimes forget that the Cranford ladies are not simply attempting to preserve a social status that is being eroded by changes in industrial society; they are upper-middle-class women trying to pretend that they are aristocrats. The competitive basis of Cranford gentility emerges in the various internecine Cranford feuds, particularly in the tactics of Mrs. Jamieson—the successor to Deborah Jenkyns's leadership—who temporarily snubs her friends for Lady Glenmire's sake and tries to cut Mrs. Fitz-Adam for being the sister of a surgeon. This aggression is demonstrated most crudely by the Miss Barkers, the former ladies' maids and milliners, who "had caught the trick of the place, and piqued themselves upon their 'aristocratic connexion'" (7.105). In general, female Cranford society is a world that aggressively pretends to be better than it is, or ever was. Its fundamental lie is that it is different from the commercial world of men in its freedom from competition, in its solidarity and compassion. For even if the Cranford ladies do promote a spirit of goodwill amongst themselves, this is to a great extent a device of mutual elevation and exclusiveness, a "kindly *esprit de corps*" (1.41) that allows them to conceal their common poverty. Their sympathy for each other often masks the essential fact that they are contemptuous of outsiders who, like Mr. Hoggins, are "content with their station" (7.108). In this context, the problem represented by Captain Brown early in the novel is not so much his "manly frankness" (1.43) about his poverty, as the affront of his indifference to rank. When Captain Brown helps a poor woman with her bundle of food, he scandalizes Cranford's "sense of propriety" (2.49). His death at the railroad station, caused by his manly, impulsive rescue of a child, is also a sign of his freedom from the selfish competition of Cranford and his moral superiority to the excessively calculating nature of Cranford's genteel pretence.

The death of Captain Brown so early in the story, however, though partly an accident of the novel's composition, also signals a disordering of male impulsiveness in the world of Cranford. One aspect of this disorder is Mr. Jenkyns's ambition and violence. But male impulsiveness degenerates and threatens social order in another way as well. In Mr. Holbrook and Peter Jenkyns, male impulsiveness endangers social order by undervaluing, rather than overvaluing it. Captain Brown's death itself obliquely points toward the danger of indifference to social rank. On his shockingly open confessions of his poverty, the narrator observes, "Death was as true and as common as poverty; yet people never spoke about that, loud out in the streets" (1.42). Captain Brown does, in fact, force people to talk about death in the streets—the Jenkyns sisters learn of his death from a public commotion outside their window. The suggestion that fatal consequences are latent in Captain Brown's breaches of social propriety, though made a narrative joke by Miss Jenkyns's senile fantasy that he was run over by a train while immersed in reading *The Pickwick Papers*, is given substance by hardships forced on the Brown family by his refusal to make economic use of his connection to Lord Mauleverer. But Captain Brown has at least a basic respect for Cranford forms and ceremonies. Mr. Holbrook and Peter Jenkyns, however, share a defiant antisocial bias, exercised in unreflecting and impulsive ways, that grows out of their parallel refusals of social climbing. These two characters are not simply models of generous, disinterested conduct; they are also men imprisoned by a self-destructive impulsiveness that includes too much, in Gaskell's view, in its refusal of social hierarchy. Peter mocks his sister when "possessed" (6.95) by his social rebellion; he is "awfully frightened himself" (6.94) when his female impersonations seem to exceed his own control. Mr. Holbrook's vehemence of character, which causes Mary Smith to think him "mad" (4.76), does as much to prevent his marriage to Miss Matty as do her father and sister, since it compels him to cultivate his "uncouth habits" (4.75). Holbrook's unworldliness makes him "Don Quixote-looking" (3.70), and even Miss Matty complains that Peter is "too easy" (5.92) in his lack of application at school. Both men are, in a sense, irresponsible social deviants. The crisis of masculinity in Cranford, then, includes impulsive male failures to uphold a necessary respect for rank. This dreaded social abnegation is acted out elsewhere in Gaskell's novels by weak men such as Mr. Hale and Osborne Hamley, and even by Mr. Thornton in *North and South*, who is ruined because of his excessive honesty. Though generations of readers have celebrated what appears to be *Cranford's* noncompetitive ethos, it is important to see that the spirit of "anticalculation," taken to extremes, is also feared by Gaskell as an irresponsible and ultimately self-destructive impulse.

At the end of *Cranford*, however, it is precisely these two opposing kinds of vices—calculating lies and uncalculating impulses—as well as their gendered inversion that produce a desirable social transformation. Most striking, the power of the lie and its ability to further social aspirations not backed by economic power prove redemptive. The tall tales Peter tells in order to captivate Mrs. Jamieson—that he "shot a cherubim" (16.217) and lived "among savages . . . some of them, he was afraid, were downright Dissenters"—reestablish social order by focusing the energies of exclusion outside Cranford (on savages, Orientals, Dissenters) rather than inside it (on Mrs. Hoggins). The disruptive potential of this mechanism is not denied in the narrative: Peter stops lying whenever Miss Matty comes near, knowing that she will recognize the symptoms of social violence in his lying.[27] But Peter's unnatural, feminine talent for lying also stresses the dangerous nature of the deceptions practiced by Matty's friends: the artificial need for tea they fabricate, the secret contributions to Matty's income, the buying up of her furniture at auction by Mrs. Fitz-Adam. Conspiracies like these "occasioned a few evasions of truth and white lies (all of which I think very wrong indeed—in theory—and would rather not put them in practice)" (15.201–2), Mary Smith tells us. Far from distressing the women of Cranford, though, "the mystery of the affair gave a piquancy to their deeds of kindness which the ladies were unwilling to give up" (15.202). Kindly feminine secrecy is linked directly to the transgressive appeal of lying, which vitalizes the compassion of the Cranford ladies with the force of desires for gentility—that is, with potentially disruptive social ambition.

The benignity of the rescue of Matty is most dramatically put into question by Miss Jenkyns's reaction, early in the novel, to the parallel ruining of Jessie Brown. Complaining indignantly of "some people having no idea of their rank as a captain's daughter" (2.59),

---

[27] Critics are generally untroubled by Peter's persistent lying. Auerbach obscurely claims that Peter "institutionalizes" lies without explaining the implications ("Elizabeth Gaskell's 'Sly Javelins,'" p. 285). Ganz sees Peter's lies as a proof of the community's new freedom from censoriousness (*Elizabeth Gaskell*, p. 152).

Miss Jenkyns vows that Miss Jessie "should do no such thing" as descend to tending shop. She willingly presides over Major Gordon's rescue of Miss Jessie, an incident that ties Miss Jenkyns's problematically elitist desires to the motives of Miss Matty's later rescuers. The parallel draws our attention to the fact that Matty's rescue, however much we are meant to wish for it, emphasizes through its narrative pleasurableness the appeal of an active acquisition of rank, as opposed to passive endowment. The providential appearance of Peter completes this emphasis, for Peter incarnates the bourgeois myth of the self-made man: having run away from home and acquired both land and a title in the colonies, Peter's redemptive capital is the capital of middle-class labor and self-reliance, only distinguished by its geographical distance from the competitive enterprise of Drumble. Gaskell also goes out of her way to make feminine deceit seem justified as a necessity of economic competition. Mary Smith lies to Miss Matty, for instance, telling her that green tea is not bad for the digestion, but that free comfits are, in order to keep her business remunerative—that is, to protect commerce itself from succumbing to the noncompetitive ideals represented by Miss Matty's kindness and honesty. Miss Pole's women's council, Martha's plan for Matty to be her lodger, and even Mary Smith's letter to Peter (a letter that adventurously leaves "familiar and commonplace" Cranford for those "strange wild countries beyond the Ganges" [14.182–83]) all signal the entrance of women into the competitive economic world, even though such empowerment is rarefied, in turn, by being identified with the feminine. In all these ways, feminine misrepresentation, rather than being simply a device of diplomacy, becomes a legitimate instrument of social ambition and authority.

In both their unexpected financial savvy and their reinvigorated capacities for deceit, the Cranford ladies reaffirm the importance of actually acquiring and maintaining rank, as against simply being honest about one's poverty. They also demonstrate the power of women to contribute to this vanguard middle-class social project. Miss Matty's friends, it is important to note, are intent on preventing her from "materially losing caste" (14.184), as well as just protecting her income. They conceal her license to sell tea; they preserve her dominant position in Martha's household. Mrs. Jamieson even concocts an official formula for guaranteeing Miss Matty's rank, claiming that "whereas a married woman takes her husband's rank by the strict laws of precedence, an unmarried woman retains the station her father occupied" (15.199). The doubleness of intent behind this formula—its defence of Miss Matty, but its attack on Mrs. Hoggins—points to the social violence underlying feminine manipulations of cultural rules. The restoration of Miss Matty to gentility is, of course, celebrated as benign by Gaskell. But the return of deceit and competition underscores an ambiguity about the innocence and order of social hierarchy, and about the social and sexual disorders that it seems to require—an ambiguity that runs throughout the narrative's affection for Cranford's charming snobbery. Indulging feminine misrepresentation turns out to be a vital sign of middle-class sophistication.

There is more than just upward-looking middle-class desire at stake in these symbolic links between lying and economic or social salvation, however. By transgressing the gendered distribution of transgression, Gaskell's male and female characters together reverse the extended sexual hierarchy that equates verbal dependability with disinterested male public power and finesse with private feminine diplomacy. Both male and female protagonists in *Cranford* reorder the public realm around a reversal of gendered vices and, by implication, around a potentially explosive displacement of large patterns of social and sexual authority. For example, Peter's legitimation of lying validates a feminine form of cultural authority by giving it an effective public dimension. Peter's public deployment of lying insinuates feminine versions of power and vitality—not just feminine moral ideals—into male spheres of authority. Its affirmation of this feminized power depends absolutely on the transgression of public/private separations made possible by Peter's institutionalizing of deceit. And in this way Gaskell's utopianism incorporates a transgressive version of gender reform, much more potent than "strengthening" women and "softening" men, into her affirmation of middle-class social ambition. In effect, Gaskell has widened elite middle-class culture to include a public function for conventionally feminine cultural strengths, by dissolving the traditional middle-class notion that public and private spheres have rigidly distinct moral rules.[28] This blurring of sexually coded moralities has far greater implications than the slight changes Gaskell made in the behavior of individual male and female characters, for it breaks up the principles of social segregation that polarize expectations about individual conduct in the first place.

Far from being a nostalgic glance at a provincial backwater, *Cranford* reaffirms a purely female, contemporary cultural authority, based on morally sophisticated feminine affiliations with misrepresentation, that it inserts into the public arena. It is largely about the "feminized" power of nineteenth-century culture (conceived in terms of its fictive abilities, or perhaps its creative idealism) to ascend the social scale, with or without the assistance of male economic power.[29] In effect, Gaskell has broken feminine culture from the ornamental, dependent role it traditionally played in the creation of signs for middle-class status and given it an autonomous, unpredictable authority over "truth" and meaning.[30] Though the emphasis on communal solidarity is unarguable at the end of *Cranford*, what is less obvious is that solidarity is accomplished through one of Gaskell's basic signs of social disorder—the lie—now transformed into an instrument of feminized public authority. For deliberate misrepre-

---

[28] I am thus at odds with the contention of Catherine Gallagher that Gaskell's novels expose public/private tensions only to "reinforce" them (*The Industrial Reformation of English Fiction: Social Discourse and Narrative Form, 1832–1867* [Chicago: University of Chicago Press, 1985], p. 113). Barbara Leah Harman charts the long history of readings of Gaskell's supposed retreat to private concerns ("In Promiscuous Company: Female Public Appearance in Elizabeth Gaskell's *North and South*," *Victorian Studies* 31 [1988], 351–74); but Harman counters that Gaskell does explore and legitimate female public action, though often in displaced terms, using conventions of private life to speak about public action—an argument with which my reading is in general sympathy.

[29] Nancy Armstrong notes that middle-class culture often embodies acceptable forms of competition in women, the better to enact competition while also denying or minimizing it ("The Rise of Feminine Authority in the Novel," *Novel* 15 [1982], 141). But Armstrong's argument also downplays the effects on sexual boundaries of this strategy.

[30] Elizabeth Langland sketches out a similar argument about Gaskell, though primarily in relation to women's control over signifiers of middle-class economics, in "Nobody's Angels: Domestic Ideology and Middle-Class Women in the Victorian Novel," *PMLA* 107 (1992), 290–304.

sentation always suggests the danger of feminine calculation run amok. This recuperation of feminine lying enacts the basic paradoxes of middle-class transgression: solidarity and refusal of competition are celebrated at the very moment when Gaskell's characters utilize the mechanisms of fraudulent social elevation. The paradoxes at work here remind us that *order* is not the exclusive goal of bourgeois culture—only its most well-advertised goal—and neither is it the primary goal of gender reformation, feminist or otherwise. The aggressive ambition bourgeois culture dreads to acknowledge in itself, but which is inseparable from the binary categories through which bourgeois culture conceives its own identity, is reintroduced carefully in *Cranford* in a celebration of signs of disordering social ambition—now identified with feminine creativity—which is presented paradoxically as the means toward a stable community in which women have prominent leadership roles.

There is another, symmetrically gendered recuperation of transgression in the ending of *Cranford*. The masculine simplicity and resignation with which Miss Matty submits to her impoverishment—even hurrying it, in acts of uncalculating generosity like her redemption of the farmer's five-pound note—is celebrated, not condemned, even though it runs counter to the efforts of Miss Matty's female friends to save her. Matty's scruples about competing with the local grocer might be threatening if they were not viewed so patronizingly. For they recall, in their "common honesty" (13.177), the dangerous social indifference of Cranford's runaway men. Once "meek and undecided" (3.67), Miss Matty becomes positively manly by confronting her ruin "so decidedly" (13.178) at the end. Her willingness to embrace poverty, and her insistence—deceptively humored by friends—that all creditors of the bank be repaid honestly out of her own pocket, is an entirely different kind of self-sacrifice than her earlier, feminine repression and self-denial. It echoes, not the socially conscious will-to-repression of her sister, Miss Jenkyns, but the luxurious abandonment of status anxiety that had driven her brother and her lover, and that had characterized the moral courage and leadership of Captain Brown. Miss Matty is hardly some kind of feminist avenger on a "Jael-like" mission of vengeance against men, as Nina Auerbach claims.[31] Nor is she simply a paragon of feminine compassion and sympathy. Rather, she is a potentially dangerous figure of excessive self-negation because she emulates masculine—not feminine—behavior in her luxuriously honest freedom from concerns about caste. Matty's benevolence is an expression of one ambivalent, uncalculating extreme of bourgeois consciousness, normally identified with male impulsiveness and honesty, but now available to feminine heroism. The sexual disorder of Matty's resemblance to the novel's men makes her a progressively disruptive figure, who appropriates the authority of masculine transgression by revising traditional images of female self-sacrifice. Matty's uncalculating economic honesty may be drained of danger because it is never fully put into practice, thanks to her own comic obtuseness, but as a revised feminine ideal it nevertheless retains its force.

In both these ways—by institutionalizing feminine misrepresentation as a benignly aggressive social force and by revising traditional feminine self-sacrifice in newly masculinized terms—Gaskell exploits the possibilities of a privileged, exceptional moral climate to allow men and women to renegotiate behavioral norms. Female characters, in particular, gain transgressive access to male behavior and to male forms of public authority, after demonstrating that feminine misrepresentation is securely inscribed in the social authority of upwardly aspiring, elite middle-class culture. Gaskell thus authorizes certain kinds of transgressive desire and authority for women by reconciling the feminine with the ambitious project of middle-class sophistication. While Gaskell has not by these means escaped the general Victorian representation of sexual or class difference, she has taken advantage of its structure to open new possibilities, however ephemeral, for thinking about transgressive exceptions to it. Most important, perhaps, sexual inversion opens up a space for female subjectivity not constrained by traditional gaps between public and private spheres. The dichotomies suggested by Miss Matty's unworldliness—between old and modern values, or between female and male virtues—are all codes for a contemporary division

[31] Nina Auerbach, *Communities of Women: An Idea in Fiction* (Cambridge: Harvard University Press, 1978), p. 87.

of bourgeois consciousness, represented concisely by Mary Smith, who had "vibrated all my life" (16.211) between the worlds of Cranford and Drumble. But Matty's transformation demonstrates how these gendered oppositions can productively converge. Gaskell herself, in attempting to define her narrative authority somewhere between the poles of social realism and domestic fiction, embodies these possibilities in more dynamic ways than her moderate sexual liberalism might seem to indicate.[32] The crucial point is that, by incorporating the symbolic potentials of transgression, Gaskell has opened the liberal ideology of strengthening/softening—incarnated quite plainly in the changes to both Matty and Peter—to exceptional energies that are considerably more expansive, both politically and psychologically, and that involve a challenge to the gendered separation of spheres which Victorian sexual liberalism usually does not.

Cranford is hardly a pious, wistful idyll about the superiority of compassion to competition. Rather, it is a fable of middle-class women's efforts to activate the threatening energies latent in middle-class principles of cultural authority, without fully unleashing their disruptive potential. Gaskell's redemptive endings covertly include the expression of disruptive desires that middle-class ideology must deny in itself, even as it holds them in tenuous, illogical harmony as signs of its own power. In terms of gender, this means that the various forms of sexual inversion itself are introduced as signs of benign eccentricity, as the mark of controlled personal depth, complexity, and sophistication. The charm of Gaskell's protagonists always takes the form of a flirtation with cross-sexual characteristics, in pleasantly frank, gently coy women (like the narrator of *Cranford* herself, who both "honestly" unravels secrets, and delights readers by remaining coyly ironic), and in moderately impulsive or manipulative men like Peter. Gaskell's delicate appropriation—and avoidance—of sexual inversion, as well as her grafting of inversion to particular class desires, should, of course, limit our sense of her as a feminist reformer. But we should remember that her limited indulgence in sexual inversion is not trivial, as it would be if understood only as a failed attempt to deconstruct sexual difference or as a limp

---

[32] Schor demonstrates that Gaskell hybridizes gender by mixing generic modes (see *Scheherezade in the Marketplace*, pp. 15, 116–17).

attempt at sexual amelioration. This indulgence signals the efforts of certain middle-class women writers to draw on the exceptional, transgressive impulses that are uncannily felt to be both their own most important desires and the most direct threats to their normative conceptions of sexual difference and social control.

CHAPTER FOUR

The Professional and the Mother:
Moral Disempowerment in *East Lynne*

L ike Wilkie Collins, Ellen Wood wrote in uneasy opposition to the professional class. Unlike Collins, however, the intraclass competition she was concerned with most was the threat professionals posed to the moral power of women, particularly within the private sphere. She expressed that concern by convicting professionals of a moral degeneration inherent in the logic of transgressive "exceptionality," upon which professionals (among others) drew for their social authority. In *East Lynne*, Wood emphasizes the dangers of such exceptionality, thus problematizing a symbolic logic that I have been describing as fundamental to mid-Victorian middle-class culture. Rather than finding possibilities for women's empowerment within the symbolic logic of transgression, as does Gaskell, Wood protests against the limited, class-bound options this logic seems to relegate to women. Ironically, however, her critique of transgression also demonstrates how closely mid-Victorian images of social authority had become tied to the dynamics of transgressive exceptionality, while leaving women writers little room to reconstruct feminine authority on other grounds.

Faithful to her culture's preoccupations with truth-telling, Wood is fascinated by blurrings of honesty/dishonesty distinctions, but she shows how such transgression consolidates the exceptional authority of professionals over women. In this sense, Wood reveals that professional control over women was not entirely a matter of knowledge and surveillance, which is the principal way in which medical and legal constructions of the feminine have been studied recently.[1] Such control also included an attack on traditional sources of feminine moral authority, an attack that complemented (without being at all confined to) the "moral management" of women.[2] This attack exploited the *disordering* of moral discourse, legitimated and ultimately controlled by professional expertise, as a sign of the sophisticated professional's authority over morally simplistic women. But Wood represents these professional moral advantages as short-term, illusory ones, paid for through a fundamental weakening of middle-class moral principles. In effect, she reads the transgressive, exceptional authority of professionals as a moral fraud.

Like Gaskell, Wood also ties ethical instability to sexual inversion. As I demonstrate in the last section of this chapter, she associates moral transgression with a reversal of gender norms that depend on polarized moral strengths. But rather than finding these inversions to be a source of desirable change in sexual roles—as does Gaskell— Wood uses them to indict the logic of transgressive exceptionality as an enemy to middle-class culture in general, and middle-class women in particular. Finding the professional to be a dangerous figure of moral and sexual confusion which her culture has mistakenly deified, Wood shows how the emergence of transgression as a general ideal in middle-class culture—modeled by professionals, but available to others as well—erodes the traditional moral power of middle-class

[1] I am thinking of a wide range of ground-breaking work on the relationship between professional discourses and the feminine. An excellent representative collection is *Body/Politics: Women and the Discourses of Science*, ed. Mary Jacobus et al. (London: Routledge, 1990). See also Jana Sawicki, *Disciplining Foucault: Feminism, Power, and the Body* (London: Routledge, 1991); Ruth Harris, *Murders and Madness: Medicine, Law, and Society in the Fin-de-siècle* (New York: Oxford University Press, 1989); Cynthia Eagle Russett, *Sexual Science: The Victorian Construction of Womanhood* (Cambridge: Harvard University Press, 1989)—though to mention these particular works is only to touch the tip of an iceberg.

[2] An excellent discussion of the moral standards of moderation promulgated by nineteenth-century medicine is Alasdair C. MacIntyre, *After Virtue: A Study in Moral Theory* (Notre Dame: University of Notre Dame Press, 1981), pp. 27–30. There are many studies of the moral management of women, but see, in particular, Ruth Harris's stimulating discussion, in *Murders and Madness*, pp. 155–242.

women and the stability that moral power once gave to middle-class culture. If sensation fiction flirts with the "subversion" of morality, as it is often said to do, *East Lynne* locates that subversion, not in its own outright attacks on official standards, but within the changing structure of middle-class morality itself.

Wood's antiprofessional, antiexceptional project cannot be dismissed as a reactionary one, nor is it rooted simply in the resentments of less-privileged segments of the middle class against elitists—though both these explanations have some weight. Wood's resistance to transgressive exceptionality is clearly related to her own social position among the petty bourgeoisie, and to the staggering popular success of her most famous novel. But *East Lynne* also articulates a complex mid-century debate about changes in middle-class moral identity, using the figure of the professional to represent increasingly widespread shifts in moral sensibility and the figure of the victimized woman to dramatize the danger of those shifts. Besides protesting against the exclusion of women from meaningful roles within the exceptional domains of middle-class culture, *East Lynne* defines a more general middle-class identity crisis, rooted in what it sees as the growing cultural role of antibourgeois transgression—a phenomenon of which sensation fiction itself was an obvious harbinger, although the preceding chapters have argued the importance of the antibourgeois in "mainstream" Victorian fiction as well.

A neglected source of *East Lynne*'s power—since most readers have focused exclusively on its concern with motherhood and the fallen woman—is the tragic atmosphere the novel's sexual drama projects onto mid-century middle-class transformations, especially the danger to traditional conceptions of moral authority that it embodies in its professional protagonist.[3] The focus of my reading of *East Lynne* is

[3] Most readers have focused on sexual conflict as the key to the novel's tremendous popularity, although there has not been much agreement about the valence of its sexual politics. Among those attacking the novel's conventionality, Jeanne B. Elliott offers the most substantial reading ("A Lady to the End: The Case of Isabel Vane," *Victorian Studies* 19 [1976], 329–44). E. Ann Kaplan claims that the novel polices Isabel's erotic desires and advocates their sublimation in repressive models of self-sacrificing motherhood (*Motherhood and Representation: The Mother in Popular Culture and Melodrama* [London: Routledge, 1992], 76–106). On the other side, Elaine Showalter has made the classic statement of the novel's "subversive" potentials (*A Literature of Their Own: British Women Novelists from Brontë to Lessing*

not the fallen woman, Isabel Vane, so much as her unassuming lawyer-husband, who aggravates sources of general middle-class distress in which class and gender apprehensions are inextricable, although some of them have been veiled beneath a conventional drama of seduction and remorse. Such a perspective can ultimately help advance the debate about *East Lynne*'s attitudes toward sexual conflict, by seeing the novel as a critique of the symbolic logic I have been defining as a dominant source of cultural authority in mid-century fiction, rather than as an assault on the supposedly stable "patriarchal" conventions that the novel is usually presumed to have targeted. Through its critique of transgressive exceptionality, and of the exceptional authority now normalized in the figure of the professional, *East Lynne* offers a more subtle analysis of women's changing position in middle-class culture than has yet been recognized. An attention to the novel's articulation of interdependent class and gender shifts is also one of the ways to read the social semiotics of popular culture without essentializing them as either liberatory, repressive, or both at once, and that theoretical project is a secondary motivation of my reading.[4]

Though *East Lynne* has often been taken to be "solidly middle class" in its ideological assumptions, the novel is centrally concerned with middle-class apprehensions about its rising political and eco-

---

[Princeton: Princeton University Press, 1977], esp. pp. 158–61). Sally Mitchell claims that *East Lynne* permitted imaginative exploration of interdicted desires (introduction to *East Lynne*, ed. Sally Mitchell [New Brunswick, N.J.: Rutgers University Press, 1984], p. xiii). Mitchell's more affirmative evaluation is hardly new. Adeline Sargeant long ago cited *East Lynne* as evidence that readers were tired of "inane and impossible goodness" in fictional heroines ("Mrs. Crowe, Mrs. Archer Clive, Mrs. Henry Wood," in *Women Novelists of Queen Victoria's Reign* [London: Hurst and Blackett, 1897], p. 181). Somewhat between these extreme positions, Laurie Langbauer inscribes both the novel's conventionality and its rebellions in a common tropological scheme—the conflation of motherhood with madness ("Women in White, Men in Feminism," *Yale Journal of Criticism* 2 [1989], 219–43). Ann Cvetkovich defines the novel's politics as "indeterminate" (*Mixed Feelings: Feminism, Mass Culture, and Victorian Sensationalism* [New Brunswick, N.J.: Rutgers University Press, 1992], p. 123). Less theoretically sophisticated readings have also defined the novel's ideological neutralization in various ways. For example, Winifred Hughes argues that Wood's novels thrive on a fascination with scandal, but also affirm standards of propriety (*The Maniac in the Cellar: Sensation Novels of the 1860s* [Princeton: Princeton University Press, 1980], esp. p. 112).

[4] One of the inspirations for my refusal of this dichotomy is Andrew Ross, *No Respect: Intellectuals and Popular Culture* (London: Routledge, 1989).

nomic fortunes, and the way those fortunes had fragmented its own moral makeup.[5] Although an upward social trajectory may not have been the universal lot of the novel's contemporary audience, the long economic boom beginning in the mid-1850s certainly induced a general feeling of affluence by 1861, when *East Lynne* was first published. The goals of the traditional professions had begun to be more widely shared by then—"great expectations" (and great nervousness about them) were very much in the air in 1861. Professions like architecture, engineering, and education (not to mention those of cultural intellectuals) expanded rapidly at this time, and the decade of the 1860s saw the founding of many of the public schools, which provided a path to gentrification for the sons of wealthy businessmen. Moreover, *East Lynne* boldly stages the political prospects of middle-class success, having Carlyle triumph over the novel's aristocratic villain when he is elected M.P. of West Lynne—a stunning public vindication that is celebrated by characters of all social classes, even as it is shown to represent the political triumph of middle-class morality.[6] From Carlyle's perspective, the novel can be read as a cathartic reorganization of social order around middle-class moral values, a project dear to the wishes of British fiction from John Bunyan through Dickens and beyond. But in 1861, when that project could begin to be contemplated as an achieved social fact, *East Lynne* displays a new self-consciousness—both narcissistic and nervous—about the meaning of middle-class success. Through the rise of the new, exceptional moral authority embodied most visibly in the professional, *East Lynne* sees mid-century transformations as a threat to the very moral identity of the class Carlyle so gloriously champions. The notorious hesitation of the middle class to assume the reins of political authority long after its social and cultural battles had been won—a loss of nerve routinely deplored by middle-class radicals (and channeled, partly, into the nostalgia for genteel social order we saw in Trollope)—owes

[5] The phrase is from Kaplan, *Motherhood and Representation*, p. 78.

[6] It is no accident that Levison, the villain, has a commission in the army. Middle-class resentment of the patronage system often focused on the military as one of the last professions still reserved almost exclusively for aristocrats. See W. J. Reader, *Professional Men: The Rise of the Professional Classes in Nineteenth-Century England* (London: Weidenfeld and Nicolson, 1966), pp. 78, 194.

something to the primal fear defined by Wood's novel: that political and social authority, when it is finally achieved, might involve a betrayal of the middle-class moral mission.[7] *East Lynne*'s stunning popularity derived from its ability to dramatize and to redefine the terms of that middle-class moral crisis without imposing a narrow ideological vision of its own. Wood continued to be preoccupied with the problematic transfer of power to middle-class hands in subsequent novels like *Trevlyn Hold* and *Verner's Pride*, though never again with the same success.

Jonathan Loesberg has pointed out that sensation fiction often worked to estrange the familiar, and he cites Lady Isabel's life as a stranger in her former home, within a family that had once been her own, as an exemplary case.[8] But *East Lynne* estranges class roles even more dramatically than it estranges familial and sexual relationships—making the magistrate's son a stable boy, ensconcing the country lawyer in the earl's mansion, turning the earl's daughter into a governess, granting impunity to the class-crossing daughter of a law clerk (who has an affair with an aristocrat, then becomes housemaid to the aristocrat's cousin, and finally marries a respectable shopman). Most important, Carlyle's self-imposed alienation from his middle-class roots and the way it disorders his relationships with women, are the primary causes of the novel's traumatic events. Class estrangements are often the source of sexual confusion in *East Lynne*, leading to emotional stresses that have been mistakenly read by critics as the effect of timeless, monolithic middle-class norms. To cite just one example, critics have usually taken Carlyle's remoteness from Isabel as the typical behavior of a well-meaning but insensitive patriarch, fully representative of middle-class manhood. But Carlyle's self-absorption can also be read as an allegory of the emasculation that seems to accompany middle-class upward mobility, an emasculation that causes his unconsciously dishonorable conduct to

[7] In 1849, for example, Richard Cobden, complaining about the difficulty of sustaining properly middle-class agitation in the face of middle-class infatuation with the captured aristocratic political parties, wrote, "We are a servile, aristocracy-loving, lord-ridden people, who regard the land with as much reverence as we still do the peerage and baronetage" (John Morley, *The Life of Richard Cobden* [London: Unwin, 1910], p. 518).

[8] Jonathan Loesberg, "The Ideology of Narrative Form in Sensation Fiction," *Representations* 13 (1986), 115–38.

his wife, especially his secrecy and deceit. Altogether, the novel's fascination with ruptured class boundaries produces an atmosphere of social anomie, represented most of all by Carlyle's transformation—which defines the dreams of many of the novel's readers—from middle-class country attorney to wealthy gentleman.

There are several reasons why Wood and other writers of the period saw the professional—a figure that "played a part out of all proportion to its numbers in both the theory and the practice of class conflict," as Harold Perkin has put it—as the quintessential figure for middle-class metamorphosis.[9] The appropriation of exceptional moral authority through transgression—as I have been arguing throughout this book—is one crucial way in which professionals established themselves as the leaders of their class. But professional ascendence was overdetermined in various ways, some of which help link professional moral exceptionality to Wood's fears about the shrinking role of women within an ascending middle-class culture. Besides the simple fact of professional success, after mid-century, at consolidating dramatic economic and social gains, professional ideology, with its remarkable power to synthesize competing class ideals, seemed an attractive formula for a general middle-class breakthrough. On the one hand, professionals seemed to exemplify the success of the middle-class entrepreneurial ideal—both in their independence and in their validation of a meritocratic reward system. On the other hand, professionals demonstrated how occupational success could be translated into gentlemanly social status through a synthetic moral idealism.[10] That is to say, professionals achieved their social gains by linking entrepreneurial competition to traditional moral values of both the middle and upper classes—to the "service ideal," or noblesse oblige, of preindustrial aristocracy, and to the moral emphasis on candor and probity of the traditional middle class. The professional thus represents a brilliant resolution

[9] Harold Perkin, *Origins of Modern English Society* (London: Routledge and Kegan Paul, 1969), p. 252.

[10] For this reason, both Pierre Bourdieu (*Distinction: A Social Critique of the Judgement of Taste*, trans. Richard Nice [Cambridge: Harvard University Press, 1984]) and Alvin Gouldner (*The Future of Intellectuals and the Rise of the New Class* [New York: Seabury Press, 1979]) find professionals to be among the most adept at transforming their "cultural capital" into social status.

of a long-standing middle-class ideological dilemma: how to blend competition with moral virtue, in a way that might represent upward-looking middle-class desire as a stabilizing social force.[11] In the figure of the professional, a contradiction that had fueled the middle-class doctrine of separate spheres (as we saw in Gaskell's work) now seemed resolvable in a single figure. Most important, by synthesizing class ideals, professional ideology made redundant the gendered public and private spheres that had once served to perform this same ideological work. Professionalism folded feminized moral ideals—service and loyalty—into masculinized public virtues of ambition and competition.

Another dimension of this synthesis of gendered public and private spheres, which further destabilizes sexual relations, is the professional's ability to ground economic, social, and political success in the innate abilities of a kind of supersubject. Middle-class opposition to aristocratic ideals often opposed virtues of selfhood (sensibility, intelligence, emotional power)—many of which were routinely identified with middle-class women—to virtues of social position or rank. The professional offered an ideal image of gentlemanly success based on these kinds of subjective competence—on abilities that are inseparable from sensibility and involve skill at interaction with other selves. As M. S. Larson puts it, "In a fusion of practical ability and moral superiority, the expert appears to be freer and more of a person than most others. Himself a choice victim of the subjective illusion, he is also, by his very existence and actions, an effective propagator of bourgeois individualism."[12] Larson extends and politicizes an insight of Eliot Freidson, writing about the phenomenon of the arrogance of physicians: "Indeed, so impressed is he by the perplexity of his clients and by his apparent capacity to deal with those perplexities, that the practitioner comes to consider himself an expert not only in the problems he is trained to deal with

[11] On the "service ideal" in professionalism, see Magali Sarfatti Larson, *The Rise of Professionalism: A Sociological Analysis* (Berkeley: University of California Press, 1977), pp. 62–63. Robin Gilmour contends that the ideal of disinterestedness is the main link between traditional conceptions of the gentleman and the new professional public servant (*The Idea of the Gentleman in the Victorian Novel* [London: George Allen and Unwin, 1980], pp. 97–98).

[12] Larson, *The Rise of Professionalism*, p. 225.

but in all human problems."[13] The superior subjective competence of the professional not only promotes the notion that professional expertise can minister to all aspects of human interiority; it also appropriates, in the process, the psychological and emotional authority of the feminized private sphere. Wood and other Victorian novelists rarely engage the more practical issues behind the professional's social ascendance—the role of professional organizations, education, certification, market control, and so on.[14] Rather, it is in terms of the ideology of the professional subject, as an intimate and universal problem-solver, blending virtues traditionally distributed across gender lines, that professional authority is represented in novels like *East Lynne*.

The figure of the detective in sensation fiction often reinforces the idea that public and private spheres can be fused in the professional abilities of specially talented men. In *East Lynne*, Carlyle's investigative work shows how the amateur detective figure of Victorian fiction was used to represent a complex of professional/subjective abilities—unusual analytical skills, creative access to information, a reserve that guards against untimely disclosures—that combine rationality and sensibility in a synthesis of gendered public and private skills. It is no accident that the most famous of all nineteenth-century detectives, Sherlock Holmes, was actually modeled on an Edinburgh physician, Dr. Joseph Bell, to whom Arthur Conan Doyle was apprenticed as a young man. What the detective role adds to the professional hero, besides excitement, is an amplification of the professional's occupational privilege to mediate between public and private spheres. Like doctors or lawyers, but in much more dramatic ways, the detective is a public functionary who ministers to the most private complaints. This kind of mediation is a large source

[13] Eliot Freidson, *Profession of Medicine* (New York: Dodd and Mead, 1970), p. 171. Quoted by Larson, in *The Rise of Professionalism*, p. 225.

[14] Since the 1980s sociological analyses have tended to de-emphasize the "ideology of professionalism" as a factor in the rising social power of the professions, focusing instead on the professions' direct reshaping of economic markets and relations, and even, in the case of Perkin, *The Rise of Professional Society: England Since 1880* (London: Routledge, 1989), their transformation of the idea of capital itself. One of the earliest and most rigorous of these studies of the professional marketplace is Anthony Giddens, *The Class Structure of the Advanced Societies* (New York: Harper and Row, 1975), pp. 177–92.

of the professional's ability to represent the middle-class culture of separate spheres as a newly reintegrated whole.

In all these ways, the professional's synthetic class virtues, which legitimate his social authority, are achieved by encroaching on traditionally feminine moral and psychological domains.[15] This encroachment can reveal the inherently transgressive nature of any attempt to combine social competition with morality—a necessarily self-contradictory project, as is evidenced by the precarious balancing of gendered spheres that often worked, in middle-class culture, to conceal or sublimate such contradictions (a precarious balancing we have seen in *Cranford*). Part of *East Lynne*'s appeal, then, was its ability to dramatize the extraordinary ambivalence professionalism could actually present, as an image of the new kind of "single sphere" ideology that seemed necessary to produce figures of (male) middle-class social and political leadership. In this sense, Wood's novel charts the way professionalism expressed and exacerbated tensions latent in middle-class culture which were gradually becoming more apparent in the course of its social ascendancy. The novel articulates its discomfort with middle-class success through a widespread moral disorientation, which it centers on questions of professional ethics, and which it sees as the cause of a catastrophic deformation of gender roles. As disturbing as the moral conundrums of Isabel's predicament are a broad range of moral ambiguities in her husband's behavior, which stem from the ambiguous standards of emerging professional codes of conduct. These ambiguities guarantee that *East Lynne*, rather than being a simple staging of the plight of domestic angels, interrogates what it sees as the changing basis of middle-class moral authority, on which female identity had traditionally depended. The chief of these interrogations turns to the increased power within middle-class culture of transgressive attitudes toward truth, which ominously underlie the growing social power over women of the professional.

[15] Lyn Pykett observes that women's authority within the private sphere is endangered in *East Lynne*, but Pykett does not explore the causes of the threat to female authority, or the general encroachment of professionalism (*The Improper Feminine: The Women's Sensation Novel and the New Woman Writing* [London: Routledge, 1992], p. 126).

Though it has always focused readers' attention on problems of female identity, *East Lynne* begins with a cautionary parable about class identity. William Vane, the Earl of Mount Severn, is revealed to have been the victim of his own unexpected inheritance and social rise. As a young Temple law student, Vane had been sober and hardworking—such a model of discipline and sobriety that he was known to his fellow students as "Judge Vane."[16] An example of middle-class moralization within the ranks of the gentry, Vane's bourgeoisification is, unfortunately, incomplete. An unlikely combination of circumstances brings him wealth, a title, and a life of aristocratic idleness—with ruin not far behind. As the novel opens, we find Vane dying of gout, fearful of his creditors, incapable of providing for his only daughter. Acts of moral impoverishment, particularly duplicity—like selling his house secretly, in order to pocket the money without his creditors finding out—are mixed with images of the earl's effeminacy: his cowardice toward creditors and the helpless physical dependence brought on by his infirmity. Emblematically, the earl mourns that he never had a son who might have cut off the entail. The bitter fruits of social mobility in this allegory turn out to be a loss of male virility, male honor, and sustained patriarchal lineage.

William Vane is not simply an icon of decadent late-Victorian aristocracy. The affinities drawn between the earl's story and the destiny of Archibald Carlyle himself are disconcerting. A simple but fabulously successful country lawyer, Carlyle acquires the earl's house at the beginning of the novel—thanks to the proceeds of both law and speculation—and then marries the earl's daughter. Over the course of the novel, he consolidates his new status and becomes, eventually, a "received gentleman" (3.11.426). Carlyle is, in fact, a spectacular example of middle-class achievement, since the social gulfs separating barristers and solicitors remained much wider at mid-century than the gap between upper and lower branches in other professions.[17] That Carlyle is eventually acclaimed as West

---

[16] *East Lynne*, 1.1.3. All references are to book, chapter, and page numbers in the Rutgers University Press edition.

[17] Reader shows that attorneys and solicitors largely left the privileges of barristers intact, pursuing their own professional advantages within a distinctly two-tier

Lynne's M.P. is an astounding social victory, and a brilliant promise
to the novel's readership of how both social advancement and
political power could be acquired through intellectual vocations.[18]
His path to success, unlike Vane's, depends on middle-class virtues—
on hard and honorable work—rather than on blind fortune. Nevertheless, Carlyle's fulfillment of the most extravagant middle-class
dreams runs certain risks that the novel identifies symbolically with
his rise into social territory formerly reserved for aristocracy.

Such fears are nervously satirized through Carlyle's sister Cornelia,
the straitlaced paragon of thrift and earnestness ("Joke? When do
you know me to joke?" [3.8.395] she deadpans). Cornelia absurdly
harangues Carlyle for spending money on the social trappings of his
new station, for letting love supplant business as his primary interest,
and for aspiring to Parliament—she regards his candidacy entirely in
terms of its cost. Yet the novel shares these and other fears, and it
expresses them overtly. At Carlyle's first dinner with the earl, for
example, the narrator offers an uncharacteristic warning: "Exceedingly great were the attractions that day, all things combined. Take
care of your senses, Mr. Carlyle" (1.7.54). Moments later, the earl
and his ambitious new friend are interrupted by Isabel's singing of a
hymn: "The conversation of the earl and Mr. Carlyle had been of
the eager bustling world, of money getting and money spending,
money owing and money paying, and that sacred chant broke in
upon them with strange contrast, soothing to the ear, but reproving
to the heart" (1.7.55). The novel's opening continually casts such
qualifications on Carlyle's sparkling success. Quite surprisingly, given
the nature of its audience, the novel thus raises vague but seemingly
fundamental questions about what seems to be the most unexcep-

---

system (*Professional Men*, p. 58). While lawyers may have made important strides
toward genteel status, Reader notes that they were not yet likely to be received in
great country houses, unlike their more "learned" brethren from the Inns of Court
(p. 68)—which makes Carlyle a real trendsetter. Larson notes that between 1850
and 1900 barristers successfully resisted attempts to create a single system of legal
education, thus preserving their institutionalized separation from solicitors and
attorneys (*Rise of Professionalism*, p. 95).

[18] The pathbreaking nature of Carlyle's social advancement is reflected in the
snide tones of reviewers: "It is perhaps a little hard to suppress a smile at the
thought that, in *East Lynne*, this king of men is a country attorney. It is odd to
reflect that the hero might have charged six-and-eightpence for the conversations
with which he charms us. But this is all prejudice" (*Saturday Review* 13 [1862], 187).

tionable kind of middle-class ambition. Carlyle's loss of his oldest son at the end of the novel symbolically expresses fears that what is at stake, ultimately, is the very continuity of the middle-class male power that has so dramatically filled the aristocratic void.

Lady Isabel herself is the most sobering counterpoint to Carlyle's rise. Though born an earl's daughter, Isabel had been raised according to the strictest middle-class disciplinary standards, in an attempt to prevent her from repeating her mother's romantic excesses. As a result of her strict training, largely at the hands of a grim governess, Isabel emerges a flower of traditional middle-class morality somewhat miscast in the earl's household—as her scornful aunt Emma never tires of pointing out. A Dorothea Brooke without intellectual pretensions, Isabel renounces ornament and opts for plain dress. She is even identified with her humble maid Joyce, in their mutual resistance to "finery" (1.16.129). Honorable, earnest, and compassionate to a fault, Isabel offers to repay her father's creditors—and is prevented only by the more worldly-wise Carlyle. Her only use of her social power is to promote a charitable concert. In the terms of Victorian gender ideology, Carlyle's middle-class moral credentials should be validated by the very choice of Isabel to be his wife, since his own pragmatic business principles are necessarily less saintly.

Yet Isabel's simple honor is not merely a rebuke to Carlyle's overreaching, nor is it represented simply as a desirable complement and corrective to a lawyer's worldliness. Carlyle is already well fortified against moral criticism: his universal admiration as a man of honor within the community of West Lynne seems to be supported throughout by the narrative tone, and Carlyle is clearly shown to embody many of the moral strengths lacking in the figures of aristocratic authority he replaces. Isabel's rigorous indoctrination in middle-class morality hardly asserts itself unambiguously—despite the heavy-handed "reproof" of her hymn—either as a critique of Carlyle or as a necessary antidote. On the contrary, Isabel's strict moral training is, ironically enough, revealed to be a fundamental reason for her fall. Her seduction is not caused simply because, as a woman, she has been raised to be timid and passive, nor because she does not love her husband sufficiently.[19] Rather, the novel uses

[19] These are the standard ways of reading Isabel's fall. See Elliott, "A Lady to the End," p. 333; and Mitchell, introduction to *East Lynne*, p. xv.

Isabel to reveal the anachronistic nature of traditional middle-class ethical standards, and to show that they are doomed values in Carlyle's new world. In Isabel, the morally simple lumpenbourgeoisie often ridiculed in Trollope and Collins is raised to the status of tragic victim, a martyr to an increasingly antibourgeois culture.

Isabel's doom is determined most of all by her simple commitment to traditional middle-class norms of honesty. Raised with a naive standard for truth-telling, Isabel is unequipped for the tangled deceptions of the socially elevated world in which Carlyle moves so comfortably, a world that—as we will see—involves Carlyle in its moral complexities as the very price of his success. "You old-fashioned child!" (1.2.12), Emma rebukes Isabel when she refuses to disguise the absence of a cross on her necklace. "If people say anything, I can tell them an accident happened to the cross" (1.2.13), Isabel replies, resorting instinctively to the truth; to which Emma laughs, " 'If people say anything!' . . . They are not likely to 'say anything,' but they will deem Lord Mount Severn's daughter unfortunately short of jewellery." Isabel's naive straightforwardness, while part of the charm of her "frank, pleasant manner" (1.1.9), becomes a liability when it makes her susceptible to jealousy. Trusting appearances unquestioningly because "her spirit was earnest and true" (2.3.183), she reads the fact of her husband's lie about meeting with Barbara as a sure sign of his faithlessness, according to a standard of strict moral consistency. Although Carlyle does lie to meet with Barbara secretly, Isabel cannot guess that he does so for purely professional reasons—whatever moral ambiguities such a phrase might entail. While Isabel may initially represent an implicit caution to the social-climbing of Carlyle, then, she ends as a moral alien in an altered middle-class world to which her naive standards of honesty are no longer appropriate.

In this sense, the lack of emotional affinity between Isabel and Cornelia—two complementary images of traditional middle-class ethics (one pacific, the other aggressive)—dramatizes the fracturing of middle-class virtue in the newly ambiguous world of the professional class. It is emblematic of both women's unfitness to exercise social authority that their strict moral standards make them reject all signs of social promotion. Isabel's principled, spiritualized rejection of ornament corresponds to Cornelia's more thrifty distaste for social display: "Miss Corny might have worn" Isabel's dress, we are told at one point, "and not have found herself too smart" (1.7.53). Given this affiliation, it is only appropriate that Isabel should be assigned Cornelia's old room when she returns as Madame Vine.

But the asceticism of both Isabel and Cornelia is only one aspect of their larger commitment to standards of truthfulness and plain dealing, even though their styles of integrity—tact and outspoken-ness, respectively—express a familiar tension at the heart of tradi-tional middle-class ethics. Although characteristically reserved and nonconfrontational, Isabel tells "home truth"s (1.12.95) only as a means of self-defense. In sharp contrast to Levison, she demands in extreme circumstances that "there be plain truth between us" (1.11.244). But her honor is expressed more naturally in the rigorous self-discipline that channels moral integrity into tact and faithful obedience. "Plain-speaking" (1.13.112) Cornelia, however, is leg-endary for her persistence in penetrating to the truth, including her passion for unearthing secrets "like a ferret" (1.5.38). Together, the two women figure the long-standing middle-class ideological contradiction between self-sacrifice and competition as a conflict between styles of honesty. To the extent that the two women are identified with outmoded standards of straightforwardness, and with an archaic clash between competing middle-class discourses about truth, the novel demonstrates how the professional world compre-hensively displaces women trained in middle-class values. But the dual collapse of these complementary—and now equally "femi-nized"—moral ideals must also be seen as a general crisis for middle-class morality. Justice Hare, for example—himself a morally severe, old-fashioned patriarch—is also shattered when he discovers that what appeared to be the simple truth about Richard, the basis for his solemn oath to bring his son to justice, turns out to have been a case of error and deception. In this sense, Cornelia represents the plain-speaking, business-like man and Isabel the trusting, domestic angel of traditional "separate-sphere" middle-class morality—two equally ineffective models of public and private truth in a world of changing values and gender roles now presided over in splendid isolation by the professional man.

The strange, new world of *East Lynne* is dominated neither by the arbitrary power of aristocratic authority nor by victorious middle-class morality, but by the legal and managerial maneuverings of an elite professional class represented most of all by Carlyle—but also by his legal colleagues and his physicians. In this shift of social authority, the chief ethical victim turns out to be the concept of middle-class honesty. Truth-telling is an anomaly in a world conditioned, it would seem, by the conspiracies of disparate and apparently antagonistic social agents which only Carlyle seems able to negotiate and bring to order through professional finesse. Nominally, the central crime of the novel may be the murder of Hallijohn. But much more prominent and more dramatic in the plot are crimes of dishonesty. Otway Bethel is paid to lie about the murder, and the exposure of this lie is eventually what unlocks Richard Hare's innocence. Levison lies to Lady Isabel in order to seduce her, claiming afterward that "all stratagems are fair in love and war" (2.11.246). Isabel's adultery itself is often diagnosed by others as a betrayal, a violation of trust. Reciprocally, Isabel accuses Carlyle of having "betrayed" (2.9.235) her. The plot is driven by numerous lies and distortions: Emma's lies to her husband Raymond, the deception of Isabel's "death," the various deceits of those working to protect Richard Hare from discovery, the innumerable lies of that "false sort of chap" (2.8.226), Levison. Even the ornament-hating Isabel is compelled to adopt a disguise in order to reenter a household in which her husband's pious frauds had misled her. In a world in which stable orders of hierarchy and responsibility seem to have become fluid—partly as the result of middle-class victories—one had better not expect to be treated with honesty, or deal too naively in honesty oneself. As the earl tells Mr. Carlyle at the opening of the novel, "If you knew half the tricks and *ruses* played upon me, you would not wonder at my suspecting all the world" (1.1.5). The earl himself is not released from such a world even by death, since his very corpse is seized by creditors through a "sly, deceitful trick" (1.10.78).

East Lynne deliberately sets itself over against these erosions of moral conduct. Unlike later writers like Thomas Hardy and Sarah Grand, Wood is hardly fatalistic about moral distinctions, or about the social viability of honesty. At the end of the novel, Richard Hare puts all to rights when he gains the courage to take the stand in court and, finally, to tell the world the truth. Earlier, Richard had persuaded a number of skeptics with the sheer force of his personal sincerity; Joyce, in particular, is convinced by the strength of Richard's personality that he is telling the truth: "Nobody could so solemnly assert what was not true" (2.17.306). The climax of the novel tends generally to restore faith in the possibility of honesty, justice, and sincerity, largely by affirming the professional skills of Carlyle and Lawyer Ball in producing certain kinds of courtroom truth. Or at least, the novel does so for its male characters. It also seems eager to show, however, that there is no comparable exoneration for Isabel. No one but the reader is ever told the complete truth about the causes of her fall. Though she is forgiven in pietistic terms, she is denied the opportunity for confession and collective understanding offered to Richard. Carlyle is "unable to form even a suspicion of [her] meaning" (2.12.255), when he reads the accusations in her note, and he is never subsequently enlightened. The much happier fate of Isabel's strange counterpart, Afy Hallijohn, seems to demonstrate that, for women, deceit is the only means of survival.

This disparity in sexual fortunes arises partly from the novel's tendency to associate self-deception with passion, which is always tied to the feminine.[20] When her publisher asked Wood for a "motto" with which to promote the book, she sent him a verse from Longfellow's "The Courtship of Miles Standish" that she felt "was so applicable to the story that Longfellow might have written it for that purpose":[21]

Truly the heart is deceitful, and out of its depths of corruption
Rise, like an exhalation, the misty phantoms of passion:
Angels of light they seem, but are only delusions of Satan

· · ·

This is the cross I must bear; the sin and the swift retribution.[22]

Many errors of perception in the novel follow the delusions of passion, particularly the passion of jealousy. Even the murder of

[20] See Cvetkovich's discussion of this point, in *Mixed Feelings*, pp. 105–12.

[21] Quoted in Charles W. Wood, *Memorials of Mrs. Henry Wood* (London: Richard Bentley and Sons, 1984), p. 208.

[22] This incident is recounted by Wood, *Memorials*, p. 207.

Hallijohn is committed in the heat of passion and is instantly regretted. These passions are strongly associated with women, or with feminized men like Levison and Richard, and they confirm the hierarchical distinction that elevates male honesty through professional control over unreliable and misleading "feminine" passion.

Though there is a disparity in the ethical fortunes of men and women in the novel, however, it would be a mistake to see this disparity outside of shifts in class identity. For *East Lynne* represents a world in which professionals in the law, in medicine, in private detection, and in politics define a new kind of exceptional morality that must actually engage in certain kinds of deceit for certain higher purposes—even though the novel is deeply skeptical about some of the consequences of this fluid, transgressive morality. The community's dependence on Carlyle's elastic skills is everywhere apparent. We are led to believe it is a common occurrence that, by imprisoning a man who weeded his garden on a Sunday, the magistrates— demonstrating their own moral literalism—have gotten themselves into a "judicial scrape" that "Mr. Carlyle alone could get them out of" (1.5.36). And, of course, justice in Richard Hare's case depends on Carlyle's going outside the boundaries of social and legal etiquette. "You are so clever," Barbara tells him, "you can do anything" (1.5.34). Though a distinctly double-edged sword, the role of the male professional turns out to be the novel's best hope for the transformation of honesty into a set of fluid ethical procedures that might hold social order together on the terms of exceptional middle-class authority, rather than on its traditional moral puritanism. In the morally anarchic environment of the novel, Carlyle proves a remarkably stable figure because his professional methods allow him to pass into the world of deception in a way that is controlled, though uncertainly, by his deep sense of professional ethics. It is this exceptional moral resilience in the midst of moral turmoil which allows Carlyle to emerge, for good or ill, as the virtual anchor of the community—a unified image of both morality and worldly know-how, androgynously gendered in the terms of separate-sphere thinking.

Stepping into the void of male power left by a decaying aristocracy (even the self-righteous and powerful new earl, Raymond Vane, is constantly thwarted by his wife's deceit), Carlyle is consistently, almost obsessively defined in terms of his honesty. The first quality assigned to him by the narrative is an "honourable, sincere nature" (1.1.5). He is a "man of truth" (1.14.116), with a "true heart" (1.15.119) and a "true and honest spirit" (3.5.366). Raymond Vane sums up the case for us quite simply: "a more truthful, honourable man than Carlyle does not exist on the face of the earth" (2.12.255). Vane proclaims the common bonds of male authority by affirming, "I could have staked my earldom on his veracity. I would stake it still," and by absurdly claiming that Carlyle's honor is a source of national pride: "He is an upright and good man; one of nature's gentlemen: one that England may be proud of, as having grown upon her soil" (2.12.257). Even Isabel recognizes Carlyle's fundamental virtue: in contrast to her lover, who is "false and heartless," Isabel realizes that, in Carlyle's case, there is "nothing false or heartless about *him*" (1.12.101). Such persistent claims are necessary to mask subtle questions that are nevertheless insistently raised about Carlyle's disinterestedness. The novelty of the opening scenes, for instance, lies in a middle-class lawyer conducting a real estate transaction *for himself*, not for another party; and Carlyle's proceedings on Richard's behalf serve the dual purpose of clearing a blot on the family name and extracting de facto vengeance against Levison.[23]

Carlyle's authority in the community rests absolutely, however, on certainties about his honor—in stark contrast to the general insecurity about matters of trust. When he is drafted to run for Parliament, as a replacement for an unscrupulous politician, Carlyle poses a giddy rhetorical question: " 'Make me your member?,' cried he merrily. 'How do you know I should not sell you all?' " (3.5.364), to which the choral reply is, "We'll trust you, Carlyle. Too happy to do it." "Carlyle and honour forever!" (3.14.442) becomes the campaign chant of his political faithful. Carlyle knowingly manipu-

---

[23] The reviewer for the *Times*, Samuel Lucas, cited this last problem—claiming it should have arisen in court—as evidence of Wood's ignorance about the law (*"East Lynne," Times of London* [25 January 1862], 6). But given the extensive legal knowledge Wood demonstrates elsewhere in this novel and in her other work, it seems more likely that these are deliberate ambiguities.

lates this reputation for honor as an instrument of his authority. In some cases, he does this professionally, by invoking his honor to deflect questions about his actions. He often silences Cornelia, for example, by attributing his secrecy to "business, you understand" (1.5.37), and he manipulates Thorn and Afy by veiling information on the grounds of professional tact. In other cases, though, Carlyle appropriates such authority for more personal uses, as when he tells Joyce that he has "good grounds" for believing in Richard's innocence, and that, therefore, "I should be glad for you to think as I do" (2.16.296); a proposition to which she accedes: "I am quite certain, sir, that you would state nothing but what is true."

This linkage of Carlyle's social authority to his honor is perfectly consistent with the ideology of professionalism, which laid particular stress on disinterestedness. The cultivation of trust was even more important to professionals than it was to other middle-class businessmen, precisely because professionals often consult with their clients on the most private matters, making expectations of candor and fidelity paramount. Yet professional ethics have always been open to suspicion, for a number of reasons. Chief of these is that the professional's authority depends on his ability to convince society that he alone is the best judge and regulator of his own conduct, since his practice explores areas in which the layman's judgment is unreliable. In that sense, professional authority depends on a communal act of faith. Persistent fears about conspiracies against the laity revolve around the suspicion that professional candor is largely a moral performance, meant to capture that faith. Further, moralists have often questioned whether professional methods, shrouded in secrecy as they are, sometimes compromise the integrity of better-advertised professional ends.[24] In general, professional honor can seem an artificial code barely disguising a number of moral contradictions that stem from its break with a more strict morality revolving around self-consistency. In *East Lynne*, these professional ambiguities are represented both as a social strength and a moral poison.

One of the innovative strategies of *East Lynne* is to express suspicion of the exceptional authority of professionals by identifying

---

[24] Perkin traces this skepticism as far back as Molière, in *Professionalism, Property, and English Society Since 1880* (Reading: University of Reading Press, 1981), p. 10n.

that authority with aristocratic, rather than middle-class, notions of honor. Carlyle's sincerity may originally seem to be a product of his class and breeding, but it also quickly becomes tied to aristocratic codes of honor, which are rooted in the importance of public appearance in ways that compromise middle-class values. Thus, while professional codes of conduct can certainly be understood to have evolved out of middle-class moral standards—and often are understood in such a way by Victorian novelists—*East Lynne* rewrites this genealogy, anticipating a more modern critique, by diagnosing professionalism's dependence on upper-class values, particularly upper-class notions about gentlemanly honor.[25] Carlyle's close affinity with the new earl, Raymond Vane, and the founding of their relationship upon several stagey professions of honor on both sides, is one sign of his moral assimilation. Another is Carlyle's parliamentary campaign, which is conducted almost like a joust—women wear the colors of their champions in the "contest," and Carlyle valorously decides not to "yield the field" (3.7.385) after he hears that Levison will be his opponent. Carlyle's presence and manner are often described as "noble" (1.1.4), and—in stark contrast to Isabel's education—he has received "the training of a gentleman" (1.1.5). Significantly, Carlyle's first major public deception is his purchase of the earl's house. While this evasion may be at the earl's request, it states symbolically the concealed nature of the alliance between professionals and aristocracy, the covert linkage between East and West Lynne. The most important element in this alliance between professionals and aristocracy is the suggestion that, like the aristocratic codes of honor disavowed in Trollope's novels, Carlyle's honor is partly a matter of public facade, having less to do with consistent moral scruples than with the performative appearances necessary to maintain authority and to disguise self-interest. The novel uses this alliance to betray its principal doubts about professional ideology: that, working in areas about which the public has no competence and which were formerly often the province of quackery, professional credibility is a show calculated to extort a leap of faith; that professional authority often claims the right to deceive clients for

[25] Such a critique can be found in the work of Larson, who draws on Gramsci's ideas about the cooptation of intellectuals. See esp. Larson, *Rise of Professionalism*, p. xv.

their own good; and that professional disinterest is actually a ruse of self-interest.[26]

Carlyle himself understands that the separation between private finesse and public decorum is integral to professional practice. When he refuses to take Richard's case, he explains that doing so would "look like" (3.9.408) self-interest on his part, even though he is perfectly willing to "pave the way" (3.11.422) secretly on Richard's behalf. And when Carlyle takes his son William to Dr. Martin, he recognizes and insists on penetrating the professional mask himself:

> "Well," began the doctor, in a *very* professional tone, "the boy is certainly delicate. But—"
>
> "Stay, Dr. Martin," was the interruption, spoken in a low impressive voice, "you will deal candidly with me. I must know the truth, without disguise. Tell it me, freely."
>
> Dr. Martin paused. "The truth is not always palatable, Mr. Carlyle."
>
> "True. But for that very reason, all the more necessary. Let me hear the worst. And the child has no mother, you know, to be shocked with it." (3.13.435)

The conflation of lawyer and detective figures in *East Lynne* further underscores doubts about professional ethics in a way that would have been well understood at the time. Margaret Oliphant's scathing attack on the morality of contemporary fiction in *Blackwood's*, for example, fastens on the prominence of the detective in sensation novels: "the science of the detective—which is by no means founded in truth-telling—[has become] one of the most largely appreciated of modern sciences."[27]

Carlyle's incidental remark to Dr. Martin about motherhood defines one of the novel's consistent protests against professional discretion: that it is used systematically to restrict women's access to

---

[26] Leonore Davidoff and Catherine Hall note that, early in the nineteenth-century, aspiring professionals were often driven to cultivate church connections as a prop for their as yet shaky moral standing (*Family Fortunes: Men and Women of the English Middle Class, 1780–1850* [Chicago: University of Chicago Press, 1987], p. 102).

[27] Margaret Oliphant, *Blackwood's* 94 (1863), 170. Oliphant also complains of Wood's apparent approval of perjury as the means of saving the hero of *A Foggy Night at Offord*.

the truth. Or, more disturbingly, that it is used to manage their very perceptions of truth. Isabel's infantilism, and to some extent Barbara Hare's, grow out of Carlyle's consistent refusal to confide in his wives. Carlyle's keeping news of William's fatal illness—as well as news of Justice Hare's infirmity—from reaching Barbara may only seem gallantly patronizing. But his habitual refusal to confide in Isabel leads directly to her ruin, and his willingness to be evasive is often presented as a key source of his power over her. One reason for this willingness to deceive is that, for all his compassion, Carlyle takes authority over his wife quite seriously—in contrast to the weakened marital control of other men from various classes. When Justice Hare complains that Barbara is "as perky as she can be now she thinks she's beyond my correction," he does not receive any commiseration: " 'She's not beyond mine,' said Mr. Carlyle, quite gravely. 'I assure you, justice, I keep her in order' " (3.3.356). Perhaps the most dramatic example of professional control over women through manipulation of the truth, though, is Lawyer Ball's questioning of Afy in court, in which he traps her by deceptively appealing to her vanity.

In a general sense, to be misled in *East Lynne* is always to be feminized—a formula confirmed strikingly when Justice Hare, upon learning the real truth about his son, collapses in a kind of feminine dependency. "As persuadable as a woman" (3.16.460) is a folk saying voiced by a minor character in the courtroom scene, and it is a sign of this logic that "in spite of his obstinacy, [Justice Hare] was somewhat easily persuaded to different views of things, especially by Mr. Carlyle" (2.17.301). Throughout the novel, Hare is one of the chief victims of Carlyle's many deceptions, and his being left "wonderfully subdued and meek" (3.13.439) at the end is an appropriately womanly fate. "Leafy Dick" (1.6.41) Hare, who is also "swayed by everybody about him," helps reinforce this pattern of feminization through gullibility. In this context, it is no wonder that the novel is in part a narrative of female exclusion, matching Isabel's spectacular estrangement within her own family with the powerless dependence of Mrs. Hare, the hopeless love of Barbara, the gradual erosion of Cornelia's influence, and even, in a sense, the exile of the "feminine" Richard from his mother. All of these figures can be seen as victims of deceit. A world amenable to professional control over truth and falsehood, the novel seems to suggest, is necessarily a world of strict male control over women. Wood thus responds on an ethical plane to the growing apprehension among nineteenth-century women that professionalism represented a new threat of gender exclusion based on occupational ideology.[28] *East Lynne* makes it clear that the threat from professionals was not solely based on the epistemic equations between power and knowledge which Foucauldian critics have noted, but that it included a moral assault, in the name of transgressive moral sophistication, against which women's traditional moral simplicity put them at a decided disadvantage.

Another element of the novel's skepticism about professional authority is its recognition that, in a perfectly circular way, the strategic use of honesty is a condition of professional authority, and vice versa. Thus, women in the novel are often exiled from the domain of truth-telling by their simple lack of authority to speak. During her jealous crisis, Isabel is often portrayed as on the verge of speech, yet inhibited by her sense of powerlessness. And while struggling against Cornelia, Isabel wishes for "the courage to speak out openly to her husband," only to be stopped by the "deep consciousness of humiliation" (1.17.142) in her dependent condition. Earlier, young William Vane had actually made her marriage possible, by voicing complaints about her unjust treatment that Isabel seemed unable to speak about herself. Richard Hare, whose feminization helps make him Isabel's double (both are exiled; both have their names placed under interdiction within their families; both are victims of Levison; both return in disguise), takes flight from the scene of the murder because of his cowardly fear of speech. "What would have been my word," he asks, "when there was nobody

---

[28] There are, as I have suggested, many discussions of professional control over women, although few have adequately recognized the moral terrain of this conflict. Mary Poovey's work on medical discourses about women, *Uneven Developments: The Ideological Work of Gender in Mid-Victorian England* (Chicago: University of Chicago Press, 1988), pp. 24–50, touches on issues of moral management, as does Jenny Bourne Taylor's excellent book on Collins, *In the Secret Theatre of Home: Wilkie Collins, Sensation Narrative, and Nineteenth-Century Psychology* (London: Routledge, 1988). In strictly occupational terms, Londa L. Schiebinger argues persuasively that there was a new nineteenth-century denial of access to scientific and technical education for women, based on increasingly polarized notions of mental ability in post-Enlightenment gender ideology (*The Mind Has No Sex? Women in the Origins of Modern Science* [Cambridge: Harvard University Press, 1989], pp. 118, 235–41).

to corroborate it?" (1.6.45). In many ways, truth-telling requires the sanction of a public role and reputation in order to be effective. Conversely, Carlyle's professional authority often depends on and licenses his concealment of knowledge. Both Isabel and Richard are victimized because they undervalue community codes of trust—or, rather, because they feel excluded from those codes and inept at negotiating them.

Most important, though, *East Lynne* exposes professional authority by revealing that professionalism's license to veil the truth leads inevitably to abuse. As the novel progresses, Carlyle's lies seem to grow in frequency and moral dubiousness. At first, his principal lies are in the good cause of Richard's defense—he lies repeatedly to Justice Hare about Richard's whereabouts, for example, and he adopts the ruse of a letter delivered by Dill in order to keep a rendezvous with Captain Thorn. But as the novel goes on, Carlyle develops an increasingly unregulated, almost pathological tendency toward deceit. His propensity for deception extends into his personal life when he lies to Cornelia about the reasons for his visits to Isabel and conceals his trip to London to buy wedding furnishings. Eventually, in his law practice, deceit comes to be an accepted stratagem that loses discriminatory power. One sign of this diffusion is that at various points, Carlyle conspiratorially uses his mansion to conceal from public view both Richard—the novel's victim—and Levison—its villain. The novel draws our attention repeatedly— gratuitously, it might seem—to the prominence of deceit in Carlyle's methods. At one point, both Carlyle and Barbara gloat, laughingly, about his routine methods of evading unwanted business: "Dill . . . has his tale ready when they miss me. 'Suddenly called away: important business; could not be helped' " (3.2.345). The contradictions between Carlyle's honor and his behavior are often presented by the narrator starkly, without any attempt at resolution: "Mr. Carlyle held deceit and all underhanded doings in especial abhorrence: yet he deemed that he was acting right, under the circumstances, in allowing Captain Thorn to be secretly seen by Richard Hare" (2.8.220). And, "Always open as to his own affairs, for he had nothing to conceal, he yet deemed it expedient to dissemble now" (1.13.103). Such condensations can be read ambiguously, either as the sign of Carlyle's intuitive professional wisdom in adjudicating moral questions or as a sign of his own moral confusion.

Carlyle's deceptions, even in the best of causes, eventually produce dire results that provoke the latter judgment. Most important, Isabel's tragedy is caused as much by Carlyle's habit of deception as by her own weakness and dependence. The most profound instance of Carlyle's increasingly pathological deceit, and its tragic potentials, is his misleading marital behavior. Carlyle's lie about his reasons for being late on the fatal evening seems to confirm Isabel's later suspicions when she sees him with Barbara—a pattern that is repeated in Richard's story and in that of Blanche Challoner, both of whom tell small lies that later inhibit their ability to cultivate general trust. Isabel's mistaken jealousy may be rebuked by several characters as a sign of her immaturity, but it is supported later on when Cornelia leaps to similarly jealous conclusions upon finding Carlyle holding a clandestine meeting with Richard. Cornelia assumes, ironically, that Carlyle is having an affair with the governess. Barbara Hare had also been misled much earlier by Carlyle's reserve, and Barbara accuses him directly of having deceived her. Cornelia, too, had felt it to be a "plot" (1.13.109) and a "conspiracy" (1.13.111) when she finds herself deceived about Carlyle's marriage. All three of the women in Carlyle's life suffer from his deceptions. Cornelia's suffering is perhaps the most easily dismissed, given her comic persona, but it is nevertheless characteristic of Carlyle's behavior that he should hide Isabel's farewell note to him ("You need not mention this," he tells his servant [2.9.235]), which results in the most devastating share of guilt for Isabel's flight being assigned to Cornelia. Thus, while Carlyle's indulgence in deceit parallels the general tendency in Victorian fiction to associate dishonesty with middle-class sexual and social ambition, *East Lynne* views that association with distress from the perspective of Isabel's tragedy. Rather than simply producing Carlyle as a figure of romantic deviance, an effect we have seen in the novels of Trollope, Collins, and Gaskell, it shrouds him in dangerous ambiguities.

The novel's critique of professional integrity goes further and includes an attack on the superior claims to knowledge which undergird its social authority. For a man who arrogates to himself the ability to play with truth and manipulate appearances, Carlyle is strikingly obtuse. Dependent so thoroughly on the power of discourse to reveal or conceal, he is abysmally bad at interpreting the unexpressed. Not only is he completely oblivious of Barbara's infatuation and his wife's jealousy, but he never has the slightest perception of the distress his sister causes Isabel, although even the servants are aware of it. He is similarly obtuse about the meaning others are likely to assign to his own gestures—as in his gift of a locket to Barbara. His own deception in harboring Levison blows up in his face because of blindness to Levison's designs on his wife, even though Isabel had given persistent indications that Levison's presence distressed her. Most disturbing, Carlyle seems to be oblivious of the tremendous power he holds over Isabel—especially when she agrees to be his wife out of sheer necessity. The traditional critical complaint that Isabel's personal flaws are proved by her willingness to marry without love overlooks the complicity of Carlyle, which is shaped by his oblivion of Isabel's dependent condition. The reviewer for the *Times*, noting Carlyle's obtuseness, interprets it, forgivingly, as a sign of his manliness: "His character is consistent with the serious preoccupations which render him so unobservant . . . he errs, but it is the error of a manly nature assailed by difficulties which a more frivolous person would have anticipated."[29] This "manly" flaw has serious consequences for professional authority, however: both Barbara's intuition and Mrs. Hare's dreams prove to be better instruments of detection, finally, than Carlyle's male rationality. In this way, *East Lynne* explicitly challenges the notion that professional power derives from knowledge.

In all these ways, the novel raises questions about the lineage, the moral authority, and the competence of the male professional, even as it celebrates the social victory of its middle-class lawyer-hero over a weakened aristocratic order. If professionalism embodies the transformed moral structure that makes middle-class elevation possible—not just for its elite, but as the model for a general class victory—*East Lynne* is not at all sure how to value that success. "Elevate him on to a weathercock!" (3.5.373), is Cornelia's persistent and sometimes difficult-to-dismiss view of Carlyle's rise. Yet it is ultimately through the reversal of gender roles implicit in the

[29] Lucas, "*East Lynne*," p. 6.

professional order that Wood raises her strongest doubts about the course of middle-class moral change, embodied in Carlyle's transgressive moral authority. By investigating the relationship between sexual inversion and professionalism, Wood goes beyond the categories typical of sociological analysis of the professions and explores an intersection of symbolic gender and class domains which is the natural terrain of the Victorian novel.

Steeped herself in the middle-class moral ideology that Carlyle is in the process of revising, Wood suggests that professional deception has fundamental affiliations with the feminine, as well as with aristocratic deceit, and that professional men who usurp the province of lying are, therefore, destined to be bad at it. Wood had strong personal reasons to associate middle-class success with the dangerous feminization of men, given the weakness and financial incompetence said to have characterized her father and husband.[30] But she also managed to give expression to a widespread mid-Victorian fear, reflected in the excesses of "muscular Christianity," the athleticism cults, and the reformation of the public schools—driven largely by a concern with manly character development—in the 1860s and 1870s.[31] If the professional flirts with effeminacy, East Lynne suggests that, at the very least, he is doomed to be inept as a woman. The sexual inversions valued by Gaskell are thus used by Wood as another means to indict professional authority.

Initially, the novel establishes a traditional opposition of feminine wiliness and male honesty in strong patterns of gendered behavior. Emma Vane, for example, is a classic instance of feminine duplicity—she torments Isabel with underhanded slights and lulls her with a "deceitful calm" (1.12.94). Emma is matched later by Alice Challoner, and to some extent by Alice's sister Blanche, when Blanche becomes a victim of her own prevarications about Levison.

[30] According to the not-very-reliable memoir written by her son, Charles W. Wood, both men were inadequate male role models—her father lost his way between glove manufacturing and gentlemanly scholarship, and her husband suffered some undisclosed financial reversal that necessitated Wood's becoming the family breadwinner through her writing. In both generations, the biography asserts, husbands found themselves under the authority of their wives.

[31] See Reader, Professional Men, pp. 129–46.

Afy Hallijohn is perhaps the most proficient and stereotypical female liar in the novel, combining skill as "an uncommon good hand at an impromptu tale" (3.15.449) with a willingness not to "let trifles stand in [her] way" (2.15.279) when it comes to such things as listening at keyholes. Though the behavior of these women stigmatizes their respective classes as well as their gender, middle-class women, too, appear to be naturally adept at deception. Barbara Hare and her sister Anne, for example, have an elaborate system of secret letters which circumvents their father's snooping. And Barbara is very acute, early in the novel, at forestalling her father, evading her mother, and concealing the state of her affections from Carlyle. Appropriately, the two prominent male liars—Richard and Levison—are both consistently feminized. Wood repeats the normative schema of gendered transgressions we have seen in Gaskell: calculating feminine vice is identified with deceit, while the more uncalculating, impulsive actions of Carlyle (in particular, his spontaneously honorable proposal to Isabel) define his fundamental manliness.

Although Carlyle may be a prototype of the wise detective, and his ethical dexterity is often appreciated by others, the novel nevertheless suggests that professional management of the truth is constrained by the ineffectiveness of deceitful men. It is partly for this reason that Carlyle is such a passive detective and that clues Barbara grasps intuitively seem to elude him. At one point, Barbara expresses surprise at Carlyle's inability to connect Levison's hair-combing gesture with Richard's description of Thorn: "I wondered you did not recognize it" (3.9.406), she tells him. And Cornelia says bluntly: "You never can see faults in anybody. You always were a simpleton in some things" (1.16.136). Other professionals in the novel come in for this kind of criticism from women as well. A female servant claims that Wainwright, the surgeon, is "as blind as any bat" (3.5.368), and Isabel is rebuked by both Wilson and Hannah for depending on the advice of medical men. Wilson tells Isabel that all the household servants know William will die (Afy knows this already when she meets Isabel at Stalkenberg), even though Isabel herself, trusting medical opinion, remains complacent.

Against this background, class transformation and the ethical confusion it evidently generates appear reflected in a number of extreme sexual inversions. To cite the most obvious examples, Richard's and Levison's feminization and affinity with deceit are countered by Cornelia's manly straightforwardness. These extreme reversals of gender roles are meant as signs of pure disorder, and they are usually presented either in a critical or a carnivalesque spirit. When Richard and Cornelia confront each other late in the novel, we are given a burlesque summary: "Sure, two such guys never stood face to face!" (2.16.293). The narrative description emphasizes a blending of masculine and feminine features in each character: Cornelia's petticoats and shawl clashing with her headdress, earlier compared to a turban—which, with a Cranfordian echo, helps in her being taken for a "female Guy" (1.15.124)—and Richard's "fustian clothes" concealing "trembling hands" and a "scared white face" (2.16.293). "I have been at many a carnival abroad," the narrator tells us, "but I assure you I never saw in the maskers a couple equal to the spectacle those two would have presented, borne along in a triumphal carnival car." In contrast to these extreme, phobic examples of gender inversion, Carlyle's feminization is much more subtle and qualified, expressing serious reservations about his conduct, even though it also distinguishes him progressively against those virile patriarchs, Justice Hare and Raymond Vane.

The range of inverted female conduct in *East Lynne* is more complex than the range of professional inversions, though in the long run the female inversions are also more disempowering. In part, the unnatural, inverted honesty of women is revealed to be a consequence of hysteria. Every woman in the novel has a moment of impulsive self-revelation, in which traditionally "feminine" reserve gives way to passionate candor. Barbara Hare's declaration of love to Carlyle at the stile is probably the most dramatic of these, but Emma and Isabel have similar scenes of violent self-revelation, when feminine constraint is shattered. Cornelia, too, is no stranger to impulsive candor. Far from simply stigmatizing passionate candor as hysteria, however, the novel seems to use it as a positive counterpoint to the atmosphere of male secrecy and deception that comes to dominate the novel. In this sense, female inversions manage to revise and represent old-fashioned candor as a reliable sign of desire—precisely because such candor violates expectations about gender roles. One of the most dramatic, but unrewarded, instances of this rewriting of female forthrightness as desire occurs when Blanche warns her sister against Levison, announcing that she must deliberately break "all the reticence that woman loves to observe as to her wrongs and her inward feelings" (3.6.379) in order to have "told you but the truth." As the novel progresses, passionate female truth-telling turns out to be a means of combatting the untruths perpetuated by men. The final scenes at Isabel's deathbed consist of three women—Isabel, Cornelia, and Joyce—united in the revelation of Isabel's identity, and in their protective initiation of Carlyle himself into their shared secret. This configuration dramatically reverses the sexual roles of power inscribed in professional conduct, making women the guardians of and guides to truth.

Female candor is not just the material for carnival in *East Lynne*. It is also the persistent force of traditional morality embodied, somewhat nostalgically, in excluded women—the rejected wife, the overpowered mother figure, the maid. In this sense, sexual inversion is exploited as a way to critique changing class ideology. If the emergence of professional authority can be made to seem an unnatural incursion of men into female domains, then hysterical female candor can be portrayed as a desperate resistance to such authority. As such, it becomes a legitimate, even heroic image of sexual inversion. Ellen Wood was powerfully attracted as a writer to such inversions, despite her resistance to the logic of transgression. Many of the reviews of *East Lynne* praised her skill at representing men, and in fact she is remarkable among Victorian women writers for the number of male narrators she employed. The *Johnny Ludlow* stories—which she worked on continuously over the last twenty years of her life, turning out over a hundred of them—are an extraordinary example of narrative cross-dressing. Her son liked to tell of her pleasure at having her collection of fictional letters, *Ensign Tom Pepper's Letters from the Seat of War*, taken as the work of a man.[32] Wood's fascination suggests a persistent need to harness the possibilities of sexual inversion for her own personal and narrative empowerment, whatever the dangers involved. The enormous power of sexual inversion as a trope of Victorian fiction certainly did not allow Wood to break cleanly with the symbolic logic of transgression.

[32] See Wood, *Memorials*, p. 280. Lucas also flatters Wood for her skill with *East Lynne*'s male characters ("*East Lynne*," p. 6).

It would be far too simple to claim that Wood reverses new, professionalized standards of ethics by proclaiming the superiority of inverted feminine candor, however. We have already seen reasons why such candor is evaluated through the novel as hopelessly anachronistic. Certainly, women's candor is shown, at best, to be limited in its effectiveness and, at worst, to be self-destructive. Rather, the concluding chapters of the novel actually foreground the ambivalent and often inadequate responses of women to their disempowerment, and to middle-class ethical confusion in general.[33] Isabel, most of all, is presented as a figure of confused roles—in terms of both her sexual and her ethical coding. While the defeminization of the governess is a standard theme in Victorian literature—Isabel replaces someone named Miss Manning—Isabel's appearance, as Madame Vine, is strikingly deformed in more ways than one. Besides being scarred and disguised, she is, of course, ambivalently gendered. "As well wear a man's collar and stock, at once!" (3.2.343), Wilson thinks, when first observing her costume, yet "she is a *gentlewoman* with it all; and looks one" (3.1.334). And as a woman conducting the most elaborate and daring deceit of the entire novel, Isabel has a dual ethical status: on the one hand, she is a more clever and a more intuitive dissembler than her husband; on the other, she demonstrates nothing in these final scenes so much as passionate rebellion against her adopted role and her inability to keep up the disguise under the emotional pressures of her desire to reveal the truth. The last third of the novel is a long, agonized staging of this internal conflict. What Isabel's various scenes of distress with her children indicate, ultimately, is the intensity of women's immediate, emotional, and finally impossible relationship to issues of truth-telling—issues that include both feminine affinities with lying and inverted feminine candor—as opposed to the distanced, professional manipulation of honesty and dishonesty that we see in Carlyle. Isabel and her tragedy are conceived, paradigmatically, as the crisis of a woman split by her inclinations toward truth

[33] Although she catalogues the range of female roles only in the simple typology of mother, wife, and governess, Helena Michie also points out the staged inadequacy of the novel's possible versions of female identity (*Sororophobia: Differences among Women in Literature and Culture* [Oxford: Oxford University Press, 1992], pp. 78–79).

and toward disguise. As such, the feminine becomes a figure for middle-class indecisiveness about its own evolving moral standards, and Isabel can just as easily be read as an antiquated, overly sensitive obstacle to Carlyle's pragmatic authority as a heroic opponent of it. Isabel's particular ethical crisis may be presented in terms of psychological divisions specific to Victorian motherhood, but such divisions also reverberate as a general middle-class identity crisis, which can be experienced in emotional terms only when it has been projected onto the feminine. Nevertheless, this internal class conflict does make middle-class mobility seem to hinge on the ascendance of men over women through their more comfortable negotiation of ethical problems. In a number of senses, the narrative of Isabel Vane is the narrative of maternal authority lost through a destabilization of feminine virtue.

Barbara Hare, also a moral hybrid like Isabel, adopts a slightly different and even more problematic approach to ethical ambivalence precisely through a transformation of her maternal role. It is through Barbara's transformation that the novel tries to imagine what a complementary feminine adaptation to Carlyle's ethically fluid world might involve. If Isabel is exiled from a world increasingly dominated by male professionals, Barbara is fully incorporated into that world. One result is that Barbara becomes much more bland after her marriage to Carlyle—there is little trace left of the "powerful will" (1.3.17) inherited from her father, or of the "innate courage" (1.3.25) that we see in her earlier in the novel. Partly, this change is a result of her coming to share in professional sensibility. That is to say, Barbara not only becomes dependent on professional management, but starts to emulate it as well. Like Carlyle, Barbara adopts a kind of emotional distance toward questions of truth and disguise. After the departure of Isabel, Barbara reconceives her relationship to Carlyle himself, as well as toward her various suitors, in what might be described as a professional manner. She plays her cards coolly in regard to Carlyle, refusing suitors but never indicating why, and maintaining her investigative ties to Carlyle without letting her emotional ties interfere. Even her fervor in aiding Richard becomes subdued, and, like Carlyle, she becomes willing to bide her time. For simple reasons of tact, she never tells Carlyle of her deductions about Levison until the time seems ripe. She even suppresses in marriage what earlier she could not contain—her sexuality: "She broke suddenly off with the name 'Archibald:' not even to Richard could she speak of her intense love for her husband" (3.11.419).

Most important, Barbara adopts a professional attitude toward the Victorian center of her femininity: her motherhood. Barbara's prescription for effective motherhood, which she outlines at length to Isabel, involves considerable distance from her children. Though critics have attributed this distance to Barbara's jealousy of her stepchildren, it is important to recognize that it extends to her own child as well. "I never was fond of being troubled with children. When my own grow up into childhood, I shall deem the nursery and the schoolroom the best places for them" (3.2.340–41). Distance is essential, Barbara argues, for her to specialize her labor in "the *training* of my children" (3.2.341). Spared the contamination of intimate contact through the help of servants, the mother may then appear gentle and pure, a model of "persuasive gentleness." In this system, motherhood is defined as work and consists of pedagogical manipulation from a position of clinical detachment. For this reason, Barbara makes the children eat separately and places her full faith in physicians to monitor their health. Most important, as an emotionally well-regulated mother, Barbara declares that she would "never give up my husband for my baby" (3.2.343)—which is, in a sense, what Isabel has done. As Davidoff and Hall have shown, Victorian women often felt intensely divided by their loyalties to husbands, to parents, and to children.[34] Barbara's simple ordering of the priorities would have shocked many of the novel's readers as a cold oversimplification of these competing claims. Anxieties about the gentrification of middle-class women were, in fact, a standard feature of the periodical press, culminating in a series of essays published in the *Saturday Review* in the late 1860s.[35] Scriptwriters certainly knew what they were doing when they emphasized Isabel's frustrated

[34] Davidoff and Hall, *Family Fortunes*, p. 348. Sally Shuttleworth has also described these contradictions over maternity in gender ideology ("Demonic Mothers: Ideologies of Bourgeois Motherhood in the Mid-Victorian Era," in *Rewriting the Victorians: Theory, History, and the Politics of Gender* [New York: Routledge, 1992], pp. 31–51). Shuttleworth finds that *East Lynne* expresses these contradictions in a fully unresolved way (pp. 48–49).

[35] See Pykett, *Improper Feminine*, pp. 68–69.

maternal love as the central emotional draw of the novel's dramatizations and de-emphasized Barbara's role.[36]

Though Isabel appears to agree with Barbara in theory, her own behavior testifies that she cannot possibly achieve this kind of emotional distance from her children. Although her original motive for returning to East Lynne—to keep her children from being "trained by strangers" (3.1.327)—matches Barbara's goals, Isabel yearns to provide far more emotional nurturance than Barbara's methods allow. Barbara herself reproves Isabel for being "too lenient" (3.17.463). Earlier in the century, however, middle-class Victorian women often scorned the aristocratic habit of leaving children in the care of nursemaids and servants, and foreign visitors were often struck by the way children of the English middle class, in contrast to those of the aristocracy, were seen as loving companions by their parents.[37] Barbara thus signifies the dawning late-century upper-middle-class "professionalization" of the mother, and as such she produces an ethical ambivalence in the domestic realm that parallels Carlyle's occupational ambiguities.[38] Although modern critics have often assumed that the novel endorses Barbara's disciplinarian systems, contemporary reviewers registered great doubts about Barbara; the *Saturday Review* wrote, "Mrs. Wood has quite avoided the fault of making Barbara too good. For so excellent a person, she is, perhaps, a shade too careless of her step-children, and too rude and harsh to her governess. Although, at the close of the story, the whole of the attorney's affections are most properly concentrated on his living wife, the reader is not sorry to feel permitted to have a slight preference for the dead one."[39] It is a striking irony throughout the third part of the novel that, while the middle-class mother has become remote and businesslike, it has fallen to the morally dubious

---

[36] This is evident not only in the diminishment of the Richard Hare story to a subplot, but in poster art that emphasized the lost mother theme. See Mitchell's comments, in the introduction to *East Lynne*, pp. xiv–xv.

[37] See Davidoff and Hall, *Family Fortunes*, pp. 335, 343.

[38] On this late-century transformation of maternal roles, see Leonore Davidoff, "Class and Gender in Victorian England: The Diaries of Arthur J. Munby and Hannah Cullwick," *Feminist Studies* 5 (1979), 87–141.

[39] *Saturday Review*, p. 187. Kaplan is fairly typical of contemporary critics, however, in seeing Barbara as a model of Victorian standards of motherhood, in *Motherhood and Representation*, pp. 84–86, calling Barbara the novel's "Ideal Mother" (p. 86).

governess to supply maternal affection.[40] For professional angels, as well as for honorable politicians, moral dichotomies are transgressively collapsed in *East Lynne* as the price of middle-class social power, and the results are meant to seem disturbing.

If Barbara is an image of the new middle-class mother, Wood makes it clear that she is still controlled by a man. In some sense, Barbara's frequent role-playing, coupled with Isabel's, suggests that women do have skills that make them fit for a professional world—or even that in some ways they are *more* fit for the demands of professionalism, given that they are naturally more versed in self-suppression, in creative intuition, and in performance. The narrator explicitly forgives many of Isabel's deceptions: "Surely the recording angel blotted out the words!" (3.20.490), we are told about one "equivocation," and the novel regularly draws attention to the great skill and fortitude necessary to Isabel's disguise. Nevertheless, *East Lynne* is plainly reluctant to endorse either Isabel's wildly emotional strategies or Barbara's "professional" motherhood, and both women's self-(re)fashionings pale in Carlyle's shadow. In the opposition of Isabel to Barbara, we are left with two versions of motherhood, old and new, which are meant to seem equally unsatisfactory.[41] Rather than reinforcing hegemonic middle-class ideals of motherhood, *East Lynne* reveals how models of mothering have been shattered and territorialized by the authority of the male professional. Ironically, the common last refuge of motherhood in *East Lynne*, for both Isabel and Barbara, is its theatricality: both women perform their motherhood rather than enacting it in some "natural" form, succumbing in their behavior to a kind of transgressive alienation from authenticity, but with none of the rewards available to Carlyle. As Joseph Litvak has shown, the theatricalization of motherhood in the latter stages of *East Lynne* deforms domestic space in a way not easily

[40] Oliphant's review was particularly severe with this narrative sympathy: "There is not a reader who does not feel disposed to turn her virtuous successor to the door, and reinstate the suffering heroine, to the glorious confusion of all morality" (p. 170).

[41] This irresolution, along with the dominant authority of professionals in the novel, ought to qualify Laurie Langbauer's argument that Wood identified a totalizing social system with the figure of the mother (*Women and Romance: The Consolations of Gender in the English Novel* [Ithaca: Cornell University Press, 1990]; see esp. pp. 171–75).

reconciled with readings that find Wood to be either endorsing or resisting available models of the feminine.[42]

The novel's ambivalence about professionalism, and about the transformations of middle-class consciousness it has produced, must ultimately be read in multivalent ways. Certainly, *East Lynne* protests against erosions of female authority. In those terms, and for other reasons that I have traced, it registers real objections to the logic of "exceptional" professional authority, which it sees as an increasingly dominant force in middle-class culture, both public and private. Simply deflecting attention away from Carlyle's success to Isabel's tragic exclusion makes this point on the level of narrative logic. The actor Edwin Forrest found this out when, playing the role of Carlyle, he attempted to divert audience sympathy back to himself during Isabel's deathbed scene—only to be booed into dropping this change.[43] The novel also clearly shows how women are forced to act like men, when men begin to act like women; and it calls attention to the absence of a strong female model as a counterpart to Carlyle's masculine authority. The novel finally expresses these protests in a tragic key, however, that could just as easily prove flattering to middle-class narcissism: success, it seems to suggest, is emotionally expansive, requiring many self-aggrandizing encounters with one's conscience. In this sense, Isabel might be seen as a cathartic sacrifice on the altar of emergent middle-class moral pragmatism. The novel might thus be read—and has most often been read—as an affirmation of Carlyle and his professional authority and as an attempt (largely through Barbara) to prescribe the kind of new woman adequate to that world—a world now widely antibourgeois, in the moral terms I have described.

Yet to read *East Lynne* this simply, as middle-class popular culture's affirmation of changes occurring higher up the social scale, is to overlook the many ways in which the novel foregrounds its distaste for the exceptional authority of the professional. *East Lynne*'s lack of clear-cut resolution deprives the novel of any singular agenda,

---

[42] Joseph Litvak, *Caught in the Act: Theatricality in the Nineteenth-Century English Novel* (Berkeley: University of California Press, 1992), pp. 138–41. Cvetkovich discusses the more empowering effects of affective performance in *East Lynne* (*Mixed Feelings*, pp. 100–112).

[43] Mitchell recounts this episode in the introduction to *East Lynne*, p. xv.

making it possible for audiences to use the story as a revolving mirror of self-understanding.[44] There is, nevertheless, one sharply defined point in its reflection of middle-class culture. With great foreboding, *East Lynne* describes a change in the sources of Victorian moral authority which has suddenly raised the stakes and complicated the prospects of middle-class social ascendance, by destroying traditional relationships between gender and class, and between public and private spheres, which had once promised to stabilize middle-class social authority on traditionally feminine moral grounds. It defines complex and long-standing moral tensions that are about to erupt in dangerous new forms, should middle-class individuals assume responsibility for social order on morally exceptional, transgressive terms. Most important, the novel critically rewrites the meaning of professional authority, formulating in the process a wish for some as yet unimagined roles for both men and women—but particularly for women—within the morally unstable social order about to be inherited by ambitious, self-admiring (male) segments of the middle class.

[44] John Fiske has argued that the more popular a text, the more likely its ideological significance will remain polysemous or "open," allowing "various subcultures to generate meanings from it that meet the needs of their own subcultural identities" ("Television: Polysemy and Popularity," *Critical Studies in Mass Communications* 3 [1986], 392).

PART III

TRANSGRESSION IN LATE-VICTORIAN FICTION

CHAPTER FIVE

Moral Authority in Hardy's Late
Novels: The Gendering of Art

One measure of our distance from the nineteenth century is our relative indifference to discourses of truth-telling, and to the symbolic power they make available through lying. The fin-de-siècle attack on authenticity—evident everywhere in British culture, from Yeats's theory of masks, to Wilde's contempt for earnestness, to various aesthetic theories of irrealism—did its work only too well. This general attack, which in some ways represents the culmination of mid-Victorian equations between anti-bourgeois dissimulation and cultural sophistication, eventually drained the moral shock out of lying itself, once the clear-cut standards of sincerity it transgressed had been devalued. Discussions of ethics among contemporary literary critics tend to revolve around very different issues—mostly questions of violence, domination, and otherness—and any serious contemplation of dishonesty as a locus of transgression is now likely to seem quaint. In the culture at large, such concerns survive mostly in regard to the credibility of politicians, an area in which the appallingly crude, unrealistic, and vacillating standards of voters and the media demonstrate the impoverishment (or the cynicism) of current attitudes toward truth-telling.

At the end of the nineteenth century, however, the breakup of the symbolic dynamics of truth-telling was a very messy affair. The flamboyant, defiant artificiality of British decadence, which often parades its desire for a clean break with Victorian ethics, obscures the much more volatile situation of late-century discourses of truth-telling. The tremendous symbolic force of honesty and dishonesty, organized in Victorian culture into a relatively stable set of oppositions and possibilities for transgression, did not simply evaporate in 1890s culture, nor was it converted into an inert sign of cultural retrogression. Rather, it was subjected to an explosive fragmentation, in which familiar ideas about truth-telling performed unfamiliar kinds of ideological work. Ethics is a system of symbolic distinctions upheld by various interrelated domains of cultural logic; it is not an isolated set of precepts. In such a system, change occurs in the form of extensive displacements and adjustments. If late-century writers disassembled certain features of Victorian ethics for their own ends, they reassembled the discursive debris of that ethics in a variety of potent deformations. Fragments of Victorian moral thought often performed unusual work within the alien framework of disparate cultural logics. In particular, notions about truth-telling played complex, often self-contradictory roles in protomodernist assaults on sincerity and authenticity. In theoretical terms, this volatility suggests that before discourses of truth-telling were marginalized, sublimated, or subjected to symbolic dispersion in twentieth-century culture, their deformations performed much more dynamic roles in unlikely discursive contexts.[1]

Thomas Hardy and Sarah Grand both contributed to the breakup of Victorian discourses of truth-telling, and the ethical contradictions that haunt their work signal the symbolically powerful incoherence of late-century representations of honesty and dishonesty. Both these writers explore a crisis in the cultural authority (or "exceptionality") that had been defined throughout the nineteenth century by certain kinds of sophisticated lying. Both Hardy and

---

[1] I have been influenced, in my approach to the historical transformation of symbolic logics, by the work of Peter Stallybrass and Allon White, *The Politics and Poetics of Transgression* (Ithaca: Cornell University Press, 1986). But I would add to their four-part model of "fragmentation; marginalization; sublimation; repression" (p. 178) a process of symbolic deformation, exemplified by the distorted rearticulation of Victorian truth-telling in a novelist like Hardy.

Grand formulate their break with Victorian culture, to some extent, through their break with Victorian conceptions of truth-telling and transgression. But both writers also try to rearticulate the grounds of social authority in ways that depend on—while at the same time dislocating—the symbolic dynamics of Victorian truth-telling. It would be futile to try to map their rearticulations of truth and transgression in perfectly coherent ways. To some degree, issues of truth-telling actually became tropes of uncertainty and confusion in the fin-de-siècle. Yet this particular ethical incoherence remains a tremendously productive one, for the breakup of the Victorian logic of truth-telling provided a number of discursive tools for turn-of-the-century writers which served very logical—if sometimes very different—ends.

In Hardy's case, we can find on the surface of his work a systematic diagnosis of honesty's inadequacy as an ethical ideal. In his fiction, Hardy typifies fin-de-siècle culture by showing how adherence to Victorian codes of honesty leads only to moral confusion. Yet Hardy's diagnosis of the death of honesty conceals a contradictory attempt on his part to reaffirm a domain of pure truth-telling that he identifies with aesthetic consciousness. Hardy's affirmation of aesthetic consciousness as the single area in which honesty can survive—and then only by candidly denying, within art, the moral possibility of truth—anticipates a pattern of ethical insularity and self-reflexiveness shared by much modernist art. In Grand's case, by contrast, the incoherence of available standards of truth-telling serves to express a crisis in feminist activism. Much less dialectical and synthetic than Hardy in her manipulation of ethical categories, Grand's confusions about truth-telling express the apocalyptic atmosphere enveloping 1890s feminism, and they signal her impatience with the moral dilemmas feminism had inherited from mid-Victorian writers like Gaskell and Wood. Grand uses these confusions to explore a series of new roles for her feminist heroines which involve radical forms of moral experimentation. Nevertheless, while ethical instabilities allowed her to articulate certain kinds of possibilities for late-century feminism, they also defined the limits of her sexual politics by rooting it in Victorian moral conundrums.

The contrasting goals and strategies of these two writers point to a kind of symbolic warfare—a pitched battle for cultural authority—

engaged by (male) modernists and late-century feminists. In this struggle, the dysfunctional remains of Victorian truth-telling are stretched into awkward but dynamic shapes, while the Victorian grounding of artistic authority in canons of moral truthfulness lent itself to resonant polemics. Recent feminist reconstructions of modernism, by celebrating the fusional, the irrational, and the unstable formal elements in works written by turn-of-the-century women, oddly repeat the ethical subtext of Victorian and modernist fiction by surrendering issues of truth-telling in art to men.[2] Assaults on New Woman fiction in the 1890s revolved very much around claims that "male" aesthetic strategies were more truthful in a moral sense (as we will see in critical reactions to New Woman fiction), and the legacy for male modernists of a writer like Hardy had a great deal to do with his ability to incorporate ethical ideals into aesthetic structures. James Joyce, for example, praised the moral integrity Hardy modeled for later writers: "It seems . . . evident to everyone that Hardy offered in his poetic attitude vis-à-vis the public an honorable example of probity and pride, which we other 'clerks' could use, especially in an epoch in which readers seem to content themselves less and less with the poor printed word."[3] D. H. Lawrence identified this integrity with a formal patterning in Hardy's work, in which "the vast, unexplored morality of life itself" is set over against "the little human morality play, with its queer frame of morality and its mechanized movement," a juxtaposition that produces Hardy's "magnificent irony."[4] Revisionist histories of modern-

[2] I am thinking, for example, of the narrative "doubleness" in the work of Kate Chopin and Charlotte Perkins Gilman, and extolled by Marianne DeKoven's groundbreaking essay, "Gendered Doubleness and the 'Origins' of Modernist Form," *Tulsa Studies in Women's Literature* 8 (1989), 19–42; and of the list of formal attributes that define "female" modernism proposed by Sandra Gilbert and Susan Gubar, in "Introduction," *Women's Studies* 13 (1986), 1: "subversive parody, disruption of linear plot, opening up of form, or fragmentation of point of view." See also Bonnie Kime Scott, introduction to *The Gender of Modernism: A Critical Anthology*, ed. Bonnie Kime Scott (Bloomington: Indiana University Press, 1990), esp. pp. 12–14.

[3] Richard Ellmann, ed., *Letters of James Joyce*, 3 vols. (London: Faber and Faber, 1966), 10 February 1928, 3:170. My translation from the French. See also Haskell M. Block, "James Joyce and Thomas Hardy," *Modern Language Quarterly* 19 (1958), 340–41.

[4] D. H. Lawrence, "Study of Thomas Hardy," in *Phoenix: The Posthumous Papers of D. H. Lawrence* (New York: Viking, 1936), p. 419.

ism, feminist or otherwise, ignore the ethical foundation in certain strains of modernist irony and self-reflexiveness at their peril. Ethical issues were closely bound up in turn-of-the-century attitudes toward the competing authority of men and women in art, and they played a significant role in gendering different modernisms. In particular, the "honesty" of modernist aesthetic rigor should be seen as the positive—and surprisingly puritanical—formulation of a certain modernist antisentimentalism that systematically alienated a range of "feminine" cultural positions from the precincts of artistic integrity.[5]

In this chapter, I attempt to unravel the convolutions of Hardyan thinking about honesty, in order to reveal the Victorian foundations of his truth-telling ethics and the strange deformations they undergo in his writing.[6] Hardy's ethical mosaic can demonstrate how modernist ethical self-reflexiveness could be anchored in persistent Victorian ideologies of gender and class. At the same time, Hardy's conflation of honesty and dishonesty in the consciousness of the artist, while it conforms in a general way to Victorian notions of exceptional transgression, remains so volatile that it requires an elaborate series of moral scapegoatings in order to shore up notions of artistic truth. In consequence, the production of moral authority in Hardy's work

[5] Suzanne Clark develops this argument in *Sentimental Modernism: Women Writers and the Revolution of the Word* (Bloomington: Indiana University Press, 1991).

[6] Hardy is usually understood to have broken with Victorian ethics in one of three relatively simplistic ways. Some readers have seen his moral views as flexible and nondogmatic, in the progressive, liberal manner of the "New Didacticism" of the 1880s and 1890s. See, for example, Kenneth Graham, *English Criticism of the Novel, 1865–1900* (Oxford: Clarendon Press, 1965), p. 73. John Holloway's famous remarks, which define Hardy's morality as organic and situational rather than prescriptive, are a common inspiration for this appraisal (*The Victorian Sage: Studies in Argument* [London: Macmillan, 1953], pp. 244–89). The extreme version of this position takes Hardy at his word, in many of his apologetic disclaimers, and simply finds him inconsistent. See, for example, David Lodge, *The Language of Fiction* (London: Routledge and Kegan Paul, 1966), p. 168. Others, less inclined to generalize in positive terms, nevertheless acknowledge Hardy's outright rejection of a few specific Victorian restrictions—mostly, sexual conventions like the double standard, taboos on divorce, and overvalued virginity. More rarely, Hardy has been celebrated for rejecting moral standards of any kind. Robert C. Schweik, for example, claims that Hardy's apparent moral inconsistencies are, in fact, an assault on "the general limitations of moral vision and the common arbitrariness of moral formulae" ("Moral Perspective in *Tess of the d'Urbervilles*," *College English* 24 [1962], 14–18).

actually reverses Victorian equations between authority and transgressive sophistication—though not in ways that critical clichés about modernism might predict. Hardy found moral complexity, including transgression, easy to represent; what he found difficult was the representation of honesty. Hardy ultimately sought to produce a precious space of aesthetic honesty over against his dramatization of moral transgression, and that production of honesty required a strenuous scapegoating of figures of moral confusion. In this sense, Hardy's concern with the power of truth-telling discourses actually had less to do with the production of transgressive sophistication than with the exclusionary distinctions of a more primitive kind of moral rigor—a project that rests uncomfortably beside the modernist moral impartialities of his work.

These scapegoatings culminate in an expulsion of the feminine from the moral identity of art. Ironically, by overlooking Hardy's fundamentally Victorian ethical commitments and focusing instead on his sexual progressiveness, critics have overlooked one of the stronger currents of masculinist bias in his work. Hardy's latent commitment to Victorian standards of honesty—which are as important to the Victorian ethical imagination as its more notorious sexual norms—may be seen as a central instance in which he perverts while preserving the basic symbolic structures of Victorian ethics, along with some of the misogynist genderings of virtue and vice that accompany them. I should emphasize that I am not attempting a blanket denunciation of Hardy's sexual politics; I want simply to isolate a particular configuration of gendered ethical oppositions, however incompletely formulated, which Hardy shared with other late-century writers, in a struggle over the moral and sexual identity of aesthetics.[7] Rather than comprehending and

---

[7] I do not dispute that Hardy struggled to resist the reduction of gender to a uniform set of ideological positions. On the strategic multivalence of his representation of gender, see Penny Boumelha, *Thomas Hardy and Women: Sexual Ideology and Narrative Form* (Sussex: Harvester Press, 1982), p. 7; and Elaine Showalter, "The Unmanning of the Mayor of Casterbridge," in *Critical Approaches to the Fiction of Thomas Hardy,* ed. Dale Kramer (London: Macmillan, 1979), pp. 99–115. Hardy was also intensely aware of the way constructions of gender difference must be read as effects of social power, an awareness that has been recognized by Margaret R. Higonnet, in the introduction to *The Sense of Sex: Feminist Perspectives on Hardy,* ed. Higonnet (Urbana: University of Illinois Press, 1993), p. 4. Linda M. Shires

labeling Hardy's sexual attitudes in some monolithic way, I want to tease out of his work a specific set of protomodernist assumptions about gender and aesthetics which draws confusedly on the Victorian symbolic dynamics of truth-telling. But before I can discuss how Hardy uses gender to produce his conception of aesthetic integrity, I must first examine a number of ways in which Hardy's overt anti-Victorianism makes the representation of honesty a seemingly intractable moral and aesthetic problem.

Buried in Hardy's high-profile challenges to sexual codes lies a basic Victorian concern for truth and honesty—at least as a virtue of artistic production.[8] Hardy often cited his own artistic honesty as the strongest rebuke to those critics who found him to be without positive values. In the general preface to the Wessex Edition of 1912, he responded to critical accusations of nihilism by claiming, "It must be obvious that there is a higher characteristic of philosophy than pessimism, or than meliorism, or even than the optimism of these critics—which is truth."[9] Whenever Hardy defended his more

---

argues that Hardy persistently destabilized the terms of gender and power relationships ("Narrative, Gender, and Power in *Far from the Madding Crowd*," in Higonnet, *The Sense of Sex*, pp. 49–65). Helena Michie amplifies this critical theme by tracing Hardy's foregrounding of class differences that fracture any unified gender identity (*Sororophobia: Differences among Women in Literature and Culture* [Oxford: Oxford University Press, 1992], pp. 81–88). Nevertheless, Hardyan "neutrality" on gender issues, no matter how studiously pursued, is disrupted by a number of controlling discursive formations. The ethical preoccupations of his work, I argue, are a central instance of his entanglement in the very same sexual ideologies he resisted. Patricia Ingham conceives this contradictory situation—too rigidly, I believe—as a dialectical encounter between a fundamentally misogynist narrative voice and the rebellious energies of the characters Hardy creates, in *Thomas Hardy* (New York: Harvester Wheatsheaf, 1989). My own argument focuses on the unique case of a particular set of discursive patterns in Hardy's work, instead of generalizing about his attitudes toward gender and power in any single, all-encompassing formulation.

[8] Criticism has been strangely silent about the recurring emphasis on questions of honesty in Hardy. Besides analyzing his sexual values, studies of Hardyan ethics have focused instead on his concepts of altruism and attacks on general social injustice. An example of the former is Virginia R. Hyman, *Ethical Perspective in the Novels of Thomas Hardy* (Port Washington, N.Y.: Kennikat Press, 1975); an instance of the latter is Ian Gregor and Brian Nicholas, *The Moral and the Story* (London: Faber and Faber, 1962), pp. 123–50.

[9] Thomas Hardy, *The Well-Beloved*, New Wessex Edition (London: Macmillan, 1975), p. 237. References to Hardy's novels are given in parentheses to chapter and

controversial material, he always invoked the seemingly uncomplicated demands of truthfulness in writing. His contribution to "Candour in English Fiction" justifies the sexual explicitness of his novels as "sincere" and "conscientious": "Life being a physiological fact, its honest portrayal must be largely concerned with, for one thing, the relations of the sexes."[10] Even when repudiating didactic fiction, he did so in the name of a more urgent compulsion to honesty. In "The Profitable Reading of Fiction," he championed the "paradox" that "the novels which most conduce to moral profit are likely to be among those written without a moral purpose," because only they will achieve a "sincere presentation."[11] The subtitle of the first edition of *Tess*—*A Pure Woman, Faithfully Presented*—goes so far as to share the novel's polemical argument about moral integrity between character and author, linking Hardy's defense of the fallen woman with his personal challenge to critical complaints that his work was "artificial."[12] Such postures are not simply the disguises of a moral wolf in sheep's clothing, for, as we will see, Hardy's convictions about aesthetic honesty had very broad ramifications.

Hardy, however, seems determined in his novels to destroy such an unstudied confidence in honesty. There is a striking contradiction between Hardy's simple claims about his own authorial honesty and his radical skepticism about that of his characters. Squarely within the thematic traditions of Victorian narrative, Hardy's plots pivot relentlessly around lies and around nagging questions about his protagonists' honesty. But in Hardy's novels, the clear standards of truth-telling and transgression which always emerge in Victorian novels are constantly revealed to be inadequate. While Dickens

---

page numbers in this edition, with the following exceptions: in *Jude the Obscure*, *The Well-Beloved*, and *Under the Greenwood Tree*, references in the form 1.11.111 are to part, chapter, and page numbers in this edition; in *The Return of the Native*, similar references are to book, chapter, and page numbers in this edition.

[10] Walter Besant, E. Lynn Linton, and Thomas Hardy, "Candour in English Fiction," *New Review* 2 (1890), 16–17.

[11] Thomas Hardy, "The Profitable Reading of Fiction," *Forum* 5 (1888), 64.

[12] On Hardy's anger at his work's being labeled artificial, see Peter Widdowson, *Hardy in History: A Study in Literary Sociology* (London: Routledge, 1989), pp. 17–18. Ann L. Ardis notes that Hardy's transformation of the fallen woman's moral identity was meant, in part, to correct English realism's ability to tell the truth (*New Women, New Novels: Feminism and Early Modernism* [New Brunswick, N.J.: Rutgers University Press, 1990], p. 60).

might have been sure, at least, of the difference in forthrightness between Oliver Twist and Fagin, Hardy's characters regularly seem to prove the impossibility of measuring conduct on any scale of honesty. The variety of the attack in itself testifies to Hardy's apparent conviction of the untenability of a morality based on truth-telling.

In *A Pair of Blue Eyes*, for example, Stephen Smith wonders if it is possible to have lied retrospectively, as it were, when he considers whether his initial failure to disclose his social origins constitutes deceit in light of his later relations with Elfride—"a nice point in casuistry" (38.354), as his mentor, Mr. Knight, puts it. In *The Mayor of Casterbridge*, among the various characters who practice deceptions out of ignorance, Michael Henchard finds he must break his promise to marry Lucetta after his long-absent wife resurfaces. In *Far from the Madding Crowd*, Bathsheba Everdene sends a fatally misleading valentine that she had intended, in as much as she thought about it at all, as an anonymous joke. The novels' plots consistently explore the gray area between deliberate dishonesty and accidental deception, partially separating lying from intentionality. Tess's famous confessional letter, which miscarries because it is slipped under Angel's carpet by mistake, is a classic example of this kind of inadvertent duplicity. On Angel's side, is it insincerity or a matter of "inconsistencies" (26.193) when he uses aspects of Tess's character that he ought, in principle, to detest (her religious ortho-doxy, for example) as a means of justifying her to his parents? In general, Hardy's uncertainties about the unity or stability of the self, provoked by unanswerable questions about intentionality, seem to render the moral axis of honesty and dishonesty hopelessly problem-atic for his characters. Hardy's various well-known convictions about the genetic transmission of psychological flaws, the mediated nature of desire, the role of chance in human events, and the interweaving of human destinies in overlapping, predetermined variations, all add to this ethical confusion by destabilizing subjectivity.[13] Such perplexity about the self finally blocks ethical judgment. It lends added resonance to Tess's protest, raised in another context, against

---

[13] Marjorie Garson reads these subjective instabilities in loosely Lacanian terms (*Hardy's Fables of Integrity: Woman, Body, Text* [Oxford: Clarendon Press, 1991]).

facile moral judgment: "suppose your sin was not of your own seeking?" (12.108).

A related set of problems arises from "lies" that are culturally conditioned. Hardy often dramatizes clashes between varying cultural standards of sincerity. Mrs. Durbeyfield's standards for honesty between the sexes differ markedly from Tess's, for example, as do Angel's. Hardy also dramatizes misrepresentations that arise from contradictory social pressures, such as the double bind facing Sue, in which her emancipation as a woman seems to depend on both sexual expression and its repression, causing her to send confused, misleading signals to both Jude and Phillotson.[14] Most problematic of all, however, are instances of lying (though "evasion" or "misrepresentation" might be better terms) which result from characters' lack of self-knowledge, their inabilities to translate themselves faithfully into discourse. Sue's vacillations, for example, much as they may look to others like coyness and flirtation, are often rooted in her inability to know her own divided mind. Though Sue is usually reviled by Jude (and by critics) for being inconsistent, Jude shares with her the kind of hazy self-understanding that can produce deceptive behavior. When Sue interrogates him about his ambiguous threat to return to Arabella, which she claims would be dishonest if "what you used to say to me is still true—I mean if it were true then," his only response is, "I don't know. I don't wish to know" (4.2.229). Such uncertainties play havoc with Angel's newfound ethical formula, at the end of *Tess*, which holds that character ought to be judged by intentions, not by deeds, and with Jude's claim that "accidental outcomes" (6.1.336) should not prejudice us against good intentions.[15] These uncertainties go to the heart of the style of characterization that Hardy pioneered, in which diametrically opposed psychological forces are set in motion within each of his protagonists.

In these various ways, Hardy's persistent critique of moral idealism—embodied tragically in characters like Jude and Angel—draws on a widespread late-century conviction about the dangerous

[14] See Kathleen Blake's excellent essay on this double bind, "Sue Bridehead, 'The Woman of the Feminist Movement,' " *SEL* 18 (1978), 703–26.

[15] Ellen Rooney argues a similar point in "Criticism and the Subject of Sexual Violence," *MLN* 98 (1983), 1269–78.

artificiality of moral systems, a conviction that Hardy found echoed, specifically, in his reading of Nietzsche and Spencer.[16] Hardy's less troubled comments about his own authorial honesty, however, suggest that his critique of honesty in the novels functions, in part at least, as an assault on particular social and sexual categories, rather than as an indiscriminate moral despair. That is to say, Hardy sought to distinguish between various realms of moral possibility—in this first case, between the kinds of honesty available in art and life—in order to create scapegoats that might carry off moral confusion from the symbolic domains he wanted to protect. His attack on concepts of honesty sometimes clears the way for a restructuring of moral distinctions and a new symbolic mapping of standards of honesty.

In one limited sense, for example, Hardy's narrative critique of honesty is often meant simply to subvert the traditional Victorian alliance between moral authority and middle-class social standing. Hardy satirizes the persistence of this middle-class linkage of social merit and morality in Angel's appraisal of Tess's social deserts: "Distinction does not consist in the facile use of a contemptible set of conventions, but in being numbered among those who are true, and honest, and just, and pure, and lovely, and of good report—as you are, my Tess" (31.224). Angel's attitude, which cracks under the pressure of Tess's history, exemplifies middle-class moral justifications of social hierarchy which structure British novels from Samuel Richardson through George Eliot. But through his skepticism about morally self-congratulating, "honorable" bourgeois men—such as Angel and Mr. Knight in *A Pair of Blue Eyes*—Hardy rejects the moral basis of bourgeois class pride. Instead, Hardy often projects possibilities for honesty into more remote social sites, with surprising intellectual simplicity—or disingenuousness. He was much more inclined to portray rural workers (Gabriel Oak, Dick Dewy) as uncomplicatedly honest, thereby relegating possibilities for honesty either to lower social classes or to the superseded "traditional" past.[17]

[16] Barbara DeMille charts Hardy's anti-idealistic affinities with contemporary philosophers in "Cruel Illusions: Nietzsche, Conrad, Hardy, and the 'Shadowy Ideal,' " *SEL* 30 (1990), 697–714.

[17] Hardy also identified disinterest with the bohemian revolts against middle-class orthodoxies carried out by characters like Jude Fawley. See Richard Dellamora,

Hardy's skeptical attacks on honesty are thus inseparable from his complex attempts to define his own relationship to class hierarchies. His attack on honesty as a viable moral concept is, in part, an instrument for undermining the moral authority of the class to which he also aspired, however ambivalently.

In general, Hardy's meditations on honesty are hardly universalizing. They are not immune to ideological inscription, either. Rather, they make use of fractured and uncertain commitments to truth-telling by differentiating the symbolic domains in which the very concept of honesty might be either affirmed or denied. Hardy's own peculiar class pride comes to depend on claims to exemplary honesty which are very similar to those of the middle-class figures he undermines, though they can survive only in a few carefully protected symbolic domains. To augment his own cultural capital as a writer, Hardy ultimately aligns a resurgent form of honesty both with aesthetic consciousness and, more generally, with masculinity. From this point of view, Hardy's surprisingly virulent stereotypes of female dishonesty are more than just unusually pronounced instances of traditional sexism. They play a crucial role in defining the resurgent moral authority of the artist, distinguished by his superior ability to speak the truth—as I demonstrate more fully in the last section of this chapter. In the course of Hardy's localized destabilization of honesty in the novels, then, some of the basic procedures of Victorian moral thinking—including its reliance on honesty as a crucial element of class and sexual differentiations—are subtly reinvoked and redefined in order to uphold the cultural authority of men and, more specifically, of an avant-garde aesthetic class gendered primarily as male.

The most important continuity between Hardy's ethical thought and that of his Victorian predecessors—and the symbolic equation that makes a masculinist semiotics of artistic honesty possible—is this: like the Victorians, Hardy cannot conceive sexual desire apart from moral violation and, in particular, from dishonesty. For Hardy, the condition of desire makes honesty impossible to define or achieve. It is crucial to understand how extensively symbolic, rather

---

"Male Relations in Thomas Hardy's *Jude the Obscure*," *Papers on Language and Literature* 27 (1991), 458–59.

than simply logical, is the association Hardy makes between desire and dishonesty. Among Hardy's characters, the affiliation of dishonesty with desire is overdetermined by a number of seemingly unrelated factors. In part, dishonesty is simply one of the desperate remedies of sexual passion. Such characters as Alec and Arabella practice deceit in the name of love shamelessly, and even more scrupulous characters regularly succumb to deceitful tactics. Jude's inability to reveal his prior marriage to Sue may be an undesigning reticence, but it is deceitful nevertheless. Sue also complains of her compulsive "craving to attract and captivate, regardless of the injury it may do the man," as well as her reluctance to let him go once she has "caught" him (6.3.361). In *Tess*, the mutual reticence of both Angel and Tess about their pasts produces the central crisis of dishonesty. Hardy's understanding of desire increasingly came to focus, in the later novels, on both the pathetic vulnerability to entrapment and the irresistible impulse to entrap others which desire generates. [18]

But deceit in Hardy is also the inevitable product of desire's division of the subject. The tendency of desire toward inconstancy is one form this self-division takes. Another form is the familiar opposition of the flesh and the spirit which plagues so many of Hardy's characters, both male and female, and which forces them to betray their own efforts at sincerity. In *The Well-Beloved*, this opposition manifests itself in Pierston's strange, impulsive proposals of marriage, which he always regrets after he has had a chance to reflect on them rationally. Jude Fawley's continual distraction from his intellectual ideals by sexual desire is perhaps the most notorious instance of this self-division. But even Tess is subject to the same internal incoherence, when her sensual desires prove too much for her vow of celibacy. Moreover, deceitfulness often seems an integral aspect of the (feminine) object of desire itself. This notion may be travestied in Alec's accusations that Tess is a temptress, but it is presented quite seriously in Jocelyn Pierston's sense that the second Avice is a "fictitious" (2.6.95) copy, or even in Angel's befuddled

---

[18] Alexander Fischler points out that Hardy's growing sense of the fatal link between entrapment and desire eliminates any of the lightness of seduction present in the early novels ("Gins and Spirits: The Letter's Edge in Hardy's *Jude the Obscure*," *Studies in the Novel* 16 [1984], 1–19).

rebuke to Tess that he had loved "another woman in your shape" (35.255), which is, after all, an accurate characterization of Angel's idealizing love.

Finally, Hardy's systematic identification of deceit with desire resists any simple or univocal explanation. Hardy (the Victorian) seems determined to create a strangely absolute symbolic gap between honesty and desire, predicated on multiple and disparate causes. This confluence forced Hardy to return obsessively in his plots to conjunctions of sexuality and dishonesty, and it compelled him to construct Byzantine ethical dilemmas involving sex and deceit—such as those of Smith and Henchard, or Jocelyn Pierston's bizarre, comic struggle to love honestly. The middle chapters of *Tess*, in particular, are staged lopsidedly around accidents and competing pressures, as if to prove how unnatural it would be to expect that Tess's "conscientious wish for candour could hold out" (29.210) against desire. Similarly, the history of Jude's vacillations between religious idealism and physical desire illustrates how much "ethical contradictoriness" is an inherent part of "human frailty" (3.1.150). Even the "happy marriages" of Hardy's earlier fiction—like Fancy Day's, for example—involve the preservation of sexual secrets.

Through his maintenance of a basic symbolic linkage between desire and dishonesty, Hardy upholds a Victorian discursive system that the modern imagination has often struggled to overthrow—a system that upholds, in turn, polarizations of virtue based on sexual identity and a gendering of art's relationship to desire. Hardy articulates the fundamental equation of desire and dishonesty most clearly in *The Well-Beloved*, especially in the 1897 version, and it is to that novel that I now turn to explore this relationship. In revising the serial, Hardy drastically reshaped the plot by eliminating his protagonist's two marriages—the early marriage to Marcia Bencomb and the marriage of the third Avice at the end of the novel. These changes freed the novel from the theme of mistaken marriage and from attacks on marriage as a legal institution, which had preoccupied Hardy in many of the later works.[19] Instead, the revised version of *The Well-Beloved* offers a relatively pure meditation on the nature

[19] Simon Gatrell notes that many short passages critical of marriage as an institution were also removed in the revision (*Hardy the Creator: A Textual Biography* [Oxford: Clarendon Press, 1988], pp. 150–51).

of desire. What this meditation reveals is that desire leads to acts of betrayal for entirely intrinsic reasons, rather than as a result of social injustice. This point of view was consistent with Hardy's pronouncements about sexuality at the time: in 1896, denying that he was an advocate of "free love," he claimed, "Seriously I don't see any possible scheme for the union of the sexes that [would] be satisfactory."[20] Hardy repeatedly sought to deny that the central subject of *Jude*, in particular, was the injustice of conventional marriage: "It is curious that some papers consider [*Jude*] a sort of manifesto on the marriage question," he wrote to Florence Henniker, later echoing the sentiment to Edmund Gosse as well.[21]

I will look closely at *The Well-Beloved* to delineate the ethical component of its apparently metaphysical meditation on the nature of desire. Then, by relocating Hardy's ethical ideas about desire in *Tess of the d'Urbervilles* and *Jude the Obscure*, I can better demonstrate his social and sexual codification of honesty, which is organized around a series of moral exclusions. In the process, I will isolate the ethical oppositions Hardy constructs in the symbolic domains of sexual desire, authorship, class, and—finally—gender, in order to show, in the last section of this chapter, how the linked ethical exclusions within these various domains coalesce around Hardy's masculinizing of the artist's moral authority. I will tease out these various entangled oppositions—in a necessarily desultory way, I confess—by proceeding through a network of incomplete relationships between dishonesty and desire, authorship, and social class, before I can show how Hardy brings these relationships together through the figure of the feminine, and through a gendering of art.

The basic pretext of *The Well-Beloved*, of course, is the notion of an ideal object of desire that takes up temporary residence in a sequence of individual women. For Jocelyn Pierston, there is no such thing as a first or a true love, since all the women he loves are ephemeral incarnations of an object of desire radically distinct from human selfhood. In this way, inconstancy comes to seem the

---

[20] Richard Little Purdy and Michael Millgate, eds., *The Collected Letters of Thomas Hardy*, 7 vols. (Oxford: Clarendon Press, 1978–88), 1 June 1896, 2:122.
[21] Purdy and Millgate, *Letters*, 10 November 1895, 2:94, 93.

inevitable consequence of desire, the more so because Pierston cannot control the shifting of his "migratory" (3.2.148) ideal beloved. Hardy may very well have been ambivalent about Pierston's quasi-Platonic theories—similar theories are invoked cynically by Fitzpiers in *The Woodlanders*. It would be an oversimplification, however, to see in *The Well-Beloved* only "contrived whimsy" or a "mock fable," as some critics have done.[22] Hardy was at pains to generalize his character's condition in the novel's 1912 preface, claiming that Pierston gives "objective continuity and a name to a delicate dream which in a vaguer form is more or less common to all men" (25). And in *The Life*, he wrote of the novel, "there is, of course, underlying the fantasy followed by the visionary artist the truth that all men are pursuing a shadow, the Unattainable, and I venture to hope that this may redeem the tragi-comedy from the charge of frivolity."[23] He also claimed, with some justification, that "the theory" of the novel was a precursor of Proust's ideas about desire.[24] Though Pierston's romantic pathology is clearly extreme and even absurd, the novel itself seeks to make him representative in some way of normal human desire. His friend Somers tells him, "You are like other men, only rather worse. Essentially, all men are fickle, like you; but not with such perceptiveness" (1.7.54).

Pierston's sense that desire migrates away from the human shapes it pursues is also strongly reflected in other late novels. Tess, for instance, recognizes love's essential impermanence when she tells Angel frankly at the end of the novel that he will outgrow his "present feeling" (58.413) for her, and when she asks him to marry 'Liza-Lu. As an attempt to contain Angel's ephemeral desire by transferring it to her blood relative, Tess's efforts to control sexual displacement oddly prefigure Pierston's destiny. More important, as Kathleen Blake has shown, certain idealizing, deindividualizing

[22] George Wing, "Theme and Fancy in Hardy's *The Well-Beloved*," *Dalhousie Review* 56 (1977), 633; Michael Ryan, "One Name of Many Shapes: *The Well-Beloved*," in Kramer, *Critical Approaches*, p. 176.

[23] Thomas Hardy, *The Life and Work of Thomas Hardy*, ed. Michael Millgate (Athens: University of Georgia Press, 1985), p. 304.

[24] Hardy, *The Life*, p. 466. In *The Captive*, through Marcel's references to Hardy, Proust makes it clear that the themes of *The Well-Beloved* are deeply embedded in his own novel. See also Peter J. Casagrande, *Hardy's Influence on the Modern Novel* (London: Macmillan, 1987), pp. 110–33.

properties of desire are more valued by Hardy in *Tess* than critics often recognize, since the attention of readers usually focuses only on Angel's oppressive distortions. These abstracting properties of desire underlie Tess's experience of souls leaving bodies, as well as various mystifying effects of nature, inebriation, and sexuality, which tend to blur human identity in "marginless" emotional states.[25] In *Jude*, Sue recognizes the unstable, impersonal aspect of desire when she admits the "insatiable" character of her "love of being loved" (4.1.222), and when she complains of expectations for constancy in the marriage vow. Arabella is blunter, answering the charge that she is "always wanting another man than [her] own" by retorting, "Well, and what woman don't I should like to know?" (5.5.305). During Arabella and Jude's first wedding, while the couple swears "they would assuredly believe, feel, and desire precisely as they had believed, felt, and desired during the few preceding weeks," the narrator comments sardonically that "what was remarkable as the undertaking itself was the fact that nobody seemed at all surprised at what they swore" (1.9.81). From this point of view, we can see it as a representative condition, and not an aberrant one, that Hardy's characters always find themselves trapped between competing romantic commitments.[26] In *The Well-Beloved*, though, Hardy creates a plot that for the first time makes inconstancy not the partial result of accident or circumstance but entirely the consequence of the nature of desire itself.

The theory of inconstant, idealizing desire that Pierston articulates—which has many parallels in late-century and modernist writing—need not logically link desire with dishonesty. Yet one unique facet of *The Well-Beloved* is that it systematically enforces this link. The association between desire and dishonesty is even increased in Hardy's 1897 revision, which gives Pierston several significant lies not found in the serial version and expands a narrative string of fatal broken promises (the third Avice causes her mother's death by eloping with Leverre on the eve of her wedding to Pierston). But the

[25] Kathleen Blake, "Pure Tess: Hardy on Knowing a Woman," *SEL* 22 (1982), 689–705.

[26] J. Hillis Miller points out that we are always introduced to Hardy's characters at the moment of a displacement in their affections (*Thomas Hardy: Distance and Desire* [Cambridge: Harvard University Press, 1970], pp. 115–16).

plots of both versions of *The Well-Beloved* are rampant with deceit and evasion. Pierston often comes in contact with conspiracies that remain opaque to him: he overhears the second Avice quarreling with her secret husband but is prevented from recognizing her voice, ironically, by the marital tone of the argument; he lends a stranger a cane, not knowing that the stranger is about to elope with his bride; he watches the islanders stare at a boat in the distance, unaware that it carries the third Avice and her lover. The tone of the narrative is also unusually stilted, not simply because of the novel's fantastic qualities and its many formal problems, but because of the cloud of reserve in which Pierston's various beloveds are enwrapped. This reserve creates a striking void of candid dialogue in the novel and constantly involves Pierston in inconclusive conversations. The atmosphere of secrecy and constraint underscores the symbolic importance of the novel's numerous lies, broken promises, and manipulations: Pierson's betrayal of his promise to marry the first Avice; his lie to Marcia that legal technicalities prevent their marriage; Marcia's startling "forgetfulness" (1.8.58) of her pledge to a former lover; the secret marriage of the second Avice; Pierston's concealment of his relationship to the second Avice's mother; the second Avice's "contrivance" (3.4.157) in engaging Pierston to her daughter; Pierston's deceptions about his age during his courtship of the third Avice. This list could be lengthened with innumerable secondary deceptions, all of them revolving around various stages of sexual desire. The well-beloved herself, the very site of sexual desire, is imagined by Pierston primarily as a duplicitous force: she is referred to as a "jade" (3.3.156) and as "capricious" (2.5.93), and she is accused of playing a "trick" (2.1.70) on Pierston and "masquerading" (1.2.34). This link between dishonesty and a feminine emblem of desire is borne out elsewhere in the novels with telling regularity.

Perhaps the most disturbing linkage between desire and dishonesty—given Hardy's championing of art's candor—is forged by the narrative's reflections about art itself. *The Well-Beloved* hints—like no other Hardy novel—at how tenuous the canon of artistic honesty is. In the first place, Pierston's art is conceived as the direct manifestation of inconstant or infinite desire. We are often told that the energy of Pierston's art comes from the ability to channel his idealistic—but morally dangerous—passion into sculptured form:

"Jocelyn threw into plastic creations that ever-bubbling spring of emotion which, without some conduit into space, will surge upwards and ruin all but the greatest men" (1.9.62–63). Pierston further confesses, at one point in the serial, to have raided his love letters in order to write lyric poetry. The resulting moral ambiguity of art is everywhere acknowledged, though often ironically: "It was in his weaknesses as a citizen and a national-unit that his strength lay as an artist" (2.7.104). The congruity between art and inconstant desire is made absolutely clear at the end, when Pierston's loss of migratory erotic desire coincides with his loss of interest and capability in art. One must respect the seriousness of this conjunction: though Hardy may have drawn Pierston satirically from the example of Dante Gabriel Rossetti—who quite literally painted one face in many shapes—his biographers have made it clear that Hardy also crafted his own art out of his erotic experience, including his sense of sexual guilt.[27] The peculiar power of Pierston's art is also identified wholly with its nature as artifice. Pierston himself condemns art as misrepresentation, as a fraudulent attempt to shadow forth the ideal, inaccessible well-beloved. Besides the latent dishonesty of his relationship to his public—for he captures "a public taste he had never deliberately aimed at, and mostly despised" (1.9.64)—his work itself is only a series of hypocritical "failures" (2.1.75), in which he "insulted" (3.8.189) the ideal. Allegorically, this connection is strengthened at the end by Marcia's abandonment of the "artifices" (3.8.188) of beauty. Her rejection of the cosmetic means of cultivating desire, which parallels Pierston's rejection of aesthetic representations of desire, prompts her to claim that at last she has become "passably honest" (3.8.189).

Moreover, *The Well-Beloved* self-consciously lays bare the artistic devices and ruses underlying all of Hardy's own work.[28] Besides the mechanical plot twists and the stylized ironies, Hardy's highly artificial repetition of the same story in three different versions suggests his fiction's characteristic tendency to "migrate" from a

---

[27] The most theoretically informed of these accounts is T. R. Wright, *Hardy and the Erotic* (Basingstoke: Macmillan, 1989). For the connection with Rossetti, see J. B. Bullen, *The Expressive Eye: Fiction and Perception in the Work of Thomas Hardy* (London: Oxford University Press, 1986), p. 236.

[28] See the comments of J. Hillis Miller, introduction to *The Well-Beloved*, p. 14.

single truth, to pursue overlapping but divergent plots and themes. Like Pierston's funneling of eroticism into aesthetic form, writing for Hardy is often dangerously inconstant or inconsistent. Although Hardy was meticulous about the realistic accuracy of his novels, he also had a persistent half-acknowledged awareness about the "falseness" of fiction. "Hence, one may say, Art is the secret of how to produce by a false thing the effect of a true," he wrote on the subject of a Royal Academy exhibition.[29] Speaking of his own work, he invoked Turner to explain that "it was sometimes necessary to see round corners, down crooked streets, & to shift buildings nearer each other than in reality."[30] He makes the same point in "The Profitable Reading of Fiction," which, whatever its claims for the truth-value of fiction, also defends imaginative transformation: "The best fiction, like the highest artistic expression in other modes, is more true, so to put it, than history or nature can be."[31]

Such remarks are more than just the concessions of a realistic novelist to late nineteenth-century aestheticism. For Hardy, writing—which he saw, in some sense, as the privileged expression of the force of sexual desire—must be associated with emotion rather than with reason. And if the essence of human emotion is its inconstancy, the unsystematic philosophy that Hardy proudly defended in his writing needs to be understood as a consequence of this identification. Writing, insofar as it parallels Pierston's ability to channel eroticism into sculptural form, must necessarily be migratory, inconstant, inconsistent. Many of the stylistic quirks of Hardy's novels, in particular their willful evasiveness, can be understood as forms of cultivated narrative deceit intimately related to the relationship between desire and dishonesty. Hardy's prose constantly tantalizes the reader with what the narrative knows but will not tell and what it knowingly misrepresents or evades. When Alec first leaves Tess, for example, we are told ambiguously that "he emitted a laboured breath, as if the scene were getting rather oppressive to his heart, or to his conscience, or to his gentility" (12.107). Earlier, just after Alec has called Tess "artful" (8.81), the narrator uses another coy simile to describe her walking beside him "thoughtfully,

[29] Hardy, *The Life*, p. 226.
[30] Purdy and Millgate, *Letters*, 12 October 1922, 6:161.
[31] Hardy, "The Profitable Reading of Fiction," p. 67.

as if wondering whether it would be wiser to return home" (8.81–82). Hardy's style always flaunts its equivocations in this manner. The novels also withhold key scenes, including Tess's rape/seduction, her later confession, and the wording of Henchard's "carefully framed" (12.106) letter breaking his engagement to Lucetta. Any writer who planned for years to pass off his own autobiography as the work of his wife had to have a somewhat developed consciousness of the duplicities of writing.

This disturbing contamination of art with deceit, though distanced by irony in *The Well-Beloved* and never directly articulated by Hardy himself, suggests, nevertheless, the urgency of Hardy's strategies for ordering moral ambivalence. It expresses, again, the dilemmas of ethical contradiction to which Hardy's thinking about honesty often led him. It also suggests, as I have been arguing, that if Hardy were ever to clarify his own practice and convince himself of his own authorial honesty, he needed to project dishonesty rather strenuously onto various scapegoats—Pierston being one. Hardy's irony about the integrity of art is, in this sense, a negative form of candor: an affirmation of the artist's ability to be honest about art's own complicity with dishonesty. Yet such irony is obviously very volatile and needs to be stabilized. The catastrophe of any full concession of art's duplicity might ultimately be forestalled by enforcing linked ethical oppositions—between art and life, between asceticism and sexuality, between one class and another, or, most important of all, between men and women—in order to scapegoat one set of these terms in tandem to the advantage of the other. Even if each of these oppositions, taken in itself, might prove to be precarious, a parallel alignment of them all serves to bolster Hardy's implicit convictions about artistic moral authority.

One such linkage of ethical oppositions is Hardy's sense that desire is inextricable from social, as well as moral, transgression. That is to say, another lingering Victorianism in Hardy's work is his tacitly expressed conviction that social aspiration always has affinities with dishonesty and—by implication—with sexual desire. Characters such as Alec, who is deceit incarnate and whose father is rumored to have made a fortune through usury, or Arabella, whose steady climb toward respectability depends on various ruses ("Don't you ask questions, and you won't hear lies" [3.8.197], she tells one of her tavern customers), or the second Avice, who admits that she would have married Pierston for his social advantages if not for her secret marriage—all repeat in almost caricatural ways Victorian tendencies to merge moral and sexual concerns with anxieties about social mobility. The fact that these figures repeatedly prey on the exemplary trustfulness, as well as the social naiveté, of Tess, Jude, and Pierston further underscores the characteristic duplicity of individuals motivated by social ambition.[32] Hardy regularly embodies the force of desire in the symbolic domains of both social and sexual transgression, commonly linked through dishonesty.

The dishonesty of social ambition is complexly intertwined in all of Hardy's sexual relationships; it is not just a flaw of his more vulgar characters. In *Tess*, for example, Tess's "gross deceit" (37.278), as Angel terms it, is magnified not just by gender difference but also by the social disparity between the two lovers. The subdued rivalry between Tess and the other three aspirants to Angel's hand—Izz, Retty, and Marian, all of whom recognize with anguish their social unworthiness—stresses the social dimension of Tess's inadvertent dishonesty. This social dimension is also emphasized by Tess's disturbingly ambiguous desires to rise above her fellow workers. Her "triumph" (10.95) at escaping the "whole crew" of workers which she had "majestically" called "a whorage," when she leaps onto Alec's horse, and her refusal earlier that evening to dance with company she considered low and disreputable, are reflected by her consistent preference for values and behavior that are symbolically coded to class distinctions. While Tess may consciously "wish for no better" name than her own (5.67), her desires are very much mediated by an awareness of class difference. At our very first glimpse of her, we find that her "pride" (2.40) cringes at social embarrassments caused by her father. After meeting Angel at the May-Dance, she spurns other partners because "they did not speak

---

[32] Patricia Alden has described the "typical" Hardy protagonist as a figure who finds that his mixed social and psychological "attempt to enlarge himself involves him in some deception, secrecy, or betrayal" (*Social Mobility in the English Bildungsroman: Gissing, Hardy, Bennett, and Lawrence* [Ann Arbor, Mich.: UMI Research Press, 1986], p. 42).

so nicely as the strange young man had done" (3.44). After her seduction, "at moments, in spite of thought, she would reply to their inquiries with a manner of superiority, as if recognizing that her experiences in the field of courtship had, indeed, been slightly enviable" (13.112–13). Such moments are less an indictment of Tess than a testament to the ineradicability of socially mediated desire. Everything about Tess's experience conditions her to filter events through social hierarchies. Her education involves her intimately in mobility by compelling her to speak "two languages" (3.46). Her guilt and shame over her parents' economic hardships repeatedly compel her to maintain the connection with Alec. No wonder, then, that she responds so guiltily to Angel's brother's discovery of her boots and to Mercy Chant's guess that they belong to "some imposter" (44.324). Hardy has created neither a social saint nor a fool in Tess, but rather a woman trapped in bad faith through the inexorable intersections of social and sexual desire.

Angel's love for Tess rests, in turn, on slightly more ephemeral signs of her social superiority. Though Angel despises "the material distinctions of rank and wealth" (18.144), he is attracted to Tess for more immaterial signs of such distinction. He relishes the fact that Tess "though but a milkmaid had that touch of rarity about her which might make her the envied of her housemates" (19.152). In reflecting on the difference between "the political value and the imaginative value" (49.364) of her genealogy, Angel "thought now that he could see therein a flash of the dignity which must have graced her grand-dames." As Angel dwells on her superiority to other women, his terms identify character traits with class hierarchies (for example, her "dignity"). The narrative itself constantly draws our attention to culturally coded signs of Tess's superiority, speaking of "the soberer richer note of Tess among those of the other workpeople" (10.94) and of her greater "eloquence" (2.39). Other characters are brought in as a kind of chorus to Tess's innate distinction. Mrs. Crick recalls that "Tess had looked so superior as she walked across the barton on that afternoon of her arrival; that she was of a good family she could have sworn" (32.231). Mr. Crick acknowledges that she is "too good for a dairymaid" (31.226). Marian admits that Tess is "more ladylike, and a better scholar than we" (31.227), and even Alec is drawn to Tess partly because she is "mighty sensitive for a cottage-girl" (8.80). The narrator himself seems erratically conscious of this mediation of Tess's attractions by class signals.[33] The rape scene, for example, employs latent class imagery that subtly fuses economic and symbolic markers: "so often the coarse appropriates the finer thus" (11.101), we are told.

Similarly, Jude's love for Sue is continually mediated by his awareness of symbolic social hierarchies, by the parallels between Sue's purity and the ideals embodied in social stations above his own. Hardy reinforces these parallels between a certain kind of sexual desirability and class ideals in various ways. He stresses Jude's perception of Sue as "elegant" (2.2.113), "elevating," and "refined" (6.3.352), not "gross" and "earthly" (4.5.259)—terms Jude uses to describe himself. He also makes it clear that Jude's aspirations in general depend on the mediation of social hierarchies: "Yet he sometimes felt that by caring for books he was not escaping common-place nor gaining rare ideas, every working-man being of that taste now" (1.10.89). Jude's outburst in the Christminster tavern reveals a kind of class contempt that conditions all of his desires: "See what I have brought myself to—the crew I have come among" (2.7.143), he complains bitterly, locating his intellectual failure in class terms. In contrast to Jude's own wish for a clean opposition between intellectual promotion and sexual desire, the entanglement of the two is dramatized by frequent comparisons of Christminster to a woman: "Like a young lover alluding to his mistress, he felt bashful at mentioning its name again" (1.3.48). Just as he imagines that Sue, that "disembodied creature" (4.5.259), will elevate him above the earthly, so, too, he fantasizes that once inside Christminster's hallowed buildings, "he might some day look down on the world through their panes" (2.2.110). Sue also reveals the elitism entangled in her war on conventionality: her conviction that marriage is "sordid" (5.1.273) and "hopelessly vulgar" (5.3.285), and that it would be "rather low to do likewise" (5.3.287) when she hears that Arabella has married. In this way, Hardy rather courageously reveals the relationship between Sue's idealistic motives for not marrying

[33] John Tudor Laird points out that later editions of the novel stripped Tess of dialect in order to lend her greater dignity (*The Shaping of "Tess of the d'Urbervilles"* [Oxford: Clarendon Press, 1975], p. 184).

and the social snobbery of her convictions—given his own opinions on the issue.

Hardy was insistent that, whatever his characters' attempts to transcend concerns of social class, the social axis is an inextricable part of their desire. His characters' blindness to this intersection only leads to various kinds of misrepresentation, including self-deception. It is not simply that Hardy seeks to dramatize the realities of class conflict by foregrounding the social barriers his lovers must overcome; rather, he stigmatizes all desire by invoking the inevitable duplicities of social mobility which it generates. The betrayal of one lover for another, for example, and therefore the violation of pledges of constancy, most often takes place upward along a social gradient. In *The Well-Beloved*, Pierston's one and only betrayal—of the first Avice—is committed for the sake of a woman who, at the time, represents an advantageous match for him. In *Jude*, Sue's eventual marriage to Phillotson is mediated by her conventional sense of social obligations. Her final commitment to Phillotson, which betrays Jude's "love of truth" (6.10.405)—even Arabella knows that any of Sue's self-justifications "won't be true" (6.11.413)—is compromised in its honesty not just by her own divided affections, but by the general return to middle-class respectability that she has chosen. Phillotson, too, confirms the connection between sexual desire and "dishonest" social aspiration when he acknowledges, at the point of Sue's return, that some "artifice was necessary" (6.4.365) to preserve respectability—a recognition that Arabella, with her false dimples and hair, has long understood.[34]

Hardy entangles dishonesty between lovers in the inequities of class partly, of course, simply to express his sense of the alienating effects of nineteenth-century social transformations. He frequently dramatized the growing gulf between self-awareness and class in his characters' sense of inner exile from their social identities.[35] This gulf, however, becomes one more division within subjectivity which

---

[34] Elizabeth Langland reads Jude's code of honor as an example of his middle-class aspirations ("Becoming a Man in *Jude the Obscure*," in Higonnet, *Sense of Sex*, pp. 36–37). Phillotson's experience, however, makes it difficult to say whether the novel positions moral idealism as middle-class, in any absolute sense.

[35] See George Wotton, *Thomas Hardy: Towards a Materialist Criticism* (Totowa, N.J.: Barnes and Noble, 1985), p. 52.

further disrupts the conditions necessary for honesty. Even those characters, such as Angel, Pierston, and Sue, who try to flaunt their downward mobility as evidence of the purity of their love, covertly undermine their claims to social disinterest by invoking signs of social distinction or aspiration. Some use the contrast of station itself, the self-conscious inversion of social aspiration, to stress the superior refinement of their love—thereby entangling themselves in even greater contradictions. For Pierston, the disparity between his social station and the vulgarity of the second Avice confirms for him that his desire is directed toward an ideal, a goddess that transcends all social classification. His pursuit of an island girl becomes proof for him of his own spiritual refinement, by underlining the profundity of his idealization. Yet the relationship of commodification between Pierston's ideal beloved and the artistic works that have elevated him socially makes it quite impossible to separate his desire from social mobility, and thus from the stigma of dishonesty always attached to such mobility.

Hardy was himself both plagued and fascinated by the guilt he associated with social desire. He insisted, defensively, on the complete lack of commercial ambition in his father and grandfather (as well as in himself), and his refusal to cultivate social connections in London was a constant source of tension with Emma.[36] Yet Hardy's gestures of social disinterest are fully consistent with both secret pleasure in his own dramatic rise and an awareness that it was made possible by the "falseness" of fiction—a situation he satirized self-consciously in *The Hand of Ethelberta*, as well as in *The Well-Beloved*. Partly because of his struggles with vocational choice—literature versus architecture, poetry versus fiction—Hardy was preoccupied with what he saw as the fundamental incompatibility of noble or lofty ideas and social success: "It is, in a worldly sense, a matter for regret that a child who has to win a living should be born of a noble nature. Social greatness requires littleness to inflate & float it, & a high soul may bring a man to the workhouse."[37] Trite as such convictions may be, one crucial corollary for Hardy is that sexual

[36] See Michael Millgate, *Thomas Hardy: A Biography* (London: Oxford University Press, 1982), p. 9; Hardy, *The Life*, p. 9; and Alden, *Social Mobility*, p. 44.

[37] Richard H. Taylor, ed., *The Personal Notebooks of Thomas Hardy* (London: Macmillan, 1978), p. 6.

desire, too, becomes incompatible with the loftiness of disinterest and is hopelessly entangled with ambition, in ways that make coming clean about one's desire a contradiction in terms. Hardy always imagines sexual desire as both morally and socially transgressive, the expression of a general, multifaceted dishonesty. As a consequence of this linkage, his efforts to fortify distinctions between honesty and dishonesty necessarily come to depend heavily on oppositions constructed around gender. In fact, gender distinctions prove crucial in Hardy's attempts to establish a domain of ethical purity that he identifies, ultimately, with artistic perception.

Although Hardy systematically banishes honesty from the domain of desire, his fundamental moral commitment to honesty is by no means weakened as a result—which suggests that honesty might depend, in Hardy, on a moral purification revolving around sexuality. Gestures of fidelity and honesty about sexuality are, in fact, a constant counterweight to Hardy's association of sexual desire with dishonesty. The novels often feature unambiguous moments of sexual honesty, and in some cases give such honesty heroic proportions: Jude's gratuitous confession to Phillotson of the exact state of his relations to Sue; Izz Huett's admission of Tess's devotion to Angel. One of the fascinating complications of *The Well-Beloved*, in fact, is its elaborate celebration of sexual sincerity. In terms of fidelity, Pierston's desire may be inherently inconstant to individual women, but he argues strenuously with Somers that he never deviates from fidelity to the ideal itself. The narrator confirms the point: "To his Well-Beloved he had always been faithful" (1.2.34). Although it may not be clear exactly what this means, Pierston seems to claim that he never allows personal or selfish desires—what he calls "wanton" impulse (1.7.54)—to divert him from his idealism. In this sense, even Pierston's initial betrayal of Avice can be understood as a form of fidelity. For in leaving Avice for Marcia, Pierston resists a wayward impulse that had nothing to do with the well-beloved, since his ideal never inhabits the first Avice, but resides in Marcia. Whatever the ambiguities here, Pierston eventually does become strictly faithful to a single image of the beloved repeated in three generations of women, which gives the notion of fidelity some tenuous physical substance. The plot is also arranged so that Pierston never technically jilts anyone, despite his dangerous desires. The women who incarnate the well-beloved always leave him, or are taken from him: "Not a woman in the world had been wrecked by him, though he had been impassioned by so many" (3.7.181). It would be easier to regard such claims as ironic if they came from Pierston himself, rather than from the narrator. The mixture of fidelity and infidelity in Pierston's treatment of the first Avice, or any of his other women, is flagrantly contradictory in ways that suggest an irresolvable dynamic between two distinct aspects of Pierston's character. The contradictions appear in numerous elliptical contrasts: in the course of his betrayal of the first Avice, for instance, what Pierston experiences emotionally is actually his scrupulous fidelity to Marcia: "He felt bound in honor to remain . . . as long as there was the slightest chance of Marcia's reappearance" (1.8.60). The apparent inconsistencies of Pierston's character are constructed around a dynamic doubleness in which constancy and inconstancy, as well as honesty and dishonesty, are in perpetual tension, but without ever disrupting each other—inconsistencies that seem to parallel the latent, inconsistent relationship of Hardyan art itself to both honesty and dishonesty. Pierston's double identity, as an islander and a Londoner, expresses this paradox neatly, for while the islanders are noted for being unusually "straightforward" (1.2.32), London society is the exemplary realm of artifice.

The double moral identity of Hardy's protagonist should remind us very closely of the moral sophistication writers such as Collins and Trollope identified with transgressive duplicity. Indeed, the public reputation of Hardy's art has a great deal to do with his ability to explore moral contamination without seeming to be defiled by it, in ways that depend on the paradigms of antibourgeois moral authority I have described in a number of mid-Victorian writers. But as I have been suggesting, Hardy complicates this paradigm—or deforms it, in a manner representative of late-century writing—by using moral instabilities as the springboard to a rarefied, precious domain of honesty, identified more closely with his art than with the human agency of his protagonists. The symbolic difficulty of this project forces him to produce an aesthetic domain of honesty through an unusually severe set of symbolic negations, some of which resurrect and amplify the crude, exclusionary strategies of mid-Victorian ethics, and all of which ultimately revolve around gendered rituals of sexual purification.

Through the linked oppositions I have been tracing between desire, class hierarchy, and lived (as opposed to artistic) experience, Hardy's performatively "candid" exploration of the moral ambiguities threatened by Pierston exploits a series of interconnected negations that are focused, ultimately, on questions of sexuality. To begin with, the odd emphasis on fidelity in *The Well-Beloved* (in the last chapter, Pierston and Marcia smugly compel the third Avice to return to her husband) is routinely made peripheral to sexual desire itself, if fidelity has not actually become the sign of its triumphal suppression or complete exhaustion. Pierston's final vow of fidelity to Marcia depends precisely on the loss of his own capacity for desire: "I have no love to give," he says, "but such friendship as I am capable of is yours till the end" (3.8.192). The couple's mutual honesty about aging puts them both beyond sexual desire, in a companionate marriage more extremely chaste than even the Victorian domestic ideal. Pierston's faithfulness here, as well as his coercive response to the third Avice's marital discord, may constitute a familiar Hardyan argument for fidelity to particularized, unidealized women, but it can follow only from Pierston's complete immunity to desire. It does not hold out the faintest possibility of constancy in love itself. Earlier in the novel, Pierston's fidelity to the image of Avice, as incarnated in her daughter and granddaughter, hinges partly on the need to make reparation for his earlier inconstancy, a motive that is quite separate from his desire for the well-beloved. And, of course, his initial proposal to Avice stems not at all from his desire, but from his sense of a special relationship rooted in their shared childhood. Thus, the image of Avice is always in a sense an image of fidelity to the past, and to prepubescent friendship. Because of this possibility of a victory over desire, *The Well-Beloved*—alone among the later works—is able to end "happily."

In other novels, Hardy suggests possibilities of a kind of fidelity beyond desire, but is unable to represent the condition of desirelessness quite so thoroughly. When Angel overcomes his prejudices and returns to Tess, for example, the quality of his love is altered, made milder. It becomes a kind of "fondness" (49.363), which contrasts sharply with Alec's reawakened "passion" (46.340) for Tess. The possibility that Angel might fulfill his vow to marry 'Liza-Lu also leaves us with the prospect of a desexualized marriage—'Liza-Lu is "a spiritualized image of Tess" (59.419). In *The Woodlanders*, the serene faithfulness of Giles Winterbourne and Marty South depends on their extreme freedom from sexual desire. Marty, in particular, "touched sublimity at points, and looked almost like a being who had rejected with indifference the attribute of sex for the loftier quality of abstract humanism" (48.375).[38] Even the occasional happy endings of the earlier novels, as in *Far from the Madding Crowd*, feature marriages of people who, as J. Hillis Miller puts it, "have outlived the time when they might have sought the bliss of full union with another person."[39] Honesty and fidelity are so imperiled by the encroachments of desire in Hardy's work—both social and sexual desire—that he can reimagine them only as a stringent distantiation from it.

The most crucial component of Hardy's resuscitation of honesty, however, is his systematic projection of dishonesty onto the feminine, as the privileged object of the sexual desire his more favored characters overcome. Readers have often commented on Hardy's negative stereotypes of women, but his attack on feminine dishonesty in particular is worth reexamining, both because of the chain of symbolic connections on which it depends, and because the figure of the feminine manages to incorporate Hardy's various concerns with the intractability of dishonesty within sexual desire, social hierarchy, and aesthetics. Hardy's representations of the feminine may be notoriously unstable, yet a few interlinked patterns seem to overwhelm Hardy's attempts to disperse them. For instance, although the assertion must be qualified in important ways, Hardy's women are regularly aligned with emotionalism, as opposed to the customary rationality of his men. Everything Sue does "seemed to have its source in feeling" (2.4.125), and Tess is "a vessel of emotions rather than reasons" (47.353). Many readers have noted that Hardy's women are further identified with sexual emotion. While the crisis

---

[38] See Mary Jacobus's comments on Marty's noninvolvement in events generally, in "Tree and Machine: *The Woodlanders*," in Kramer, *Critical Approaches*, esp. p. 121.

[39] Miller, *Thomas Hardy*, p. 54.

in Hardy's novels for men is often intellectual, for women it is always sexual in nature.[40] And as we have seen, the nature of Hardyan sexuality is inherently inconstant and duplicitous, the enemy of sincerity. Hardy's narrator persistently generalizes about women's linked affinity with both the emotions and with dishonesty. In *Jude*, commenting on one of Sue's incomplete confessions, he observes that "a contrite woman always keeps back a little" (6.9.402). In *The Return of the Native*, we hear of "the fact of the indirectness of a woman's movement towards her desire" (4.2.258). As a result of this conjunction, women are more consistently associated with the pattern of sexual entrapment in Hardy than are men.[41] Instances of entrapment by men are often made to appear aberrant, or are qualified by greater male capacities for self-consciousness and self-renunciation. In addition, female passivity tends to add to woman's inconstancy, in Hardy's view. Sue, for example, is "a harp which the least wind of emotion from another's heart could make to vibrate as readily as a radical stir in her own" (5.3.292). Male characters often echo these generalizations about women, and even the women themselves sometimes acknowledge their moral incapacity. Sue is ashamed to let Phillotson know "what a slipshod lack of thoroughness, from a man's point of view, characterized her transferred allegiance" (4.6.266), and at another point speaks of "the rule of women's whims" (4.5.253). In morals, Sue claims, men are "so much better than women" (3.4.168).

Hardy's men, by virtue of their greater distance from emotion and from sexual desire, acquire an aura of truthfulness by contrast. The novels consistently feature men who, however passionate, transcend the temptations of passion and resist the contaminating influence of their desire. Hardy could not, of course, draw an absolute distinction between the sexes in their capacities for dishonesty. His sense of the link between dishonesty and desire was far too strict for that. The novels do feature male characters who are also identified with emotion and with deceit—Wildeve, Fitzpiers, and Sergeant Troy, among others. Yet such men are often diagnosed as the source of

---

[40] See Boumelha, *Thomas Hardy and Women*, p. 48; and Patricia Stubbs, *Women and Fiction: Feminism and the Novel, 1880–1920* (Sussex: Harvester Press, 1979), pp. 58–87.

[41] See Fischler, "Gins and Spirits," p. 2.

great social and sexual disturbance, and the deviance they represent is often ritualistically purged from the novels, either through their deaths or through other persistent signs of fatality (as in Grace Melbury's ominous reunion with Fitzpiers). Many of these men are also explicitly feminized—both in physical description and in terms of a certain impulsiveness that Hardy often uses to align the feminine with inconstant behavior.[42] Most important, fundamentally dishonest men are always closely paired and contrasted with almost preternaturally honest male characters—Giles Winterbourne, Diggory Venn, Gabriel Oak—as a way to objectify their deviance. Moreover, Hardy permits even his morally anguished male protagonists greater opportunities than his female characters to overcome, finally, their own weaknesses for desire and the dishonesty it entails. Consider the compulsive, morally compromised acts of Tess and Sue at the conclusions of their narratives, in contrast to the long trajectory toward philosophical clarity and detachment that marks the moral progress of Angel and Jude.

All these strategies help to project onto women the ethically problematic qualities of desire. What often results is simply a more negative interpretation of the inflexibility of female dishonesty in desire, or an excessively stark delineation of feminine dishonesty. The second Avice, for example, who shares more than anyone else Pierston's addiction to inconstancy, is derogated as "common" (2.7.104), as a "very wicked woman" (2.12.130), and even as an "elf" and a "witch" (3.2.146). In opposition, the symbolic terrain of the masculine—rather than each of Hardy's male characters individually—becomes a theater of charged moral ambivalence that can lead to resurgent moral purity, either through self-resistance or through resistance to the deviant examples of other, vilified men or of unregenerate women. In these ways, masculinity comes to partake of the same dynamic ethical ambivalence—as well as possibilities for purity through the strenuous expulsion of that moral confusion—that conditions Hardy's sense of authorship itself. In general, by regularizing female deceit and by positing male ambivalence as an

---

[42] On the feminization of Sergeant Troy, see William Mistichelli, "Androgyny, Survival, and Fulfillment in Thomas Hardy's *Far from the Madding Crowd*," *Modern Language Studies* 18, no. 3 (Summer 1988), pp. 53–64.

arena of dynamic resistance to dishonesty, Hardy creates ethical standards in severely gendered terms.

One inevitable correlative of this sexual stigmatization of women is their greater identification with social ambition.[43] Early heroines like Fancy Day, Elfride Swancourt, and, of course, Ethelberta Petherwin, give dishonesty in service of social mobility a distinctly feminine stamp. In the later novels, Arabella and the second Avice are the most glaring instances of this equation, but even Tess's evasions are linked to her social gain. Sue's dishonesty about the nature of her desire, as I have noted, takes the form of a grasping for respectability as well. While Jude's sexual desires, like Angel's, may also be associated with social hierarchies through the mediation of symbolic forms, they are never graphed in terms of achieved economic or class gains. In these ways, women are more consistently and more overtly tied to the practices of class, and thus more compromised in their cultural and erotic idealism than men—not an uncommon pattern of male fear in late-nineteenth-century writing. In *Under the Greenwood Tree*, Fancy Day's letter of confession to Maybold makes the association clear: "It is my nature—perhaps all women's—to love refinement of mind and manners; but even more than this, to be ever fascinated with the idea of surroundings more elegant and pleasing than those which have been customary. . . . Ambition and vanity they would be called; perhaps they are so" (4.7.176). We might very well wonder that this stigmatization of female ambition is so routinely echoed, by Hardy and by his biographers, in the projection of social aspiration onto the women in his life, particularly his mother and Emma.[44]

A comparison of the distribution of ethical action in *Jude* and *Tess* offers the most revealing contrasts along these lines, for the schematic configurations of gender are neatly reversed in the two plots.[45]

---

[43] Widdowson notes that Hardy tends to gender "rising" class forces as feminine, although Widdowson sees this tendency as part of a general assault on liberal-bourgeois society, which, he claims, victimizes rising women as well as static men (*Hardy in History*, pp. 214–15).

[44] Millgate follows Hardy in identifying his mother as the source of the family's social ambition (*Thomas Hardy*, p. 21). Emma's disappointed social-climbing is a persistent theme of the Millgate biography. See also Robert Gittings, *Young Thomas Hardy* (London: Heinemann, 1975), p. 136.

[45] Some of these reversals have been noted by Kathleen Rogers, "Women in Thomas Hardy," *Centennial Review* 19 (1975), 249–58.

The atypically innocent character seduced by a schemer is female in *Tess*, male in *Jude*. The naive lover who is later shocked by confession of the seduction is male in *Tess*, female in *Jude*. In both novels, too, the plot pivots around an occasion of symmetrical reticence between the two lovers. But there are immense differences in the moral stigmas attached to male and female behavior in these similar circumstances. Whereas Sue's reaction to Jude's confession is to falsify her affections by throwing herself at Phillotson, Angel confronts such temptation, in the form of Izz Huett, and resists it. Jude never actually wins his lover through concealment of his sexual past, but Tess, of course, does. Most important, Tess both marries upwardly and is seduced by an aristocrat. Jude, on the other hand, marries a woman who sees herself as beneath him, and although Sue may be superior to Jude in manner, she is his equal in social origins. In both novels, too, the female characters are most strongly identified with vacillation—Sue, because of her "perverse" constitution, and Tess, because of her inability to negotiate the dilemma of Angel's marriage proposal. Finally, at the end of each novel, it is the women who live a lie, having surrendered themselves in marriage to men they do not love—Jude's resigned, semisuicidal return to Arabella, we must remember, hangs entirely on Sue's betrayal. In all these cases, female duplicity is relatively magnified, despite the universal contamination of desire by dishonesty, thereby constructing a space of male honesty if only by contrast, by negation.

Most important, in the chain of ethical scapegoatings encompassed by sexual difference, Hardy's stigmatization of the feminine with sexual and social desire incorporates the most crucial opposition in his rearticulation of honesty: his attribution of honesty to artistic observation—that is, to the vantage that art holds over life. The moral basis of Hardy's authorial distance and neutrality, his intention to produce "an impression, not an argument" (*Tess*, preface, p. 28), is the implicit honesty that comes of having no special agenda to pursue, no authorial desire to impose. But in Hardy, the desirelessness achievable within artistic perception always depends on confining desire to the (feminine) object of observation. While the detached, spectatorlike posture of Hardy's narrators seems to correspond simply to Hardy's own faith in the documentary qualities of fiction, the honesty that accrues to artistic consciousness finds its symbolic foundations in Hardy's sexually coded representation of the act of observation itself.

Observation in Hardy is always represented as distinctly double. Much has been said of the appropriative gaze of desire in Hardy and of its primary affinity with male desire.[46] Self-consciously, the novels consistently feature scenes of male observation of women which suggest the projective, inaccurate perspective of observers who are contaminated by desire. But Hardy doubles the trope of a misrepresenting male gaze by postulating certain male observers who have escaped their desire and have presumably achieved truthful perception as a consequence.[47] No doubt, these fantasies play a compensatory role in what Hardy's biographers have described as his own compulsive voyeurism.[48] In any case, the novels repeatedly dramatize privileged moments of honest and accurate observation, in which men are imagined to oppose themselves successfully to the sexuality they survey in women. Jude's sudden, sympathetic recognition of Arabella at the end of their life together, for instance, takes shape as a moment in which he observes her hysteria without desire: "Jude was exasperated, and went out to drag her in by main force. Then he suddenly lost his heat. Illuminated with the sense that all was over between them, and that it mattered not what she did, or he, her husband stood still, regarding her. Their lives were ruined, he thought" (1.11.93). Later, Jude watches her with "the eye of a dazed philosopher" (3.8.198) when he encounters her unexpectedly in a Christminster tavern and finds her flirting with a customer. He is

---

[46] An excellent account is Kaja Silverman, "History, Figuration, and Female Subjectivity in *Tess of the d'Urbervilles*," *Novel* 18 (1984), 5–28. See also Boumelha, *Thomas Hardy and Women*, pp. 32–36, 120–22; and Rosemarie Morgan, *Women and Sexuality in the Novels of Thomas Hardy* (London: Routledge, 1988), pp. 35–37, 44–46. Feminist film theory has refined this perception of narrative voyeurism, as demonstrated in Silverman, "History, Figuration"; Wright, *Hardy and the Erotic*; Dianne Fallon Sadoff, "Looking at Tess: The Female Figure in Two Narrative Media," in Higonnet, *Sense of Sex*, pp. 149–71; and Jeff Nunokawa, "*Tess*, Tourism, and the Spectacle of the Woman," in *Rewriting the Victorians: Theory, History, and the Politics of Gender* (New York: Routledge, 1992), pp. 70–86.

[47] Julie Grossman, in "Thomas Hardy and the Role of the Observer," *ELH* 56 (1989), 619–38, shows how observation in Hardy is divided into interested and detached categories, the latter being the condition of objectivity. Though she points out that observation in Hardy is often eroticized, Grossman does not address the gendering of this perceptual dichotomy.

[48] See Wright, *Hardy and the Erotic*, esp. pp. 22, 29–30.

able at that point to decide the course of his relations with her as a matter of principle. In a related fashion, when Phillotson spies on Sue's meeting with Jude, he is freed of his own desire for her and gains an honest appreciation of the two cousins' love for each other that convinces him, disinterestedly, to dissolve his own marriage to Sue. Hardy thus adopts a sexual strategy for distinguishing between interested and disinterested observation—a strategy that is central in the work of James, Conrad, Forster, and other male modernists.

Throughout Hardy's novels, male characters occasionally attain this plane of accurate observation, on condition that they free themselves of desire for the sexually active women they observe. Gabriel Oak spies protectively on Bathsheba's trysts, motivated by his constancy. Diggory Venn, who has put himself outside social and romantic relations entirely, is an accurate, clandestine, almost choral observer of both Eustacia and Thomasin. Never do women observe men in Hardy with the same transcendence of desire at stake.[49] Hardy's narrators implicitly echo this sexually coded objectivity, in a form of detachment that Miller has described as outside of desire and, indeed, "outside of life."[50] To the extent that Hardy intended his novels to represent "a sincere school of Fiction," as opposed to what he called the current "literature of quackery," it is "through a procedure mainly impassive in its tone and tragic in its developments."[51] But Hardy's characteristically tragic or pessimistic vision must be understood in both moral and sexual terms, as a perspective of honest (male) recognition of sexual fatality, which may be focused on the impossible contradictions of dishonest (female) desire, thereby gendering the relation of art to life.

[49] Kristin Brady astutely associates the specular promiscuity of the second Avice with Hardyan representations of hysteria ("Textual Hysteria: Hardy's Narrator on Women," in Higonnet, *Sense of Sex*, pp. 87–106). Though Shires calls attention to the powers of female observation in *Far from the Madding Crowd*, she does not recognize how Bathsheba Everdene's visual powers are figured as masculine and deviant, or how they are framed and corrected by Gabriel Oak's supervision ("Narrative, Gender, and Power," pp. 54–55). Sadoff shows how the erotic gaze of the female in Hardy is always controlled by a logic of masculine desire, in which woman's own desire "wounds" her ("Looking at Tess," pp. 153–54).

[50] Miller, *Thomas Hardy*, p. 7. Mary Jacobus describes Hardy's narrative posture of seeing and speaking as if from beyond the grave ("Hardy's Magian Retrospect," *Essays in Criticism* 32 [1982], 258–79).

[51] Besant et al., "Candour in English Fiction," p. 16.

The real moral hero of the late novels is aesthetic perception. And for Hardy, the honesty of art—which must be achieved through an act of energetic resistance, given the potentials for aesthetic duplicity that I have traced—is constructed mainly through a series of linked negations that are comprehensively figured in observation of the feminine: negations of sexual desire, of lived experience, of social ambition, and even, in a form of ironic doubling, of art itself.[52] This production of artistic honor through sexually coded acts of negation, it should be noted, is an ethical subtext not unique to Hardy but latent in much modernist self-reflexiveness. Proust's affirmation of art in *Remembrance of Things Past*, for example, parallels Hardy's very closely in its sense that all sexual love is deeply treacherous and that desire is subject to a process of temporal decay reversed only through art—Marcel's sense of loss at Albertine's death is the stimulus to his own transcendence of desire through art. The ironic doubling of Joyce's detached authorial consciousness with Stephen Dedalus's sexual obsessions in *A Portrait of the Artist as a Young Man* similarly identifies aesthetic integrity with linked negations of sexual desire, class angst, and female sexuality.[53] It is a short step from this kind of moral purification, achieved over against the feminine, to claims that women writers themselves could not achieve a similar impartiality. William Courtney, a prominent late-century reviewer, expressed this widely shared sentiment in *The Feminine Note in Fiction:*

Recently complaints have been heard that the novel as a work of art is disappearing. . . . [T]he reason is that more and more in our modern age novels are written by women for women. . . . It is the neutrality of the artistic mind which the female novelist seems to find it difficult to

[52] Kevin Z. Moore cites this pattern of aesthetic negation when he defines Hardy's work as "a literature of cancellation" and "a purely specular literature without future returns" (*The Descent of Imagination: Postromantic Culture in the Later Novels of Thomas Hardy* [New York: New York University Press, 1990], pp. 9, 47).

[53] Recent feminist criticism has been deeply divided about Joyce, as Bonnie Kime Scott makes clear in *Joyce and Feminism* (Bloomington: Indiana University Press, 1984), esp. pp. 116–32. But for a classic statement about his negation of female otherness see Florence Howe, "Feminism and Literature," in *Images of Women in Fiction: Feminist Perspectives*, ed. Susan Koppelman Cornillon (Bowling Green, Ohio: Bowling Green University Popular Press, 1972), pp. 263–64.

realize. A greater creator like Shakespeare or Dickens has a wise impartiality towards all his puppets. Sometimes Thackeray shows a personal interest in one rather than another, but he does so at the peril of his own success. If a novelist takes sides, he or she is lost. Then we get a pamphlet, a didactic exercise, a problem novel—never a work of art.[54]

In Hardy's case, the process of aesthetic negation is most visible in the moral progress of Pierston, in whom sustained aesthetic concentration leads finally even to the rejection of art as a career. But all Hardy's late protagonists are affiliated with aesthetic sensibility—though not, pointedly, with artistic vocations—through their emphatically peripheral forms of artistry: Angel's harp-playing and study of musical scores; Jude's stonework, urban model design, interest in music, and creative pastry. More important, all exhibit a kind of immaterial aesthetic perception through their self-negating visionary tendencies. And all aspire ultimately, like Pierston, to move beyond both sexual and social desire, even if there is always a shortfall between their persistent worldly involvements and the narrator's implicitly perfect removal. These equations suggest that, if Hardy had not found sufficient reasons for embitterment in order to justify his rejection of fiction-writing as a professional career, he would probably have had to invent them.

Aesthetic consciousness, once defined as impassive distance—rather than as the production of artistic works themselves—acquires moral authority in Hardy not simply through a naked appropriation of middle-class Victorian standards of honesty, but by making honesty a negative condition. Honesty in Hardy is available only to those who, like artists, are in some sense able to negate the pressures of their desire. Moral authority, then, is representable only as an act of refusal that must oppose and judge the desires of others. The will-to-honesty lies outside any reconciliation between self and others, which is one reason Hardyan honesty relies so much on acts of exclusion and scapegoating. Aesthetic consciousness also surrounds the detached observer in a specific aura of classlessness, by opposing his observation to the worldly involvement he reports in others. In

[54] W. L. Courtney, *The Feminine Note in Fiction* (London: Chapman and Hall, 1904), p. xii.

effect, while Hardy's radical destabilization of honesty makes it possible to subvert the moral authority of middle-class ideals, it allows him to exalt instead the moral authority of those whose class positions appear unresolvable, as a sign of their distance from desire. The fantasy of social indifference this distance involves is played out in Pierston's utter disdain for advantageous matches, as well as in his contempt for commercial success, which parallels Hardy's publicly staged disdain for social standards about art. But all the late protagonists range themselves against the sordidness of social ambition and aspire to escape social classification completely. All aspire as well to the perfect distance from themselves that Hardy claimed to have acquired, perhaps as an enabling condition of his autobiography: he once told his friend Sydney Cockerell that he could "think with almost complete detachment" about his youthful self.[55]

Art's special relationship to honesty, as we have seen, is dynamically, dangerously entwined with the moral ambivalence Hardy identifies with every form of human aspiration. Yet through a process of self-reflexive negation, in which the dishonesty of desire is objectified through clear self-perception, such dishonesty can be distanced or expelled. The resulting contradictoriness about art's ethical status typifies much modernist irony. Such irony allows art to indict art, in a doubling of aesthetic consciousness that establishes moral oppositions even as it contests them. While Hardy appropriates Victorian bourgeois ethics, then, as a crucial device of his cultural authority, he refuses to subscribe to it simplistically, in the name of a more rarefied consciousness of the transgressiveness of all human experience. This transgressiveness forms a limit to bourgeois capabilities for honesty: that is, aesthetic honesty recognizes the impossibility of any worldly honesty. Yet it allows the artist honestly and objectively to represent, from the vantage of an aesthetic distance, the ethical failures of all human activity, even—in some way restricted by irony—of art itself. In this sense, the goal of art is the transmutation of an epidemically transgressive moral universe into detached, purified forms of aesthetic integrity. Hardy's general pessimism, which was loudly rejected by Lawrence, Joyce, Proust, and others, nevertheless conceals a puritanical moral idealism about

---

[55] Quoted from a manuscript by Millgate in *The Life*, p. xi.

aesthetic consciousness which prefigures their own. Such idealism typifies a characteristic paradox of modernist art, in which the apotheosis of Victorian culture's antibourgeois, antitruth-telling sophistication coincides with a desperate return to simpler bourgeois mechanisms of exclusion, which were designed to shore up norms of moral self-righteousness as the justification for aesthetic authority.

For Hardy, the social distinction of aesthetic consciousness is grounded ultimately in the dynamic, performatively "candid" apprehension of both desire and morality, dishonesty and honesty, worldliness and detachment, as well as in the possibilities for the distantiation of dishonesty which this candid apprehension makes available. Unfortunately, such distantiation depends fundamentally on a kind of symbolic scapegoating that uses gender difference, in particular, as an instrument for ethical purification. Hardy's ethical imagination may be complex and contradictory, but it is hardly diffuse. Its chief innovation is the grafting of a traditional middle-class Victorian moral discourse onto the separate cultural authority of aesthetic observation, and the subtle transformation of nineteenth-century standards of honesty—which Victorian culture also identified primarily with men—by focusing them on the detached recognition of their opposite, that is, on the inherent transgressiveness of worldly experience. From a middle-class perspective, it is this appropriation that ought to have seemed scandalous, not Hardy's sexually explicit material itself. From a critical perspective, it is this appropriation that underlies the moral authority of modernist distantiations of both subjectivity and desire, as well as the underlying masculinist current that such aesthetic detachment often sustains.

CHAPTER SIX

Feminism's Ethical Contradictions:
Sarah Grand and New Woman Writing

L ike so many other works of late-century fiction, Sarah Grand's feminist blockbuster *The Heavenly Twins* raises issues of truth-telling in self-consciously contradictory ways. A revealing instance is Angelica Kilroy's apology, after she has perpetrated one of the more bizarre episodes of cross-dressing in English literature. Having disguised herself as her own twin brother to gain the intimacy of a character known as "the tenor," Angelica is unmasked and accused of simply playing a "trick."[1] But even though she had fanned the flames of the tenor's infatuation with the "real" Angelica (the tenor not suspecting that Angelica is, in fact, already married!), Angelica begs him, somewhat fantastically, to believe in her under-lying sincerity. Her meandering self-defense includes a claim that she had faithfully performed her brother's character "in very truth" (4.15.456), as well as an analogy between her principles of veracity and those of the author of a work of fiction. She prefaces her self-justification with a "candid avowal" of her uncontrollable habit of embellishment (the tenor tells her, perhaps overconfidently, "I ought to know your method sufficiently well by this time to enable

---

[1] Sarah Grand, *The Heavenly Twins* (New York: Cassell Publishing, 1893), 4.15.461. Further references are to book, chapter, and page numbers in this edition.

me to sift the wheat from the chaff" [4.15.449]). Most important, Angelica cites an inevitable gap between the purity of moral consciousness and the impurities of human behavior, a formula that resembles what we have seen in Hardy's aestheticization of honesty:

> "I see"—she broke off—"I see all the contradictions that are involved in what I have said and am saying, and yet I mean it all. In separate sections of my consciousness each separate clause exists at this moment, however contradictory, and there is no reconciling them; but there they are. I can't understand it myself, and I don't want you to try. All I ask you is to believe me—to forgive me." (4.15.461)

Angelica's urgent and, in the event, tragic appeals for trust, despite her evident unreliability—like Hardy's authorial honesty about the impossibility of honesty—define a cultural moment in the breakup of Victorian ethical systems, a breakup that plagues both protomodernist and New Woman fiction. In turn-of-the-century writing generally, the socially productive dynamics of Victorian truth-telling and transgression are subjected to a radical deformation. The dynamic interdependence of honesty and dishonesty in mid-Victorian fiction, with its mechanisms for accommodating social order to various kinds of social and sexual desire through legitimated forms of transgression, is fragmented and redeployed in a number of more unstable forms—one of which we saw in Hardy's morally ironic aestheticism. This instability includes both enabling and disenabling features for such writers as Hardy and Grand. But for late-nineteenth-century feminists, uncertainties about truth-telling largely paralyze the development of certain kinds of thought—both ethical and political. A discursive fragmentation lending itself to new kinds of symbolic order in Hardy's work becomes for Grand a sign of feminism's moral confusion and powerlessness, an inability to formulate its own cultural authority in easily comprehensible or effective terms.

Though they are little read and seldom treated with the critical attention they deserve, Grand's novels vividly demonstrate the debilitating fragmentation undergone by Victorian ethics within the early stages of British feminism. Although Grand has been seen as typical of a retrograde emphasis on female virtue among late-century feminists, her moral universe is, in fact, deeply split by uncertainties about the status of truth-telling.[2] New Woman fiction generally, in stark contrast to Hardy's transformation of ethical confusion into a dialectic between art and life, develops catastrophic ethical contradictions by repudiating and embracing the Victorian discourse of truth-telling at the same time. On one level, it dismisses honesty as socially ineffective or as psychologically damaging. On another, it affirms honesty in extreme and increasingly abstract terms as a domain of ideal feminist consciousness, however imperfectly realizable in individual behavior. Yet again, it affirms transgressive lying in the form of a flamboyantly overt performativeness. The elaborate ethical convolutions of characters such as Angelica—which are explicitly presented as instances of moral confusion, not as images of successfully achieved aesthetic distance—reveal a crippling incoherence within late-century feminism. Such incoherence has been obscured by viewing New Woman writing too narrowly in terms of its explicit sexual politics and by taking its moral self-righteousness at face value. In fact, one of the neglected continuities between Victorian and New Woman fiction is the growing struggle among nineteenth-century women writers to locate themselves satisfactorily either within or against discourses of truth-telling. One might say that Sarah Grand tries to build a positive feminist program on the shattered foundations of truth-telling bemoaned by Ellen Wood, although the apprehensions of the earlier writer seem to be confirmed by Grand's tortured, unsuccessful efforts to reconstruct feminine moral ideals around deeply fragmented conceptions of honesty and dishonesty.

Beneath the preoccupation of New Woman fiction with sexual morality, which has led many critics to structure it around the axis of a "purity school" and a "bachelor-girl" (or "neurotic") school, lies an obsession with questions of truthfulness which saturates feminist ideology of the 1890s.[3] Critics have recognized that late-century feminist writers were plagued by numerous contradictions about

[2] Even Grand's contemporary, Hugh E. M. Stutfield, praised her for believing in the "moral and mental perfection of the modern incarnation of the feminine spirit" ("The Psychology of Feminism," *Blackwood's* 161 [1897], 107).

[3] On these two schools, see A. R. Cunningham, "The 'New Woman Fiction' of the 1890's," *Victorian Studies* 17 (1973), 176–86.

gender ideology, which kept them from galvanizing activists as later suffragist writing did.[4] But criticism has not yet recognized how the general ethical dilemmas of late-century culture helped produce, exacerbate, and express those contradictions. Attention to such contradictions can play a positive role in sexual politics, by revising many of the stereotypes that persist about the literary and ethical puritanism of early feminist fiction. It can also forestall critical tendencies to blame New Woman writers for internal contradictions that have a very broad, intractable cultural basis. Separating feminist ethical uncertainty from more general cultural confusions, and seeing it only as the product of flawed feminist theorizing, contributes to the marginalization of New Woman writing. Such writers as Hardy and Grand actually meditate on very similar ethical issues with comparable philosophical rigor and integrity, although Grand was less successful at appropriating late-century ethical instabilities in positive forms.

Hardy and Grand are a useful pair in which to observe the play of late-century ethical confusion, not simply because their work in the 1890s shares the terrain of the New Woman and particularly the cultural debate over candor in relation to female sexuality.[5] They also share other similarities that make the divergent fates of truth-telling in their work even more striking. For example, both writers explore a narrative form that was later central to modernist writing— the semiautobiographical *Kunstlerroman* (Hardy in *The Well-Beloved*, Grand in *The Beth Book*).[6] Both use this form to dramatize the

[4] Joseph Allen Boone discusses the internal contradictions of New Woman thinking about gender identity and monogamy, for example, in *Tradition Counter Tradition: Love and the Form of Fiction* (Chicago: University of Chicago Press, 1987), p. 131.

[5] Grand helped coin the term "New Woman," as recounted by David Rubinstein, *Before the Suffragettes: Women's Emancipation in the 1890s* (Brighton: Harvester Press, 1986), pp. 15–16. Hardy disingenuously claimed to have invented the fictional prototype, in the postscript to *Jude the Obscure*, New Wessex Edition (London: Macmillan, 1974), p. 30.

[6] The aesthetic parallels between these two writers are generally striking, in ways that mitigate the gap that used to be drawn between masculine and feminine fictional camps of the period. Despite her strident defense of traditional notions of realism, Grand's work actually shares much of the interest in formal experimentation usually ascribed to late-century male writing. The most comprehensive reexamination of these debates to date is Ann L. Ardis, *New Women, New Novels: Feminism*

incompatibility between moral consciousness (particularly the distinguished consciousness of the artist or "genius") and ethical behavior. Most important from the perspective of a history of literary ethics, both ambiguously repudiate (or have their fictional spokespersons repudiate) art itself as a form of "untruth."[7] This attack on the ethical truthfulness of art is a gesture that later modernism incorporates as a crucial form of ironic self-awareness. But in Grand's work, the emphasis falls slightly differently. Rather than anticipating an ironic aesthetics, Grand tries to engineer an ironic feminism. That is to say, she tries to construct a feminism that is willing to finesse questions of veracity fluidly, without entirely resolving them. Nevertheless, the dismantling and reassemblage of Victorian notions about honesty are fundamental to both enterprises, and these processes form the basis for one of the central projects of cultural modernity: a search for post-Victorian ethical models that might sublimate or rarefy issues of truth-telling.

Both Hardy and Grand also define themselves explicitly as iconoclasts in relation to Victorian culture, and their iconoclasm depends in large part on charting the discursive breakup of Victorian sincerity. Both diagnose and repudiate what they see as oppressive features of Victorian honesty, associating moral strictness about truth-telling with a repressive cultural past. Both demonstrate, as well, how controlled transgressions against norms of honesty—of the kinds I have explored in preceding chapters—are available but no longer consistent means to what I have called social "exceptionality," given

---

and Early Modernism (New Brunswick, N.J.: Rutgers University Press, 1990). See also Linda Dowling's pathbreaking essay, "The Decadent and the New Woman in the 1890's," *Nineteenth-Century Fiction* 33 (1979), 434–53. The conventional view, formulated by, among others, Elaine Showalter (*A Literature of Their Own: British Women Novelists from Brontë to Lessing* [Princeton: Princeton University Press, 1977], p. 193), is that New Woman novelists were too activist and polemical to be interested in aesthetics and that they grounded themselves instead in an antiquated didactic realism.

[7] Certainly, some of these concerns underlay Grand's acknowledgement of her debt to Hardy. See Gillian Kersley, *Darling Madame: Sarah Grand and Devoted Friend* (London: Virago, 1983), p. 74. Hardy, in his turn, may have been snide about the quality of Grand's fiction, but he deeply respected her for the candor and integrity of her work. In a letter to Florence Henniker, he wrote, "having decided to offend her friends (so she told me) . . . she can write boldly, & get listened to" (*The Collected Letters of Thomas Hardy*, ed. Richard Little Purdy and Michael Millgate, 7 vols. [Oxford: Clarendon Press, 1978–88], 16 September 1893, 2:33).

the loss of symbolic coherence around questions of truth-telling. Angelica's "prank" with the tenor, for instance, frustrates comic expectations that the novel had developed in relation to the peccadilloes of the twins, leading not to moral sophistication but instead to a dual fatality: the tenor's death and Angelica's lapse back into conventional marital obscurity. Moreover, both writers self-consciously explore the ethical inconsistencies of their own fiction and validate them as signs of a transitional age. Inconclusiveness about honesty becomes an overt theme for Hardy and Grand, an explicit attempt to define cultural liminality. The interdependence of honesty and dishonesty becomes a fictional subject, rather than an operative cultural logic, and this interdependence is presented as urgently, even apocalyptically, problematic.

At the same time, both novelists also appropriate and even inflate vestigial Victorian moral distinctions in order to ground social hierarchies on the terrain of honesty—Hardy, as we have seen, to serve the authority of the disinterested (male) writer; Grand, to bolster that of the feminist. The breakup of Victorian notions about honesty generates new discursive and ideological opportunities for each writer. For Grand, and for feminism generally, fragments of that discourse occasionally even justify willful "dissembling" with gendered cultural signs, a dissimulation that is presented—however provisionally—as a form of moral sophistication. Although New Woman novelists—and Grand in particular, who has been relegated exclusively to the "purity school"—are commonly thought to have endorsed a conservative view of female "nature," Grand actually justifies a new permissiveness about the tactical manipulation of representations of the feminine, a permissiveness that depends, somewhat archaically, on revoking the cultural cachet of honesty.[8] In this sense, Grand plays a role in an early stage of the long-standing twentieth-century opposition between essentialist and

[8] The reduction of Grand to the "purity school" is maintained by Ardis, *New Women, New Novels*, p. 93; Showalter, *A Literature of Their Own*, p. 183; Gail Cunningham, *The New Woman and the Victorian Novel* (London: Macmillan, 1978), p. 57; A. R. Cunningham, " 'New Woman Fiction,' " pp. 180–82; and Barbara Caine, *Victorian Feminists* (Oxford: Oxford University Press, 1992), p. 253. Ardis does discuss the "antinaturalism" of what she sees as a minor strain in New Woman fiction (pp. 98–114), but she does not include Grand in this category, nor does she discuss the "antinaturalism" of New Woman performativity.

nonessentialist feminisms.[9] In the 1890s, this opposition was constructed largely around moral categories—a significant point of origin that has been omitted from histories of the debate over essentialism.[10] That is to say, the question Grand brings to the foreground of her work is this: when are women justified in "dishonestly" defying received ideas about female nature through various kinds of deceptive self-invention and performative artifice?

Formulating the question with this Victorian moral emphasis, however, means that Grand's work is haunted by her inability to escape or control ethical confusions about female "nature." Rebellious, self-inventing women in her novels—such as Angelica—are often critiqued in strict moral terms as deceivers, which reinscribes them in Victorian clichés about ingrained female mendacity. Their failed rebellions are understood as the result of a fatal contest between sincerity and insincerity. This conflation of ethics with gender politics contributes, symptomatically, to Grand's Ruskinian defense of traditional marriage, which she saw primarily as an issue of honor. In an approving review of Elizabeth Rachel Chapman's *Marriage Questions in Modern Fiction*, for instance, Grand highlighted Chapman's argument against sexual freedom as a form of deceitfulness: "We should diligently nurture the growing opinion which ranks unchastity *in either sex* with the anti-social and contemptible vices, such as theft, or fraud, or cowardice, or falsehood. Then, having trained our children, especially, in this opinion, we should, I venture to think, educate them together, and generally promote more *camaraderie* and freer intercourse between youths and maidens thus prepared to enjoy each other's society in honesty and honour."[11] The equation of monogamy with honesty was widespread in New Woman writing. Eleanor Marx and Edward Aveling, in *The Woman*

---

[9] In the context of George Egerton's work, Lyn Pykett points out that New Woman novelists often alternated between presentations of a "real self" and performance of a staged female selfhood (*The Improper Feminine: The Women's Sensation Novel and the New Woman Writing* [London: Routledge, 1992], p. 173).

[10] Perhaps the most thorough of these overviews is Ann Snitow, "A Gender Diary," in *Conflicts in Feminism*, ed. Marianne Hirsch and Evelyn Fox Keller (New York: Routledge, 1990), pp. 9–43.

[11] Quoted in Sarah Grand, "Marriage Questions in Fiction," *Fortnightly Review* 375 (1898), 387. In "The New Woman and the Old," *Lady's Realm* 4 (1898), 470, Grand defines monogamy as a matter of being "loyal," and exercising "sincerity" as well as a sense of "fair play."

Question, drew a similar parallel: in their elaborate defense of fidelity, the "two great curses that . . . ruin the relation between man and woman" are said to be "the treatment of men and women as different beings" and "the want of truth." Marx and Aveling saw monogamy as an escape from "the hideous disguise, the constant lying, that makes the domestic life of almost all our English homes an organized hypocrisy."[12] A typical convolution of this equation is articulated by the narrator of George Egerton's "A Cross Line," who claims that monogamy makes a woman "an unconscious liar," given the "untamed primitive savage temperament that lurks in the mildest, best woman," but that adultery is inconceivable because "it is not loyal."[13] The free-thinking heroine of Olive Schreiner's *The Story of an African Farm* is less sanguine about these distinctions, finding that her sexual freedom is in fatal conflict with her conscience because it forces her to deceive: "I hate lies. I tell them if I must, but they hurt me," she says.[14] Unfortunately, the equation of monogamy and honesty, meant to be a stabilizing one in the absence of traditional ideals of female chastity, disguises the explosive potential of the discourse of truth-telling itself in feminist writing. In this sense, the incomplete political commitments of a writer such as Grand need to be understood as the result, not simply of a moderate or transitional ideological stance, but of the capacity for fragmented Victorian notions about sincerity and its opposites—reserve, secrecy, masquerade—to disrupt and confuse questions of sexual oppression.

What Grand shows us, then, is how the unraveling discourse of Victorian honesty is refracted—disastrously—through late-century feminist activism. The entrance of women into political activism necessarily created a tension between traditional ideals of personal sincerity and new feminist attitudes toward the performative nature

[12] Eleanor Marx and Edward Aveling, *The Woman Question* (London: Swan, Sonnenschein, Lowry, 1887), p. 16. See Showalter's comments in *Sexual Anarchy: Gender and Culture at the Fin de Siècle* (Harmondsworth: Penguin, 1990), p. 54.

[13] George Egerton, "A Cross Line," in *Keynotes* (Boston: Roberts Bros., 1893), pp. 30–32. Similarly, Mona Caird, though arguing strenuously for women's liberation from the marriage contract, does so only in order to make possible a new basis for "honourable union," one that is to be based on "private contract" and will herald a "moral renaissance" (*The Morality of Marriage and Other Essays on the Status and Destiny of Woman* [London: George Redway, 1897], pp. 58, 110).

[14] Olive Schreiner, *The Story of an African Farm* (London: Virago, 1989), p. 217.

of public roles, which only exacerbated general cultural uncertainties about candor. New Woman writers often address this intersection of the personal and the political by foregrounding in their work an unresolved debate about principles of honesty—a debate that ultimately victimized the New Woman novelists themselves. Their inability to negotiate widespread late-century ethical confusions by withdrawing into disinterested specularity, as Hardy and other protomodernists did, has much to do with the noted absence of successful women writers during this period. While the protomodernists managed, more or less efficiently, to identify aesthetic honesty with a detached perspective on moral entanglements—that is, with the kind of Hardyan self-distantiation Angelica gropes for, unsuccessfully—the more confused assemblage of both candor and performativity in New Woman fiction was vulnerable to a double attack. On the one hand, even from the perspective of the anticensorship movement of the 1890s, New Woman honesty about sex was seen as excessive—a reduction of art to polemic, and therefore a violation of the disinterest necessary to artistic truth-telling.[15] James Ashcroft Noble, in an important attack on the "erotomania" of New Woman fiction, objected that microscopic attention to one narrow aspect of human life was a misguided stab at realism: "Is it even a clear, truthful seeing of that part of life which it unnaturally isolates?"[16] Arthur Waugh attacked the excesses of feminist frankness for producing an "age of effeminacy," which he contrasted to the moral superiority of male artists who attempt to view life as an "impartial spectator," a viewpoint that understands the moral and aesthetic importance of reticence.[17] On the other hand, the New Woman writers' performativity encouraged later feminist critics to accuse them of having indulged deluded and even hypocritical fantasies. Elaine Showalter writes, "Given the freedom to explore their experience, they rejected it, or at least tried to deny it. The private rooms

[15] For a good discussion of the links between New Woman fiction and attacks on censorship launched by George Meredith, George Moore, Hardy, George Gissing, and others, see Gail Cunningham, *New Woman and Victorian Novel*, pp. 45–79.

[16] James Ashcroft Noble, "The Fiction of Sexuality," *Contemporary Review* 67 (1895), 493. Noble complained in particular about *The Heavenly Twins*, calling it "a flagrant violation of the obvious proportion of life."

[17] Arthur Waugh, "Reticence in Literature," *Yellow Book* 1 (1894), 212, 210. See also Stutfield, "Psychology of Feminism," pp. 116–17.

that symbolize their professionalism and autonomy are fantastic sanctuaries, closely linked to their own defensive womanhood."[18] The absence of "great" women writers in the 1890s is not something that happened "quite accidentally," as Patricia Stubbs has notoriously put it, nor was it entirely because New Woman writers were too polemical or too pessimistic, nor was it purely the result of a professional battle over the marketplace.[19] A fundamental cause of this gap is late-century feminism's inability to resolve questions of truthfulness in both personal and aesthetic domains, a failure that prevented it from achieving a moral foundation within fiction, or a satisfactory relationship to the changing moral status of the aesthetic itself in early modernist culture.

To trace the diffusion of Victorian truth-telling in Grand's work, and the various stalemates it generated within feminism, I focus primarily on her enormous popular success, *The Heavenly Twins*, and to a lesser extent on her experiment in aesthetic self-fashioning, *The Beth Book*, as well as the first novel of this trilogy, *Ideala*. Though I often read these three novels as pieces of the same ethical puzzle, it is important to see *The Beth Book* as a failed attempt to resolve some of the ethical inconsistencies that the earlier works indulge less self-critically. Consequently, in the final section of this chapter I address *The Beth Book*'s instructively inadequate moral synthesis.

Angelica and Diavolo are not the only "heavenly twins" of Grand's most famous novel. The plot is also structured around the opposition

---

[18] Showalter, *A Literature of Their Own*, p. 215. Showalter speaks with disdain of a feminism that saw itself as "cosmically grandiose" (p. 183), when in her view it merely extended concepts of innate female virtue. In the process, according to Showalter, New Woman writing misrepresented feminine sexuality by sublimating it into maternity, which "stripped it of all its less acceptable associations" (p. 187), and by indulging in other "naive" fantasies (p. 192).

[19] Patricia Stubbs, *Women and Fiction: Feminism and the Novel, 1880–1920* (New York: Barnes and Noble, 1979), p. 120. Showalter objects to the fiction's propagandistic narrowness, *A Literature of Their Own*, p. 193. Many critics have faulted the novels for gloominess, including Gail Cunningham, *New Woman and Victorian Novel*, p. 49; and David Rubinstein, *Before the Suffragettes*, p. 26. On late-century marketplace conflicts among writers, see Gaye Tuchman, *Edging Women Out: Victorian Novelists, Publishers, and Social Change* (New Haven: Yale University Press, 1989).

of two competing models of "angelic" womanhood: an old-fashioned moral ideal represented by Evadne and a new, morally self-inventing womanhood represented by Angelica. In a sense, the "purity school" meets the "bachelor-girl school" in the novel's twinned heroines. These opposing models of virtue center the novel on an implicit debate between Evadne's extended Victorian commitments to truth-telling and Angelica's cavalier explorations of performance, disguise, and fabrication. Although the two women's moral experiences ulti-mately converge in disturbing ways, discrediting old and new ethical alternatives together by having them both lead to disease and death, they are polarized at first as equally admirable forms of moral resistance.

Evadne, known for being "fearlessly upright and honest" (6.11.619) and "almost peculiarly frank" (6.14.640), transforms Victorian candor, usually identified with men, into a feminist weapon. In this way, she represents the moral strategy of earlier Victorian writers, such as Ellen Wood, to reconstruct feminine moral ideals along the lines of traditionally male standards of truth-telling. From a very early age, Evadne insists on knowledge at all costs, and her diligent, plainspoken pursuit of it allows her to expose various kinds of hypocrisy. These range from the invidious social conspiracy of disinformation that plagues all marriageable young women to the petty slandering of an innocent couple at Malta. Angelica's moral status, by contrast, is marked by an unpredictable destabilization of standards for honesty, which is much more in tune with late-century moral sensibilities. Although she and her twin brother are fiercely loyal to each other and are noted for their scrupulous adherence to promises, neither has any compunction about subverting standards of truthfulness—whether for the pursuit of a higher moral good or simply for the sake of mischief. The twins defend the opening of others' letters, for example, by claiming that snooping is justified if it leads to knowledge. They cleverly trick their tutor about their respective intellectual abilities in order to secure a nongendered education for themselves. Their tricks and pranks are often intended to flush out the hypocrisy of others, although the twins deeply value what they call "talking it out" (1.19.128) between themselves. But the twins' willingness to violate the truth also has a life of its own, which verges away from principled uses toward random devilry: they tell fibs to commandeer a hansom cab for a wild ride in London; they mislead their hosts to get a double serving of cake. There is, at times, a decadent aesthetic cast to this taste for deception: the twins are amused, rather than dismayed, when they find their own parents have tricked them in order to get away for a year, and they contemplate their parents' strategy with detached, connoisseur-like appreciation.

The twins have, of course, unmistakably moral dispositions that are perfectly apparent to the more perceptive and sympathetic characters of the novel, who strongly approve of them. Their innate moral intelligence suggests that the twins are not so much in rebellion against morality itself as deliberately remaking and redefining its terms. During the course of her bizarre religious dream, Angelica dismisses the pope and his assembled bishops by telling them, "We're very busy in here, and you disturb us. We're revising the moral laws" (3.8.295). The narrator sums up the twins' moral creativity about truth-telling by noting that "they made a point of keeping their word, but in their own way" (1.6.30). Nevertheless, the new moral principles the twins seem to be heralding are never precisely defined. The enigmatic status of the twins' conception of honor, as well as its occasional abandonment, suggests a moral code that is still evolving, that is constantly being improvised: "The Heavenly Twins never worked on any regular plan; their ideas always came to them as they went on" (3.10.303). When Angelica accounts for her adventure with the tenor, she makes a similar claim: "I had no object. I am inventing one now because you ask me" (4.15.449). It seems crucial, however, that the heavenly twins' moral extemporaneousness should reject any stable relationship to features of conventional morality, particularly truth-telling. Angelica presents herself as the vanguard of a new morality precisely by refusing to adhere to traditional standards of honesty: "I don't see why I should be severely consistent," she says; "Let me be a mixture—not a foul mixture, but one of those that eventually result in something agreeable" (5.2.482).

The opposition between truth-telling and its destabilization in the novel's double plot reinforces and expresses late-century feminist dilemmas of various kinds. For instance, in Evadne and the twins' moral opposition, sociological and scientific feminism conflict with literary feminism: Evadne rejects literature in general (and several classics in particular) as being untrue to life, morally dubious, and systematically misogynist, whereas the twins read voraciously, improvise theatricals, and display the kind of inventive powers that culminate in Angelica's "romance" (5.2.479) with the tenor (which she converts into a narrative that her husband takes to be fictional). Formally, the two plots of *The Heavenly Twins* juxtapose seriousness and comedy, moral purpose and entertainment, linear plotting and narrative disjunction, in ways that raise questions about the proper form of political art (Grand called the twins' plot a sugarcoating to help the medicine of the other story go down—though this formula seems far too glib).[20] That both women's stories end bleakly and inconclusively is a sign that, despite her evident admiration for the kinds of resistance modeled by both Evadne and Angelica, Grand wished to problematize both strict honesty and its abdication as alternative moral ideals for feminist art. In this way, Grand fractures the widespread convention of Victorian narrative which defines moral distinctions by opposing honest and dishonest female protagonists—Amelia Sedley and Becky Sharp, Dinah Morris and Hetty Sorrel, Agnes Wickfield and Rosa Dartle, Lucy Morris and Lizzie Eustace.[21] Instead, she suspends the moral hierarchy that this standard opposition is meant to serve. But Grand's moral ambivalence is hardly a liberating iconoclasm, since it keeps her from resolving the questions about realism and fantasy, scientific knowledge and literary artifice, which her twin protagonists raise. Rather than distancing moral ambivalence as Hardy does, Grand's narrative remains constrained to an already disrupted ethical field, leaving her to vacillate inconclusively about the political and literary choices she has filtered through ethical conflicts. This kind of irresolution helps her instead to inaugurate a popular twentieth-century feminist narrative form in which dual protagonists model equally unsatisfactory choices—a dialectic in search of synthesis, and, thus, a bleak variation on the twin-heroine format that had been a staple of feminist fiction since the eighteenth century. While criticism of the 1990s has been eager

---

[20] Grand claimed that she added the twins to the novel "so that it would be mistaken for a bonbon and swallowed without a suspicion of its medicinal properties," in the foreword to *The Heavenly Twins* (London: Heinemann, 1923), p. ix.

[21] See Alexander Welsh, *The City of Dickens* (Oxford: Clarendon Press, 1971), p. 169, on the prevalence of this pattern.

to validate the disjunctive form of the female *Bildungsroman*, Grand's double plot generates counternarratives that are self-cancelling— both overtly, in their thematics of failure, and in terms of the symbolic structures they define.[22]

Grand's dissatisfaction with Evadne's standards of truth-telling— with the rigidities of "this straightforward nineteenth century young woman" (3.12.322)—is an important counterpoint to the fiasco of Angelica and the tenor, and it needs to be unraveled in some detail. As is the case for many of the honorable women in Wood's *East Lynne*, Evadne's experience ironically demonstrates nothing so much as the importance of a healthy reticence and distrust. Grand's critique of Victorian honesty, like Wood's, begins in a perception that Victorian standards of sincerity are incapacitating—although this failure is presented far less nostalgically in the later novel. Evadne's saving characteristic—a trait that Lady Isabel tragically lacked—is her instinctive, but strangely nonantagonistic, suspicion of others.[23] As a child, Evadne is characterized by a systematic distrust of authority, particularly of her father's opinions, and she believes nothing that she is not able to test empirically. Noting her capacity to hold her own contentious conclusions in reserve, how-ever, the narrator acknowledges a seeming inconsistency in her character: while questioning her father's patriarchal opinions, Evadne oddly retains her love, respect, and dependence on him. Her father "often contradicted himself, and the fact never escaped her attention, but she loved him with a beautiful confidence, and her respect remained unshaken" (1.1.6). Evadne's deep instincts for trust and honesty correspond to a dangerous passivity in her charac-ter, which is balanced only in some precarious, dissociated way by her intellectual and moral skepticism. The dissociation itself, while symptomatic of Grand's own inability to synthesize honor with suspicion, ultimately leads to a psychological crisis from which Evadne never fully recovers, and to her custodial marriage with Dr.

---

[22] For example, Susan Fraiman generalizes that the multivalent narrative lines in the female novel of development offer progressive feminist possibilities (*Unbecoming Women: British Women Writers and the Novel of Development* [New York: Columbia University Press, 1992]).

[23] Grand's advice to young women about courtship revolved obsessively around the need to be on one's guard against deceptive male appearances. See, for example, Sarah Grand, "On the Choice of a Husband," *Young Woman* 7 (October 1898), 1–3.

Galbraith. In *The Beth Book*, one sign of this same dissociation is that the necessity of suspicion is a lesson that Beth is repeatedly said to learn for the first time.

The premium that *The Heavenly Twins* places on suspicion extends beyond Evadne's particular differences with her father and with other men, acquiring a genuinely paranoid dimension that grotesquely parodies Victorian fearfulness about women's vulnerability. The novel's paranoia, in contrast to the more desultory suspiciousness of *East Lynne*, sees women as the sole and permanent victims of social fraud. Its central theme, of course, is the danger of women's infection from syphilis—a danger that is systematically concealed from them, and that requires an active vigilance about their prospective partners. It is certainly true that the issue of syphilis was a pressing one among 1890s feminists, as fears that syphilis had become rampant drove feminist calls for male chastity and for the public availability of information about the disease. Even though Grand's formulation of the problem sometimes confined itself to earlier frameworks of debate associated with the Contagious Diseases Acts (abolished in 1886), her novels, along with notorious works by Emma Frances Brooke and George Egerton which followed *The Heavenly Twins*, fueled the "social purity" movement so interwoven with suffrage a decade later.[24] Nevertheless, the theme of contagion in *The Heavenly Twins* extends well beyond physical disease to include intellectual and moral contamination as well. Throughout the novel, Edith, Evadne, Mrs. Malcomson, and Mrs. Orton Beg complain about the debilitating influence of close contact with morally or intellectually degenerate men. In *The Beth Book*, Grand makes this problem central to female self-development by documenting the various defects of character Beth's "genius" owes to the influence of men. In numerous essays, too, Grand complained about what she saw as the social conspiracy to impose upon women and the consequent necessity for women to live in a perpetual state of distrust: a woman must, she wrote, "be for ever on guard against

[24] See Kersley, *Darling Madame*, p. 8. To put the timeliness of Grand's work in perspective, it should be remembered that Ibsen's *Ghosts* was banned in 1889 simply for referring to venereal disease. Nevertheless, several reviewers objected to what they saw as Grand's anachronistic passion in relation to the Contagious Diseases Acts. See, for example, *Nation* 57 (1893), p. 374.

fraud and deceit; her life is one long look-out! And this, of all her trials, is the most warping, the hardest to bear."[25]

At times in *The Heavenly Twins*, the metaphor of contamination is applied so universally that it seems to empty feminism itself of any claim to moral purity. Feminism is often spoken of by the novel's misogynists as a kind of creeping disease. Lord Groome complains that when women "begin to have ideas they spread them everywhere, and all the other women in the neighbourhood catch them, and are spoiled by them" (2.13.230). The novel's odd equations between feminism and disease, rather than being a simple satire of antifeminists, are intended to cast a certain kind of feminist rebellion as a holy scourge—an avenging force that is morally implicated in the corrosive evils it destroys. This suggestion is made very clearly about Angelica's improvised ethical and feminist principles: while Edith Beale goes mad with syphilis, Angelica swells with rage against men and catches a dementia of a different kind: "All this filth will breed a pestilence . . . and I shouldn't be surprised if that pestilence were ME!" (3.8.296). Fittingly, Angelica begins her career as holy scourge by carrying out Edith's diseased, murderous impulses, breaking Mosley Menteith's phallic nose with a Bible. Angelica's impressive vitality, however problematic, suggests that male moral decadence might be fought not simply with Evadne's brand of moral righteousness, but with a kind of counterdecadence, free of conventional ethical norms. Grand's tendency to conceive feminist scourges like Angelica in terms of dishonesty may have deeply constrained her ability to embrace them. Nevertheless, Angelica's pestilential self-awareness explores the possibility that feminism might see itself as demonic and transgressive, rather than as simply congruent with the Victorian moral ideas embodied by Evadne.

Grand and other New Woman writers were not simply interested in transposing Victorian ideals of the sacred mission of womanhood into an activist key, despite critical stereotypes to the contrary.[26]

---

[25] Sarah Grand, "The Case of the Modern Spinster," *Pall Mall Magazine* 51 (1913), 55. Such complaints were a theme of early nineteenth-century conduct books as well, but they take on inflated dimensions in Grand's work.

[26] Showalter argues this position in *A Literature of Their Own*, p. 184. In general, Showalter's dismissive reading claims that New Woman novelists dreamed of "withdrawing from the world" to "find a higher female truth" (p. 215).

The Heavenly Twins strenuously critiques the passivity of Victorian moral idealism through the fates of Evadne and Edith. Edith's simple faith in others, which causes her to accept the syphilitic Mosley Menteith as her husband, shows how excessive trust can be suicidal. And Evadne's own unfortunate marriage—though placed on a new footing by her penchant for finding things out for herself—is also the result of her unwarranted confidence in her family. Repeating Lady Isabel's tragedy in newly militant terms, Grand shows how a woman's trust can imprison her in a relationship with a morally degenerate man. Evadne's strange susceptibility to promises (such as the promise to her husband that she will not join the women's movement) also suggests that, in this climate of persecution, female honesty is driven to extremes of purity which make it a monstrous caricature of Victorian norms. *The Heavenly Twins* parts company with *East Lynne* in its insistence on the repressive extremism latent in ideals of feminine honesty. Evadne's outsized earnestness is found discomfiting by a number of characters, including the twins themselves, who enjoy her company only because she is so easy to shock. Evadne's moral rigidity is a general one: her censorious dismissal of literature carries an ambiguous charge, and her eugenic view of vice reflects a popular, puritanical feminist view that the novel explicitly refutes through Angelica—who is not at all bound by the ancestral vices that she often frets over ("Well, I exaggerate," Angelica ultimately admits about these fears [5.7.536]). Evadne's idealism illustrates the debilitating repression that Victorian standards for sincerity demand.

In its most important departure from *East Lynne*'s nostalgia for ideals of feminine truth, Grand's novel demonstrates how feminine honesty, driven to extremes of self-defense, is actually compelled to become its opposite, to devolve into a performative caricature of itself. Evadne's moral purity, too strict for compromises, forces her to adopt a set of masks, beginning with a reserve before her father and culminating in a sham marriage to Colquhoun. Evadne's duplicity begins at a very early age, when she adopts the "trick" of "veil[ing] the penetration" of her gaze (1.6.32), and Colquhoun often complains that he had been misled by her manner into thinking she was docile and conventional—"you have played me a—ah—*very* nasty trick" (3.14.341), he later tells her. Dr. Galbraith notes that there is something unhealthily "artificial" (6.1.556) about Evadne, and the observation is borne out by the mental collapse that her sense of honor ultimately provokes.

The etiology of Evadne's illness is presented by the novel in several ways, all of which help to undermine her moral identity. From one perspective, Evadne's masks, however repressive and dissociative, turn out to have been integral supports for her sanity. When Colquhoun dies and the necessity for her masquerade is lifted, Evadne loses her sense of self and begins to degenerate—as if her commitment to truthfulness depends on the ability to reserve herself, to preserve a certain boundary between her inward honor and the corrupting conditions of the world. From another perspective, her repression degenerates into a hysteria that the novel defines as ambiguously performative. For Dr. Galbraith, at least, Evadne's hysteria makes her a mysterious object that he must uncover, a "text" (5.3.566) whose truth always eludes him (as it had eluded Colquhoun). Galbraith's scrutiny of Evadne's hysteria follows all the classic patterns of late-century psychoanalytic colonization of the feminine—at one point, he even compares his observation of Evadne to the exploration of a cave. But Galbraith's sense of the hysteric as a performer, although treated with subtle narrative ironies, is unchallenged from within the world of the novel itself, and his professional observations even gain a certain credibility through his steadfast support of feminist issues and social groups. Galbraith's lengthy discussion of hysteria during a fashionable dinner party revolves around hysteria's affinities with shamming. The story he tells of a former patient who admits having feigned hysteria gains significance when Evadne herself points out that the patient was shamming illness in order to gain his love. Galbraith's attitudes reflect a widespread sense in late-century psychiatric circles, absorbed uncritically by Grand, that hysterics were manipulatively performative. S. Weir Mitchell's work, for example, repeatedly insists that practitioners need to dominate the hysteric to constrain her performativeness. In France, the debate over the relationship between hypnosis and hysteria focused very much on the performative aspects of hysteria—particularly Charcot's claims that susceptibility to hypnosis (and thus to certain kinds of hypnotic performance) was a sign of incipient hysteria or a disposition to hysteria.[27]

In Evadne's case, hysteria is represented as the debilitating mask that must be "cured" and removed through psychiatric confession—the telling of the truth about the self. Yet the ending of the novel makes it clear that Evadne's therapeutic self-confessions are always incomplete and unreliable—both because complete confession would coincide with complete submission to the doctor, and thus, in a sense, with Evadne's death, and because her confessions always seem to be a performance of her inescapable hysteria, which leaves them maddeningly circular. In Evadne's illness, honesty and insincerity become blurrily related, a confusion that, among other things, marks the novel's attempt to exit from Victorian ethical idealism about truth-telling.

The relation between Evadne's honesty and loss of identity—her decline into an unreadable, masklike illness—only confirms certain advantages in Angelica's more extemporaneous behavior. The novel gradually makes it clear that all identity is in some important moral sense a mask. That is to say, Grand shares the doubts about the epistemology of self and sincerity which are readily found throughout late-century fiction, including Hardy's, anticipating contemporary arguments that "identity politics" itself is always already a form of performance.[28] If Evadne's honesty and her hysteria are presented as masks, so is Angelica's histrionic rebellion, as well as her later acceptance of the role of the model wife. All conceivable female roles are presented by the novel as performative ones. For a feminist such as Grand, deeply committed to the principle that women can be empowered through access to empirical knowledge, this perception leads in ambiguous directions. But it suggests, at least, a degree

[27] Charcot's discussion of hysteria and hypnosis runs throughout Jean-Martin Charcot, *Lectures on the Diseases of the Nervous System*, trans. Thomas Saville, 3 vols. (London: New Sydenham Society, 1889). Weir Mitchell's novels often revolve around the domination of hysterics by physicians. See also S. Weir Mitchell, *Lectures on Diseases of the Nervous System, Especially in Women* (Philadelphia: Lea Brothers, 1885).

[28] On this problem, see Diana Fuss, *Essentially Speaking: Feminism, Nature, and Difference* (New York: Routledge, 1989).

of epistemological sophistication in New Woman feminism which is usually ignored by those who categorize it simply as a form of late-century naturalism.

If Evadne allows her identity to be constructed by a man (which may not necessarily be a catastrophe, given Galbraith's charter membership in the feminist society that flits through the background of the novel), then Angelica mobilizes energies of self-construction through a deliberate project of fraud and fabrication which Grand tentatively enshrines as the progressive counterpoint to earnestness.[29] Through her cross-dressed self-invention before the tenor, in particular, Angelica achieves a view of the world as seen by men, an intimacy with a man not limited by bias about gender, and, most important, a new assertiveness made possible by the mixture of sincerity and artifice. Grand's evaluation of Angelica may ultimately be limited by her sense of self-construction as a form of lying. Angelica's plot does pivot, at least superficially, around her renunciation of artifice and her conversion to truth-telling—Angelica's relationship with the tenor shows that, because the effects of both performance and moral experimentation cannot be controlled, falsehood can kill. Lady Fulda passes this judgment explicitly: "You had not chosen *honestly*. . . . You wanted to bring yourself nearer to him" (5.7.538). Nevertheless, assigning this moral valence to feminist performance also allows Grand to think in productive new ways about the antirealist potentials of representation in feminism, however Angelica's individual failures might be understood.

In Grand's journalistic writing, she returns again and again to the necessity for feminists to craft appearances for strategic purposes—to sugarcoat the feminist pill, and more. Symptomatically, Grand's first involvement with the suffrage movement grew from her prior engagement with the Rational Dress Society. And with particular emphasis, Grand urged late-century feminists to transcend the dowdy earnestness of their predecessors—along with the cultural

---

[29] See the affirmative reading of Angelica's performative strategies of empowerment in Sandra Gilbert and Susan Gubar, *No Man's Land: The Place of the Woman Writer in the Twentieth Century, Vol. II: Sexchanges* (New Haven: Yale University Press, 1989), pp. 347–48. But Grand's ambivalence—her view of Angelica as a warning against the anarchy of experimentalism—is teased out convincingly by Dowling, in "Decadent and New Woman," p. 439.

clichés that earnestness had inspired: "When you describe a woman as earnest, ninety-nine people out of a hundred will immediately conclude that she is also a fright. And in this way earnestness is discredited. . . . Then consider: is it dishonorable to be prepossessing in manner and appearance?"[30] Her emphasis on the usefulness of cultivated charm is openly at odds with the emphasis on candor with which New Woman fiction is always identified, and it led to occasionally strained compromises between sincerity and tactics: "By being inelegant, an earnest woman frustrates her own ends," Grand claimed.[31]

Grand's crusade against naive, direct self-expression took its strongest form as a rather obsessive call—typical of many New Woman writers—for women to take care with their physical appearance. In one sense, this crusade was simply a politically savvy attempt to deflect attacks on feminists by encouraging women to appear conventionally feminine:

> We women would have had the suffrage long ago had not, unfortunately, some of the first fighters for it—some of the strong ones—been unprepossessing women. . . . These two or three were held up everywhere as an awful warning of what the whole sex would become if it got the suffrage . . . "A lot of old harridans seeking notoriety. If you just saw them! their dress! their manners! If women are to look like that when they get the suffrage, then defend me from it." This idea is the origin of the rooted objection which many people who would otherwise have sympathized with us have to the suffrage.[32]

Gillian Kersley comments usefully on the "poetic poses" Grand habitually struck for photographers, and on her deliberate attempt to cultivate a "delicate and dumb" look—that is, to aspire to traditional ideals of feminine prettiness.[33] An acquaintance commented on Grand's dexterity with appearance, in the light of several photographic portraits: "Each picture might have represented a different person. In some she looked fifty years of age, in others she

[30] Sarah Grand, "The Morals of Manner and Appearance," *Humanitarian* 3 (1893), 89.

[31] Ibid.

[32] Ibid., pp. 92–93.

[33] Kersley, *Darling Madame*, pp. 79–80.

did not appear to be more than twenty, yet all had been taken within the last two years."[34]

Another component of Grand's crusade for appearances, however, was her attempt to blend Victorian ideals of feminine beauty and reserve with a model of traditional upper-class behavior that depended on the social authority of the mask—a cultivated and principled sense of deference. In this way, Grand's concern that women refine their manner and appearance was an attempt to empower women by appropriating an outmoded but still resonant upper-class code of performativeness. The class-coding of this performative model thus functioned to counter attacks on the supposed vulgarity of the New Woman, as well as to negate old-fashioned stereotypes of innate and debasing feminine deceit.[35] Though she often rebuked contemporary women for being too assertive, seeming to play into the hands of the antifeminists, Grand's strategy was to encourage women to combine their powers of self-assertion with the refined manners that would make for a recognizably upper-class display of social authority: women need to be "both refined and independent," she argued.[36] In some cases, Grand makes the connection between the mask and aristocratic bearing perfectly explicit. She once wrote, approvingly, that French women of all classes had acquired a kind of cultivated deference "which in England is only associated in our minds with the manners of people of the highest birth."[37] Her contribution to a volume on the reformation of British political parties, *The New Party*, deviates entirely from political questions to advocate that society be "leveled upwards," specifically by fusing concepts of honesty with refinement and reserve: "Those who offer roughness as a proof of honesty, if they are not to be suspected, are at all events to be avoided."[38] After detailing the horrors of contemporary poverty in this essay, Grand recommends as

[34] Athol Forbes, "My Impressions of Sarah Grand," *Lady's World* 1 (1900), 880.

[35] Attacks on the lower-class identifications of New Women were common. One of the most virulent is Elizabeth Lynn Linton, "The Wild Women as Social Insurgents," *Nineteenth Century* 30 (1891), 596–605. See Dowling's comments, in "Decadent and New Woman," p. 443.

[36] Sarah Grand, "The Modern English Girl," *Canadian Magazine* 10 (1898), 300.

[37] Ibid.

[38] Sarah Grand, "What to Aim At," in *The New Party*, ed. Andrew Reid (London: Hodder Bros., 1895), pp. 248–49.

her solution a universal aspiration toward upper-class moral codes that combine sincerity with the cultivation of polished manners.

Though the biographical information we have about Grand is too paltry to allow for much speculation, it does reveal that she often viewed her own public life as an artifact that could be manipulated, often for purposes of upward class identification. The pseudonym itself, "Madame Sarah Grand," pretends to a personal and social authority that is deeply at odds with her own humble background (her father served in the coast guard in Ireland). Several striking lies mark her own accounts of her life, including the history of her choice of the pseudonym itself—she imputed its origin alternately to a dream, her stepson's suggestion, an acquaintance of that name, and pure whim. Grand lied in several interviews about her birthplace, claiming that she had been born in Bally Castle in Ireland when, in fact, her birthplace was an ordinary middle-class house. She irritated friends who allowed her to live in their Bath mansion by encouraging rumors that she owned it.[39] It is perfectly fitting that Grand should have spent six years later in her life as Mayoress of Bath—an honorific post in which she supplied the social graces to civic occasions.

Grand's interest in performance carries over in fragile ways to the novels, even though they are as likely to problematize performance as to endorse it. Characters such as Mrs. Malcomson in *The Heavenly Twins* often trigger this ambivalence and suggest Grand's discomfort with her own tendencies to validate feminist misrepresentation: "If she had not been a good woman she would have been a dangerous one, since she could please eye and ear at will, a knack which obtains more concessions from the average man than the best chosen arguments" (2.2.180). Like Angelica in her affair with the tenor, Grand confusedly dabbled in exploiting the power of female sexuality, while at the same time struggling to denaturalize gender. Tellingly, her two most exalted characters, Beth and Ideala, are characterized by both an aversion to ostentation and an obsession with it. Nevertheless, a clear affirmation of performance does crystallize at the climax of *Ideala*, the first novel in Grand's trilogy. Having resisted the narrator's every argument against an extramarital liaison

[39] See Kersley, *Darling Madame*, pp. 65, 19, and 133.

that tempts her, Ideala finally relents when the narrator points out
that she will damage her public reputation in ways that will keep her
from serving the cause: her "honor," the narrator tells her, is "the
sign of [her] superiority."[40] But perhaps the most moving argument
in defense of manipulated appearance is Angelica's discovery that,
in order to experience equality in a relationship with a man, she
must dress as a man. The tenor himself is struck by "what a
difference it made" (4.15.446) when he discovers Angelica's real
gender, and how impossible it is to recover their egalitarian relationship without the benefit of artifice.

Because of her profoundly ambiguous structural opposition of
honesty to dishonesty, the power and appeal of performance in
Grand's novels transcends any simple public relations strategy. An
aesthetics of deceit might even be said to govern the novels—an
aesthetics more indebted to sensation fiction than to the English
realist tradition with which New Woman fiction is usually compared.[41] Grand's narratives frequently manipulate the reader rather
flamboyantly, temporarily concealing crucial information or using
narrative conventions in misleading ways. For instance, the narrator
of *Ideala*, who maintains an intimate relationship with Ideala herself
throughout the novel, does not clearly reveal his masculine gender
until very late in the narrative. In effect, the novel does to the
reader exactly what Angelica does to the tenor. Besides the new
ambiguities that arise retrospectively when one realizes that the
narrator's nonerotic intimacy with Ideala had, in fact, occurred
across a gender gap, this revelation complicates the framing of
Ideala as a spokeswoman for Grand herself. The oddly equivocal
introduction to this novel, in which Ideala's thoughts are bracketed
as "the mere effervescence of a strong mind in a state of fermenta-
tion" (preface, p. iii) is severely qualified by the revelation that this
narrative distancing is carried out by a male narrator.

All three novels are infected with unconcealed narrative manipulation. In *The Beth Book*, the early chapters seem to be narrated from

---

[40] Sarah Grand, *Ideala* (New York: Optimus Printing, 1894), 26.125. Further
references are to chapter and page numbers in this edition.

[41] It is important to remember that New Woman novelists were at first compared
by contemporary reviewers to French decadents, rather than to English realists. See
Ardis, *New Women, New Novels*, pp. 30–33.

a point in time beyond Beth's achievement of feminist liberation, a promise belied by the novel's more qualified ending. In *The Heavenly Twins*, the persona of the "Boy" is carefully maintained during the episodes with the tenor, as is the secret of Angelica's prior marriage. These narrative manipulations, which are so extravagant as to call attention to themselves as authorial performances, are matched by Grand's more subtle tendency to render the literal as metaphorical, and the metaphorical as literal. In *The Heavenly Twins*, for example, madness and contagion are, in the early chapters, developed extensively as metaphors that later become literalized through the infection of Edith with syphilis; real instances of syphilitic madness are later converted into symbolic significance—as in Angelica's claim to be pestilence incarnate. This interrelation of the literal and the metaphorical is crucial to the novel's efforts to perceive sex as gender—as performative and unstable.[42] Moreover, Grand's occasional, conventionalized opposition to modernism often takes the form of an insistence on aesthetic honesty—she continually exalts the educational value of life over books; the novels crusade against stylists; and her creative heroines develop into writers of nonfiction. But as both an activist and a novelist, Grand repudiates simplistic claims for honesty with performative strategies that she herself regarded as instrumental, if morally problematic.

The most positive form this aesthetics of deceit takes is Grand's use of a kind of pastoral utopianism, one not so very different from that employed by Yeats or Wilde, which puts in the service of feminism the decadent, fin-de-siècle writer's means of transcending nature and culture at the same time. The strikingly artificial pastoralism of the tenor and Boy episodes in *The Heavenly Twins* and much of the baroque sensuality of Beth's childhood in *The Beth Book* express the desire of late-century artists to escape established culture by deforming that culture's view of nature. It is this kind of pastoral artificiality, and the outrage it inspired among mainstream readers, that prompts Linda Dowling to observe, perhaps a bit too generously, that the "New Woman was recognized as a full participant in the fin-de-siècle revolt against nature."[43] What we tend to forget, though, is

---

[42] I am indebted for this point to my student Erin O'Connor.
[43] Dowling, "Decadent and New Woman," p. 450.

how much this New Woman revolt is fractured by anxieties about honesty which are inscribed into its aesthetic and behavioral performativeness. Thus, the idyll of the tenor and the Boy, as a narrative form, yields at the end of *The Heavenly Twins* to the dominant culture's narrative of truth, the psychological case study, and *The Beth Book*'s evocative childhood scenes yield to the conventions of a romance plot.

One of the most important of Grand's ambiguities about performativeness is that lying is always presented both as a sign of her heroines' distinguishing genius and vitality and as a stage of moral conduct which they must overcome. However misguided Angelica may sometimes be—and perhaps for precisely that reason—her inventiveness is regarded by others as the sign of great potential for leadership within the feminist cause. While events may wean her away from the "hateful deception" (5.5.517) of her cross-dressing, the narrative is ironic about her consequent loss of vitality, and particularly about the general consensus that her experiment had been caused only by "mischievous energy," unnaturally bottled up in "the requirements of the life to which society condemned her" (5.7.551). Whatever the tragic outcome of her romance with the tenor, several of Angelica's goals, especially her quest to see the world as men see it and to establish an egalitarian relationship with a man, seem to carry Grand's strong approval. In *The Beth Book*, all of Beth's important stages of self-assertion involve her inventive power: her fiction about the "Secret Service of Humanity"; her many "wild fancies"—which are often the prelude to visionary insight; her poetic discoveries in what is called the "acting-room"; her "pious fraud" with Brock's money; her ruse of going by the name Miss Maclure; and her refusal to correct the prevailing assumption that she writes for fashion magazines.[44]

Nevertheless, one sign of her deep-seated moral ambivalence is that Grand tends to associate the productive power of lying with female adolescence and to demand that her mature heroines reject it. The heavenly twins make deceit seem an acceptable stratagem of revolt largely by confining it to youth. And in *The Beth Book*, Beth's

[44] Sarah Grand, *The Beth Book: Being a Study of the Life of Elizabeth Caldwell Maclure, A Woman of Genius* (New York: D. Appleton, 1897), 28.292; 23.231; 15.142; 50.551. Further references are to chapter and page numbers in this edition.

progress involves a gradual renunciation of the "servant's tricks" (20.209) of her childhood. The high jinks of juvenile tricksters in Grand's work correspond to the widespread fin-de-siècle compartmentalization of adolescence as an insulated space of rebellion which, as John Neubauer has shown, is "largely hollowed out psychologically and socially."[45] In both novels, too, heroines abandon their creative vocations—Angelica her violin and stories, Beth her aspiration to become a novelist—in favor of more prosaic work, as if to suggest the sterile incompatibility between Grand's moral conception of aesthetics and feminism. Beth's mature discovery of her oratorical powers and abandonment of the creative fantasies of her youth sublimate her performativeness into a nonfictional mode. It is crucial, too, that Beth's speeches are always the efflorescence of her "natural bent" (52.571) for oratory, as opposed to the "cultivation" (52.570) of writing talents that had "misled" her. To escape the stigma of guile (Beth is accused throughout the novel of acting in order to call attention to herself), she must not simply reject a literary vocation, she must also renounce all conscious control of herself as a feminist agent.

Despite her various efforts to legitimize feminist performativeness, Grand's fiction always seems to insist on the unbridgeable disjunction between honesty and falsehood. In *The Heavenly Twins*, the stories of Evadne and Angelica, so promising at first, both end in destructive excess: a rigidly held sense of honor leads to submissive hysteria, and lying ends in neurosis and manslaughter. Given the novel's preoccupation with murdering the master—Edith's murderous fantasies are echoed by the infected Frenchwoman and by Angelica, and they are literalized in the tenor's story—honesty and dishonesty are perceived as producing intolerable relationships, either of submission or rebellion, to masculine authority. Grand's two heroines seem to be on opposite courses of moral transformation as well, becoming perverted images of each other: Evadne, the rock of sincerity, becomes "unlike herself" as a hysteric; Angelica, the fabricator, lapses into a conventional and extremely limited sincerity. In one of Grand's more bitter echoes of George Eliot, Angelica gains only the

[45] John Neubauer, *The Fin-de-Siècle Culture of Adolescence* (New Haven: Yale University Press, 1992), p. 11.

small victory of having her husband read some of her speeches in Parliament (one sore spot among 1890s feminists was the stock argument that an ability to manipulate their husbands was the only political power women needed).[46] Both characters continue to be marked by a deep ethical split, and the absence of passion in both their marriages suggests a permanent gap between vitality and respectability.

The most striking expression of the impossibility of a synthesis between truth and falsehood in *The Heavenly Twins* is the death of the tenor. In an odd reversal that may be intended to distance moral dilemmas, Grand casts her male figure as a tragically inaccessible moral ideal. The tenor is represented as the Christ-like man Evadne had earlier tried to imagine, and, given the path of Angelica's later repentance, the tenor even seems to have died for her sins. The "romance" of the Boy and the tenor parallels the moral opposition of Angelica and Evadne, with the Boy enacting a facetious, open-ended moral experiment and the tenor holding on to an ascetic religious faith that shocks the Boy in "the grand simplicity of it all! the wonderful solemn earnestness!" (4.11.414). In this sense, the romantic meeting of old Victorian values and vanguard moral experimentalism ends not in marriage but in death. But the tenor is also idealized because he represents the perfect combination of earnestness and role-playing that the novel as a whole has sought to synthesize—he exemplifies what it might mean to unify sincerity of purpose with a permanently manipulable identity. From his very first appearance, the tenor is described as both preternaturally "earnest" (4.1.365) and a "clever imposter" (4.1.361). The odd mixture that is his social identity—he lives above his social origins, but perhaps beneath his genealogy; he maintains an impression of good breeding while spurning all material pretensions—stresses moral transcendence by neutralizing his relationship to social conflict. And his apparent victory over passion—he lives a "calm and passionless existence" (4.1.367)—together with his susceptibility to infatuations, casts him as an idealized image of Grand's contradictory feminist ideals about sexual love. But in the tenor's case, synthetic

---

[46] See Stubbs on this point (*Women and Fiction*, pp. 44–45). Stubbs misses the irony in *The Heavenly Twins*, however.

idealism can only be achieved through a withdrawal from life, through his decision to "bury himself alive" (4.1.361) in Morning-quest. As a kind of cross-dressed Lady of Shalott—a figure referred to repeatedly during this episode—the tenor is destroyed (literally, by floating downriver in a boat) when he attempts to enter the world for love, a coming-out precipitated, ironically, by Angelica's efforts to bring his moral virtue into the public realm.

In her insistence on ethical disjunction, Grand inhibits her own ability to formulate a moral foundation for feminism. No wonder that the New Woman ideal is always represented in her fiction as remote and unrealized and that even the character she named "Ideala" is exalted for being "full of inconsistencies" (*Ideala*, 1.7). *The Heavenly Twins* stresses the suffocation of feminist energies in many obvious ways: by leaving the final book of the novel to be narrated by a man, as the case history of a hysteric; by allowing both Angelica and Evadne to be saved from suicide by disturbing figures of social authority—the religious zealot, Lady Fulda, and Dr. Galbraith, respectively. But this suffocation does not have its sole roots in overt oppression. Rather, its primary source is feminism's own internal moral dilemmas. Grand's novel is structured so prolifically around character pairs that figure the disjunctive opposition of truth to falsehood—Evadne and Angelica, the tenor and Angelica, Galbraith and the newly evasive, hysterical Evadne—that twinship, rather than contagion, becomes the central structuring metaphor of the novel. Not at all a figure for complementarity, twinship in *The Heavenly Twins* defines the permanent dissociation of the New Woman's moral identity.

Despite her attempts to keep ethical alternatives in a state of balanced negation, Grand could not help but maintain commitments to some of the broken fragments of Victorian moral discourse. Her novels are indebted to Victorian ethics in specific and fairly rigid ways which are often politically counterproductive, even though she subjected these ethical fragments to significant transformations and displacements. It is important to analyze Grand's more regressive ethical commitments carefully, in order to understand the sources of her inability to break free of Victorian ethical discourse and its late-century convolutions.

For one thing, Grand is as absolute about the connection between sexual desire and dishonesty as is mid-Victorian culture, although she redescribes this symbolic linkage for purely feminist purposes. In Grand's novels, love is always presented as a lie, even though this supremely Victorian idea is newly inflected in relation to the oppression of women. Like Hardy, and like many other late-century writers, Grand had her own theory of "migratory" erotic desire, in the sense that her heroines' multiple romantic attachments result from their pursuit of an ideal object of desire which can never be fully embodied. *The Beth Book* offers the most extended treatment of this pattern, shamelessly applying to women this familiar, tragic topos of male desire: Beth's desires diverge from Sammy Lee, Alfred Cayley Pounce, and Dan Maclure in a way that often alerts her to the idealistic quality of her own desire, while the novel mischievously plays with Beth's yearning for a Lancelot-like dream figure on horseback. In this sense, individual, inadequate male objects of desire are always represented as dangerously deceptive for Grand's heroines. Grand's attack on conventional marriage, as a conspiracy against the freedom of young women, also begins by exposing the misguided choices that women make when emotional life is allowed to predominate over intellectual life. Evadne's unfortunate choice of a husband comes at a time in her life when she "revelled in sensations" (1.11.53), and Edith, too, marries when caught by "the glow of sensation" (2.6.284). The novels routinely identify men with outright deceitfulness, which only adds to love's fatality. Finally, the novels insist that focusing one's desire on sex is a channeling of human passion in overly narrow, reductive ways, and thus a surrender to misrepresentations of sensuous nature. Even Dr. Galbraith recognizes that "it is stupid to narrow [life] down to the indulgence of one particular set of emotions" (1.15.98). Given the rigidity of Grand's association of sex with deceit, it is no wonder that Beth yearns for "some one to trust . . . more than some one to love" (50.542).

New Woman refusals of sex were not intended simply to forge an alliance with the culture of decadence—though both New Woman and decadent writers do explore "artificial" sexual relations. Nor is it the case, as Elaine Showalter and others have argued, that

New Woman writers were "disgusted by sex" and refused biological femininity as part of a "wish to be male."[47] It is true that many feminists did see celibacy as a way to strike back at men—a tactic that culminated in Christabel Pankhurst's militant crusade for chastity.[48] But Grand always complicates questions of sexuality by refracting them through problems of truth-telling, and her inability to resolve problems of marriage and monogamy are rooted, not in her flawed feminism, but in widespread ethical confusions. The distancing of sex in New Woman writing has everything to do with a kind of ethical struggle that is relatively remote from sexuality: an attempt to arrive at a sensuality free of overdetermined cultural connections to dishonesty. By distancing sex, New Woman writers were attempting to appropriate male moral authority for women. Such distancing refigured chastity as a kind of honor, a sacrifice of self-interest that strengthens valor and authority, and resisted the dishonor and deceit affiliated with sexual desire. That is to say, New Woman sexual renunciation should be seen, not simply as a continuation of passive Victorian feminine ideals but also as an attempt to rewrite the meaning of honesty and to gender it as female by defining a triumph over sexual self-interest as the sign of feminine warrior virtues.

Grand did not aspire to sexual abstinence so much as to the production of an honorable, alternative sensuality. A crucial post-Victorian project of her novels is their frank exploration of the life of the senses apart from sexuality, and Grand's characters repeatedly insist that British culture's emphasis on sexuality blinds women to the range and power of their sensual experiences. This sentiment informs the narrator's view of Evadne: "She was too highly tempered, well-balanced a creature to be the victim of any one passion, and least of all of that transient state of feeling miscalled 'Love' " (2.12.226). Despite Evadne's repression, the narrator firmly rejects the notion that she is "cold" (2.12.227) simply because she is a sexual ascetic. Her moral opposite, Angelica, when disguised as the Boy, also rails against "the intrusion of *sex* into everything" and claims he is "sensuous, yes; not sensual" (4.13.423). The narrator of *Ideala* argues, somewhat defensively, that de-emphasizing sex actu-

---

[47] Showalter, *A Literature of Their Own*, pp. 191–92. A critique of Showalter's condescension can be found in Ardis, *New Women, New Novels*, p. 6.

[48] See Showalter's comments, in *Sexual Anarchy*, pp. 22–23.

ally expands the range of sensual feeling: although "the world will call her cold," Ideala is in fact "a snow-crowned volcano" (30.191). In sometimes shocking contrast to earlier nineteenth-century fiction, Grand writes explicitly about female sensuality, and this candor is itself an attempt to rewrite female sensuality as honorable. *The Beth Book* breaks new ground in this regard in its attention to Beth's childhood sensations—an attention to physical detail which anticipates the microscopic dissection of childhood in Joyce's *A Portrait of the Artist as a Young Man.*

Nevertheless, there is inevitably a tension between these characters' discovery of their sensuality and the threatened reduction of that sensuality to sex. Although Grand's project is in some sense a strategic reversal of the common accusation that feminists are puritanical, one of the liabilities of her strict identification of sexual passion with the symbolic complex of falsehood is that she traps her characters in narratives of renunciation and self-sacrifice which maintain the very puritanism she seeks to escape. Sensuality and sexuality remain opposed, as honorable and dishonorable, paralyzing the conventional narrative trajectories of the novels and producing disturbing self-contradictions for Grand's characters. Both Angelica and Evadne in *The Heavenly Twins* reinforce this narrative paralysis through their problematic nonmarriages, and the conclusion of *The Beth Book* resorts to conventional economies of self-sacrifice and reward which are straight out of *Jane Eyre*: Beth tends her lover and proves herself capable of giving him up, only to be rewarded later with his chastened love, though her ability to consummate that love is deeply in doubt. In *The Heavenly Twins*, the adulterous "romance" of Angelica and the tenor is displaced and played out affirmatively in the last book of the novel, when Evadne escapes from a loveless marriage (through her husband's death) and finds consolation with her real lover. But this consolation is desiccated by the clinical nature of their marriage. In the long run, Grand's novels do not seem to escape the contradictions dramatized by Angelica's ambivalent interest in the tenor. Grand's efforts to use sexual renunciation as a bulwark for female honor is doomed by its grounding in Victorian contradictions that cannot be appropriated and extended without cost.

Another vestige of Victorian symbolic dynamics is Grand's

grounding of social hierarchies in an exclusionary moral code. This anachronistic moral snobbery is carried out most clearly in class and ethnic terms. The Irish in *The Beth Book* are routinely vilified for their inbred mendacity, as are Roman Catholics and the French. The behavior of servants is also regularly scorned as deceitful. One ambivalent sign of this association of class with dishonesty is the role servants play as Beth's initiators into the world of creative narrative. Her servant Harriet, in particular, has a "brilliant imagination" (15.133), and she often induces Beth to help with her housework in exchange for access to her narrative gifts. As noted earlier, Grand also identifies women fairly strictly with sincerity and men with falsehood. The great villains of *The Heavenly Twins* are Mosley Menteith, whose surname identifies his fundamental crime as a lie told in France, and Colquhoun, who is constantly defined by his "inscrutable bearing" (1.13.66), his obsession with concealing domestic trouble from public view, and his inconsistencies. Beth feels "a certain contempt for her father's veracity" (6.50), and Dan Maclure, Uncle James, and Alfred Cayley Pounce are so deceitful as to be pasteboard villains. Even Arthur Brock is lacking in trust, as he demonstrates when he discourages Beth from confiding her story in him.[49] However innocuous some of these moral hierarchies may seem, as attempts to *épate* the male reading public, they run counter to Grand's more democratic and egalitarian tendencies. While it is "not Beth's nature to be exclusive" (16.154), it is the occasional nature of Grand's texts to reinforce moral structures of exclusion.

At the same time, Grand's novels draw, provisionally, on the dynamics of transgressive exceptionality to elevate characters who have a mixed experience of honesty and falsehood. Much of the interest of Grand's female protagonists, with their checkered, complex moral experience, draws on their difference from characters who are simplistically identified with either truth or falsehood. The desire to mix morality and transgression is always part of the

[49] Grand abused the truthfulness of men in numerous essays, notably "The Man of the Moment," *North American Review* 158 (1894), 622 ("weak-willed, inconsistent"); and "The New Aspect of the Woman Question," *North American Review* 158 (1894), esp. p. 275 ("But where are our men? Where is the chivalry, the truth, the affection, the earnest purpose, the plain living, high thinking, and noble self-sacrifice that make a man?").

enchantment of New Woman feminism—revulsion from the pruri-
ence of interlopers such as Grant Allen, author of *The Woman Who
Did*, notwithstanding. It is no accident that Grand repeatedly
highlights suspicions about her heroines' sinfulness, in sexual matters
as well as in questions of the truth. Evadne, for example, is distinguished socially by being the victim of the Brimstons' insinuations:
it works to her credit that Maltese society cannot tell whether she is
"nasty-minded" or a "prude" (2.9.216). Later, her oblivious tramp-
ing through Regent Street piques the interest of Dr. Galbraith.
Gratuitous flirtations with sin, while functioning partly to reinforce
the trustworthiness of characters like Evadne, also signal the distinc-
tive proximity of Grand's heroines to vice. Such flirtatiousness,
raised to a fever pitch in Angelica's manipulation of the tenor's
desire, is jarringly at odds with New Woman emphasis on moral
rectitude, and it clashes with the moral absolutism manifested
occasionally by initiates such as Beth: "The plea of exceptional
character, exceptional circumstances, exceptional temperament,
and what not, is merely another way of expressing exceptional
selfishness and excusing exceptional self-indulgence" (48.507).

One indication of the fragmentary nature of Grand's various
borrowings from the discourse of Victorian ethics is that her sporadic
appeals to moral authority are anchored in the merits of wildly
disparate social groups. Both the authority of honor and the enchantment of transgressive lying are tied to the heroine's identification with conflicting social groups and ideological foundations.
Evadne's characteristic verbal precision and candor, for example, are
appropriated directly from her father as a means of supervening
traditional claims about male honor. Angelica, too, imitates the
"extreme precision" (5.2.488) of her father's speech. But the twins
also borrow a code of honor that has aristocratic, rather than
gendered overtones. Their constant fighting over their patrimony,
conducted in chivalrous style, is not just narrative whimsy—the
twins' ideas about loyalty, as well as their sense of moral license,
have affinities with the patrician attitudes we have seen in Grand's
journalism. The aristocratic authority of honor is also strongly
suggested in Beth's history, especially in the moral model furnished
jointly by her mother—who emphasizes courage as the test of one's
honor—and by her father, who admires Beth's "noble nature"

(10.81) and whose moral sermons lean rather valorously upon "loyalty" to both self and others: "Be loyal, be loyal to yourself, loyal to the best that is in you; that means, be as good as your friends think you, and better if you can. Tell the truth, live openly, and stick to your friends; that's the whole of the best code of morality in the world" (9.76). At the same time, however, "loyalty" is often identified with the solidarity of oppressed groups. At St. Catherine's girls' school, in *The Beth Book*, honesty is considered more important than class status, and one of the unspoken compacts that solidifies Beth's rapport with servants is that they disdain to snitch on each other. Middle-class moral codes are not absent from the novels, either. Honesty is often starkly allied with middle-class emphasis on sincerity, as opposed to aristocratic valor—Angelica unfashionably defends "bourgeois" values to her genteel friends: "Sincerity and refinement make good manners, and principle is the parent of both" (47.489).

The contradictions New Woman writers are often accused of harboring—ambivalent attitudes toward maternity and childbirth, uncertain nostalgias for Victorian moral and sexual ideals—are seriously complicated, and partially explained, by the inability of writers like Grand to integrate the various pieces of Victorian discourse about honesty. Grand's novels do not seem altogether self-conscious about these various borrowings and transformations—rather, the effect is that of a moral system frantically groping for new foundations. Without a coherent system for integrating the disjunctions of Victorian honesty and vanguard moral performativeness, Grand's use of the discursive features of honesty could result in only an awkward pastiche of social codes and values. In these various ways, New Woman honesty remains ill defined and opportunistic in its attempts to provide a foundation for feminist ethics. While it would be reductive to evaluate Grand's moral code as a whole in the light of her fragmentary treatment of either sexuality, moral hierarchies, transgressive enchantment, or social anchoring, the dispersion of her thought in all these areas reveals the disorienting effects on feminism of the disjunctive climate for truth-telling in late-century culture.

One unmistakable sign of Grand's own dissatisfaction with the ethical inconsistencies of both *The Heavenly Twins* and *Ideala* is that she attempted a more satisfactory integration of truth-telling and performance in the persona of Beth Maclure in *The Beth Book*. Grand's project of ethical integration in this later novel is all the more significant because, with the exception of Edith Johnston's *A Sunless Heart*, *The Beth Book* is the only late-century novel to present an optimistic account of a New Woman's artistic success. Yet Beth's moral integration seems, finally, only to defer the various ethical contradictions I have outlined. The same reviewer who noted that Beth was "a kind of Angelica and Evadne rolled into one" also saw that the novel ultimately chronicles the sacrifice, rather than the fulfillment, of Beth's potential: "It is like watching the decay of some one whom we loved in life."[50]

In this later novel, Grand tries to minimize in a number of important ways the contradictions between honesty and performance which had been so exacerbated in *The Heavenly Twins*. For example, Beth's skill at performance is nearly as well developed as Angelica's, but it is wedded much more soberly and strictly to the pursuit of truth. While Beth is fairly addicted to games of "assumption" (3.21), even as an adolescent her impersonations are consistently presented as a form of knowledge. She tells Aunt Grace Mary, in defense of her mimicking of a workman's speech, "How am I to tell you what he said if I don't say what he said?" (12.108). And when, at one point in her childhood, she falls into a steady pattern of impersonations, the narrator explicitly defends her on the grounds of veracity: "She was generally somebody else in these days, seldom herself; and people who did not understand this might have supposed that she was an exceedingly mendacious little girl, when she was merely speaking consistently in the character which she happened to be impersonating" (16.142). More important, Beth's skill at lying is often linked to higher moral purposes of various kinds. "Being so sensitive herself," for example, "she was morbidly careful of the feelings of others, and committed sins of insincerity without compunction in her efforts to spare them" (3.28). More aggressively, she pretends to be dead to teach Harriet a lesson; she tricks Bernadine

[50] *Review of Reviews* 16 (1897), 619, 621.

out onto the roof to instruct her about disloyalty; and she poaches on her uncle's land to serve her family and to develop her own principles of economic usefulness—she "poached on principle" (23.233). Often, too, Beth conceals secrets out of loyalty to others. Most dramatically, when she commits "pious frauds" in the Brock episodes, it is for lifesaving reasons. Because of this kind of scrupulous integration, Beth can confirm to her appropriately named spiritual tutor, Aunt Victoria, "I am always in earnest" (17.160), without striking a false note. One of the remarkable things about this novel, in fact, is that Beth feels no conflict between the moral guidance of her Aunt Victoria and the more performative moral models in her life: Count Gustav, Harriet, and the sensation fiction she reads and sometimes imitates.

Grand also tries to synthesize Beth's allegiance to both old and new moral values by describing Beth's "genius" as a psychologically expansive force. That is to say, Grand explains the mixed ethical tendencies of Beth's character as the result of her involuntary and erratic "further faculty" (3.31). Because her genius compels her toward greater individuality, while her native tendency, we are told, is to submit, Beth "appeared to be a singular mixture of weakness and strength, courage and cowardice, faith and distrust" (3.31). It is not at all clear which phases of Beth's character correspond to faith and which to distrust (the symmetry of the first two oppositions of this series is strategically transposed), but the instabilities of Beth's moral character are nevertheless attributed to her extraordinary psychological makeup. At various points in the novel, Beth's "genius" does, indeed, erupt in ways that link creative vision to performance, in contrast to those stretches of her life characterized by a more earnest submissiveness.

Finally, Grand distributes instabilities in Beth's moral nature to the vagaries of her growth, attempting to reconcile them within a narrative of feminist self-development. In this narrative, external forces develop one or another side of Beth's nature in an uneven but ultimately progressive sequence. For example, we are told that "the same faculty made Beth either the naughtiest or the best of children; the difference depended on her heart; if that were touched, she was all sympathy, but if no appeal was made to her feelings, her daily doings were the outcome of so many erratic impulses acted on without consideration merely to vary the disastrous monotony of those long idle afternoons" (16.152). In dark phases of her life, Beth resorts to concealments as extreme as those we saw in Evadne, often with the narrator's explicit approval: Beth learns "the futility of discussion" with men of a certain stamp, for "such heavy things as theories, opinions, and arguments must be kept carefully concealed from [them]" (18.168–69). But when conditions allow her confidence to blossom, she can be brutally candid. These vacillations are explicitly presented by the narrative as part of a progress: "It was by intimacy with lower natures that she learned fully to appreciate the higher; by the effect of bad books upon her that she learned the value of good ones; by the lowering of her whole tone . . . that she was eventually confirmed in her principles" (22.220). In these terms, Beth develops a dialectical moral sense that is always firmly attuned to principle and to progress: Beth's experience teaches her the wisdom that "there is no crime but has some time been a virtue" (27.265).

Despite all of Grand's efforts, however, Beth's moral development suffers from the same constraints that we have seen in the other novels. Beth's marital quandaries, for example, are presented almost entirely in ethical terms, so that questions of sexual politics are reduced to a blind moral impasse. Whether or not to divorce Dan and accept true love from Brock is made entirely an issue of honesty and dishonesty—a strict reduction of the issues that Beth elaborates in her long lecture to Alfred Cayley Pounce. Tellingly, however, the end of the novel leaves the question of marriage and adultery completely unresolved, with Brock melodramatically riding toward Beth on horseback like the white knight of her Lady Shalott daydreams (significantly, she dreams of her rider as "a man to be trusted" [45.471]), even though Beth seems firmly committed to honor her promises to Dan—many of which seem gratuitously designed to emphasize the association of marital fidelity with honesty. Beth's earlier argument with Aunt Victoria about monogamy culminates in a moral double bind rooted precisely in the code of honor she learned as a child: "Loyal! . . . that was my father's word to me: 'Be loyal.' We've got to be loyal to others; but he also said that we must be loyal to ourselves" (21.219). One profound reason Grand could never overcome her ambivalence about marital bonds, then, was that, like Beth in her argument with Pounce, she defined marriage as an ideal that "depends on loyalty" (48.508). If Grand had had settled convictions about loyalty, this kind of formula would not have been so problematic, but, as we have seen, Grand's unresolved attitudes toward honesty do not prepare her to understand monogamy as some kind of clear-cut choice between truth and deceit. The sexual quandaries of late-century feminism need to be understood, not just as the culmination of a nineteenth-century emphasis on the empowering nature of female chastity, but as the result of a linkage between problems of sexuality and problems of truth-telling.

Conflicts between literature and activism, filtered through ethical quandaries, are also left very much in abeyance by *The Beth Book*. It is, indeed, striking how much less settled these conflicts are than the conventional New Woman diatribes against "art for art's sake" have led many critics to believe. Beth "lived upon books" (15.134), we are told, at the very same time in her life that she supposedly finds consolation in the "practical experience of life rather than from books" (15.131). The novel seems to support Galbraith's theories about the creative power of representation: "catch-words are creative; they do not prove that a thing is—they cause it to be" (38.381); yet the novel also militantly attacks antirealist literature. Beth is nourished upon fiction, yet at a crucial phase of her reading she scorns art for philosophy and ethics. Beth expresses her own ambivalence about the moral status of literature during a discussion in which Galbraith much more reductively condemns fiction as "the opium of the West" (40.404). Beth counters, "I notice in all things a curious duality, a right side and a wrong side. Confusion is the wrong side of order, misery of happiness, falsehood of truth, evil of good; and it seems to me that novel-reading, which can be a vice, I know, may also be made a virtue. It depends on the writer." On some occasions, Grand overtly sides with the anti-aesthetes, with those who believe that "right thinking, right feeling, and knowledge are more important than art" (40.407), and her antimodernism revolves relentlessly around calls for honesty in literature. Yet Grand also insinuates in *The Beth Book* that didactic art is not entirely sufficient for a creative, experimentalist visionary such as Beth. Beth derives a sense of "artistic accomplishment," for example, from the frauds she practices upon Brock, and she muses on "a certain wonderment at the very slight and subtle difference there is between truth and falsehood as conveyed by the turn of a phrase" (50.552). The form of *The Beth Book* itself is morally skewed. On the one hand, it is presented as a narrative of overcoming, a kind of "Pilgrim's Progress," in which Beth's worst traits—for example, her relapses into lying—are gradually repudiated. On the other, it is presented as a narrative of self-discovery and self-affirmation, in which signs of Beth's genius can be found throughout her life, including in her adolescent experimentalism and in her "wild fancies."

Most important of all, though, Beth's struggle with sexual politics is completely subjectivized around these moral questions. In the manner of nineteenth-century domestic fiction, Beth's personality is meant to fascinate, ultimately, because it is so deeply riven by contradictions of various kinds: she is self-sacrificing but self-assertive; she is her father's "ardent temperament" at war with Aunt Victoria's "Puritan principles" (36.363); she is indifferent to personal appearance but preoccupied by it; she craves independent work but fears a career (she retreats from public view while her book is published anonymously, and loses all her sewing money to Dan with a curious sense of relief); she is nervous but fearless; her body is sometimes represented as starved and sometimes as a model of health. One of the novel's persistent themes is the uniqueness of Beth, set over against the common herd, and this uniqueness is defined, to a great degree, by the psychological multidimensionality created through these internal contradictions. In this sense, if Grand refused to resolve moral questions, it was to displace moral authority onto the complexly textured interiority of the "genius," rather than to use the figure of the "genius" to define moral systems. Beth herself concludes that morality lies not in acts themselves but in the "character" (50.547) of the people who perform them.

Feminism's inability to negotiate the late-century breakup of Victorian discourses of truth had disastrous consequences for women writers of the period. Unable to resolve the relationship between Victorian ideals of honesty—which had never been identified with women in the first place—and the demands of a new, performative morality that threatened to reinstate Victorian clichés about female lying, New Woman novelists were unable to develop a unified image of feminist moral authority appropriate to the publicly performed sexual and social activism they so urgently desired. The progressive social forces traditionally and transgressively identified with deceit offered too jarring a clash with ideals of honesty which seemed both anachronistic and indispensable at the same time. These ideals themselves had to be treated ironically, in the spirit of a decadent antinaturalism, even as they formed the basis for feminist demands for public candor and for knowledge—rallying points for feminism since early in the nineteenth century. For the New Woman novelist, the pressing ethical dilemma was not only imagining the virtue of an ideal heroine, but accommodating the ambiguities of truth-telling within fiction itself to the demands of feminism, especially at a time when early modernist aesthetics was moving—in New Woman writing as well as in the work of male writers—away from the ideals of truth-telling cherished by Victorian realism. It is because women writers could not negotiate the truth dilemmas of post-Victorian literature, not because of their lack of talent or their ideological single-mindedness, that they made inevitable their own exile from a canonical tradition that had begun to treat honesty as an issue that could only be resolved through aesthetic rarefaction. The finely maintained, aesthetic "reticence" that the Arthur Waughs of the literary establishment preferred to either feminist candor or feminist dissimulation was a far more efficient means to transgressive sophistication.

Afterword

For several years now, as I have groped toward an understanding of what this project is really about, I have evaded casual inquiries by saying, vaguely and simply, that I am writing a book about lying. People generally assume that I must have some quirky, personal interest in deceit and that I must be writing some kind of theoretical defense of it—the scholarly version of those recent self-help books that tell us a certain amount of lying is actually good for our psychic health. I have shamelessly indulged both assumptions—making jokes about my family and my ancestry and letting the conversation slide toward interpersonal topics, rather than mustering the courage to try to articulate the truth about my work.

In fact, however, my object of study has been a fairly remote and historically specific practice. I have been trying to describe the peculiar ways in which flaunted acts of dissimulation shaped Victorian notions about prestige, rather than trying to describe personal or contemporary practices of deception (both of which, it goes without saying, are numerous). A primary objective of this project has been to locate a point of difference between the Victorians and ourselves, a way in which Victorian models of sophistication took a unique and now outmoded cultural form. Lying, or risking the appearance of lying, is just not as sexy as it used to be—not so much because everyone is doing it as because it has been disinvested of the interlocked cultural and ethical forces that undergirded Victorian social power. "Image is everything," we are too often told, or "we live in a culture of surfaces." The validity of such ideas is less important, in this context, than the fact that they have lost their shock value. Though we have our own repertoire of transgressive sophistications, and our own favored tropes for exploiting the reversibility of good and evil (addiction, consumption, cultural appropriation, and so on), deception does not have a prime place among them.

In this sense, I have attempted to explain thematic, psychological, and formal patternings in Victorian novels which have struck me as both persistently strange and strangely persistent—especially in the light of twentieth-century inclinations to take the Victorians at their word when it comes to their supposedly lofty standards of candor. Lying did not decay in Victorian England. It enjoyed a remarkable, unique, and now largely extinct life. The last two chapters chart the early stages of this extinction, showing how transgressive powers based on deceit began to wither away as truth-telling norms themselves became precarious. But the very explosiveness of questions about honesty and dishonesty in late-Victorian culture testifies to the breakup of a coherent way of thinking about the power of the lie which flourished in the middle of the nineteenth century.

At the same time, there *are* contemporary and personal motivations for the work I have done. The most sustaining of these has been my interest in the competitive use of socio-symbolic dynamics. Perhaps the most inspirational reading behind my project—the book I have always wanted to respond to and have always wished that I had been temperamentally suited to write—is Richard Sennett and Jonathan Cobb's *The Hidden Injuries of Class*.[1] I read Sennett and Cobb's book many years ago, after I had first been told by the University of Michigan that I had expectations, and its vivid account of internalized class violence has haunted me ever since. My project

---

[1] Richard Sennett and Jonathan Cobb, *The Hidden Injuries of Class* (New York: Random House, 1973). A more recent source of inspiration in the same vein has been Carolyn Kay Steedman, *Landscape for a Good Woman: A Story of Two Lives* (New Brunswick, N.J.: Rutgers University Press, 1987).

seeks to expose transgressive sophistication as a hidden social and sexual injury, one that shaped the antagonisms of Victorian men and women of various social locations. While I have concentrated, overtly, on defining the various discrete or generalized powers mobilized by Victorian dissimulation, I have also been at pains to show how self-limiting these powers become in the context of the status wars that pit one faction of the middle class against another. This is not a moral judgment so much as a recognition of the many ways disguised forms of social power can divide those who, in other ways, share a community of interests.

More broadly, then, my project seeks to define a long-standing, internal middle-class struggle in which the conspicuous appropriation of the "antibourgeois" is one of the most powerful weapons of social competition—a dynamic that remains very much a characteristic of contemporary culture. In a sense, the culture of postmodernism, with the special premium it places on transgressing the boundary between high and low culture, might be read as the glorious fulfillment of this bourgeois symbolic dynamic. At no other time in history has it been so classy to violate class lines, and at no other time has antibourgeois behavior been so obviously bourgeois.[2]

It is not news to say that contemporary culture (including literary theory, which has opened up new vistas of transgressive sophistication through cultural studies) makes the "in-your-face" parading of one's "antibourgeois" behavior a way of life. What my six chapters seek to show, however, is how widely shared mechanisms of cultural privilege—like antibourgeois transgression—are relentlessly and competitively appropriated by various social subgroups. When "insiders" pretend to be "outsiders," as a sign of their cultural authority, their targets are very often other "insiders" behaving in distressingly similar ways. The result is an epidemic of disguised conflict. Mechanisms of socio-symbolic power are often abstractly shared, but this sharing conceals the divisiveness of privileged groups. It is easy to forget that people with opposed social interests often claim the same

[2] At least it is now possible to define the cultural style of the professional-managerial middle class as one marked by its radical ambivalence toward the "middling" social identity in which that class finds itself wedged firmly between capital and labor. See Fred Pfeil, " 'Makin' Flippy-Floppy': Postmodernism and the Baby-Boom PMC," in *Another Tale to Tell* (London: Verso, 1990), 97–125.

kinds of symbolic legitimacy for themselves. It is very difficult to restore a historical and politicized legibility to these claims.

In this sense, the dual goals of my project—to define a shared mechanism of cultural privilege and to situate it in directly competing social locations—respond to what many people have seen as the most urgent of problems in contemporary theory. The homogeneity we have come to expect in socio-symbolic logics of domination can too easily blind us to important internal differences in the way these logics are appropriated. Not all sophistications are equally powerful; not all social exclusions are equally damaging. It is much easier to measure these differences concretely in a culture that is relatively remote. But it is my hope that the study of social competition taking place within and through shared mechanisms of socio-symbolic authority can contribute to the new, more nuanced, less monolithic models of cultural power which contemporary theory is plainly working to develop. Ethical reversibility—like the social productivity of the lie—is simply one kind of transgressive symbolic power that deceptively appears to be the same for everyone.

Index